HORIZONS
OF SCIENCE

CONTEMPORARY EVANGELICAL THOUGHT Series

HORIZONS OF SCIENCE

Christian Scholars Speak Out

Edited by

CARL F. H. HENRY

1817

Published in San Francisco by

HARPER & ROW, PUBLISHERS

New York, Hagerstown, San Francisco, London

FIRST EDITION

Designed by Jim Mennick

Library of Congress Cataloging in Publication Data
Main entry under title:
HORIZONS OF SCIENCE.

  (Contemporary evangelical thought series)
  "Partly an outgrowth of the International Conference on Human Engineering and the Future of Man
held in Wheaton, Illinois, July 21–24, 1975."
  Bibliography: p.
  1. Religion and science—1946- —Addresses,
essays, lectures. I. Henry, Carl Ferdinand Howard,
1913– II. International Conference on Human
Engineering and the Future of Man, Wheaton, Ill.,
1975.
BL240.2.H67 1978   234   77–7849
ISBN 0-06-063866-4

Contents

Preface

The contributors to this symposium are gifted and respected scholars; all have gained national and some even world eminence in their fields of professional expertise. They are distinguished by a shared conviction that our generation will inevitably pay a high penalty for ignoring the spiritual and moral guidance proffered by biblical Christianity and by a common confidence that the Christian view of God and the world has nothing whatever to fear from empirical science. Indeed, they affirm not only that the Judeo-Christian revelation supplied the framework within which Western science has found much of its stimulus, but also that biblical theism remains the intellectual context within which the scientific enterprise can find continuing illumination and moral norms for its profoundest endeavors.

This volume, fifth in the series on Contemporary Evangelical Thought, is partly an outgrowth of the International Conference on Human Engineering and the Future of Man held in Wheaton, Illinois, July 21–24, 1975. Five of the contributors participated in that conference, which closed with the drafting of a statement of "Evangelical Perspectives on Human Engineering" (see Appendix A). Some wider window on the world of evangelical engagement with science is needed, however. This volume provides Christian scholars that more extensive opportunity to delineate crucial issues and concerns in this field.

Among the popular notions today is the idea that the more one knows about science the less one needs God. These essays refute such snap judgments. The naturalistic literature inundating our radically secularistic culture often gives the impression that its credo ("I affirm the ultimacy of natural processes and events") has once and for all displaced the opening articles of the Apostles Creed ("I believe in God, the Father Almighty, Maker of Heaven and Earth . . ."). But such declarations merely prejudge what needs to be argued on a reasoned basis.

No attempt has been made to impose rigid uniformity upon the convictions of the contributors. Nor is this volume to be considered a completely definitive and systematic statement of evangelical theological positions. Rather, it contains the disciplined reflections of prestigious evangelical scholars on the implications of the newly emerging horizons of science, together with numerous theological excursions. The writers do not claim to speak on all points for all evangelical believers; in fact, at places they question views now prevailing in Christian circles and present alternatives among which evangelicals themselves must choose. But every contributor will be found to share the historic Christian faith not only in an unapologetic way, but also in full confidence that it explains the nature of reality and illumines the predicament and prospect of modern man far better than does any contemporary alternative. The purpose of the writers is not to give a comprehensive statement of the Christian world view; it is, rather, to concentrate specially on broad areas of present-day scientific concern and controversy from the Christian perspective. The writers maintain God to be at the center of the cosmos and life, and seek to win thoughtful support of their position at a time when the dilemmas posed by science and technology unnerve a generation often unsure about moral goals and imperatives.

Some differences of view are far-reaching and no effort has been made to resolve them. To defuse what might be controversy over epistemological concerns, the editor has postponed certain essays to the latter pages of the volume, in particular the contributions by Professor Thorson and Professor Clark. In any symposium an editor must be prepared for a certain diversity of conviction on the issues represented, and essayists should be allowed some contextual comment without either compromising the volume or inviting rejection. The placement of these valuable essays together at the conclusion of the book will, it is hoped, encourage productive discussion on the important issues they raise. With that conviction in mind, we offer the following summary comments.

The rise and development of modern science, according to Professor Thorson, shows that the medieval ways of thinking about the problem of the physical world and the problem of knowledge are inadequate. Yet even today the churches (both Roman Catholic and Protestant), he holds, still retain the medieval thought patterns, being either unaware of their inadequacy or choosing deliberately to ignore it. Rejecting science as an irrelevant episode in history thus becomes a perilous ecclesiastical possibility.

Thorson believes that science deals potentially with 'real truth,' part of a single fabric encompassing also the truths of the Christian religion, even though the source of the latter is revelation rather than creation. He argues that a proper epistemology of science therefore has relevance for theology. He finds in Michael Polanyi's approach to epistemology "an essentially biblical" emphasis on the role of commitment in knowledge, rather than a final or anticipative expression of subjectivism, despair, and scepticism. The medieval notion that scientific theories merely "save the appearances" reappears in positivist philosophy (Ernst Mach, for example, says that scientific theories are merely convenient descriptions of the facts, and have no other significance). For Thorson, as for Polanyi, this is a symptom of modern man's loss of confidence in the value or reality of scientific truth; such loss of confidence he considers unfortunate and unnecessary, since he insists that "scientific truth is *real truth.*" Yet he points out that the scope of scientific truth is of course deliberately limited by the scientific *intention* and by the nature of scientific methods of investigation, which can recognize as significant only patterns of causal relationship (on the idea of the limitation of science by intentionality and method, see John Macmurray, *Religion, Art, and Science,* Liverpool, Liverpool University Press, 1961).

Thorson agrees that scientific knowledge is indeed subject to falsification, revision, and reinterpretation, but he holds that the significant fact about this process is that from it there emerges a body of knowledge that grows in substance, coherence and generality. He asserts that true knowledge survives this process and our confidence and understanding of it grow thereby.

Thorson takes the view that Christian theology is a rational construct in much the same way as scientific theory. He distinguishes, however, between *theology* and God's *revelation* (in Christ or in Scripture); the latter he considers the source of empirical reality from which theology is properly to be constructed. Truth is an intrinsic property of reality itself; but Thorson argues that it becomes a property of knowledge only in the process of commitment and responsible action, and the ongoing manifestation of reality which results from that.

Thorson affirms that we can know universally valid truth, and that this knowledge can (and should) be stated in rational terms. He finds in the eternal God Himself the continuing guarantee of that universal validity. He views Christian theology properly based on the Word of God like a reasonably mature and complete scientific theory; in principle its assertions are open to falsification, while in practice it exhibits universal validity and durable stability. To assert that our own knowledge is coextensive with a faithful representation of truth involves a responsible and intelligent commitment, that is, an act of faith. Readers familiar with Polanyi's analysis of the epistemology of science will find here its analogous application to theology.

The implication here seems to be that Christian theology retains the *goal* of faithful representation of objective reality in intellectual terms, but must renounce indubitable and rational certainty as a medieval mistake and intolerable philosophical burden. Ultimately the faith by which the Christian lives is rooted for Thorson not in divine propositional revelation but in the character and work of God. As an alternative to a divine revelation of unshakable truths he affirms a revelation of God's nature and work "in Christ and in Scripture as the Word of God."

In the theology of the recent past the correlation of God's personal confrontation and inner faith has yielded to increasing scepticism. Thorson, by contrast, insists that both scientific and theological knowledge are sustained by faith in the Other, in accord with the universal necessity of responsible faith directed toward the object of knowledge. In brief, one cannot have knowledge of the truth without responsible commitment to what one believes to be true. True knowledge of God and of His creation—theological and scientific knowledge—is manifest as true by acts, choices, and changes in the history of the world, or it will not be manifest at all, Thorson contends.

In a volume of this kind theological excursus is more a background than a forefront discussion. We should note therefore that in these arguments Thorson does not claim to present a complete understanding of theology. He is using scientific knowledge as a paradigm of theological knowledge, but that paradigm he readily acknowledges to be incomplete. In particular, he does not presume to present here a complete or even adequate view of the doctrines of Scripture or of revelation in general. Thus his views need not be considered final, except for the insistence on the fundamental parallel between scientific and religious knowledge.

Professor Clark's view differs notably with many of these emphases. He does not touch upon certain of the theological aspects because this symposium was intended to focus on empirical scientific concerns; those familiar with Dr. Clark's other writings know well that he does not view theology within this category. In numerous of his books Clark insists that faith must be answerable to reason precisely because the Reason, or Logos, of God is the supportive center of the universe. But what Thorson considers a positive biblical conclusion, namely that knowledge of truth is impossible without responsible commitment, Clark considers an unwitting invitation to scepticism.

The two chapters therefore present a contrast between divergent philosophies of science. Dr. Thorson's view descends from Aristotle and Newton. They hold that the laws of physics are fixed, unchangeable, absolute truths based on experimentation. Around the beginning of this century W. I. Clifford, Karl Pearson, and, a little later, the Chicago biologist A. J. Carlson promulgated this view in their attack on Christianity.

Dr. Clark's quite different view derives from Plato: science is always tentative and always changing. In modern times Ernst Mach broke with Newtonianism and anticipated further developments; Einstein stated the position succinctly; Henri Poincaré and Percy Bridgman of Harvard worked it out in considerable detail. Although the nonscientific general public has long regarded science with divine awe, today even these laymen recognize, to some extent, the basic and all encompassing revolution that leaves no law of physics fixed and absolute. Thus Clark insists that every law of physics—if regarded as a description of natural processes—is false. From this he derives the conclusion that science is no logical threat to Christianity.

Clark's aim is to defend absolute, fixed truth against any basic relativism. Yet this is not something that science can do, he insists, since scientific laws are constantly changing. The Newtonian synthesis, he observes, was exploded along with the atom; much that Clark was taught in college physics classes has changed, and the end of change is not yet.

Clark is not on this account hostile to science; he is much in favor of basic research. But he cannot accept the argument that Christians should support "pure science" as a bulwark of Christianity. Christianity was propagated and it overthrew the pagan civilization of Rome, he observes, without supporting or even knowing the basic research of the twentieth century; its survival into the future does not depend on any vindication of the truth of science. Induction and description never attain universality nor fixed truth. Anything less than fixed truth can hardly serve as a bulwark of Christianity. In fact, anything less would sooner or later erode Christianity. Precisely because revealed religion affords certain fixed truths and changeless norms—which are just what empirical science cannot supply—its transcendent superiority is evident.

From the outset of the symposium the reader will be challenged by equally interesting and important differences. In the opening essay by Professor Boyd, the alert reader will note that the distinguished space scientist thinks that Genesis 1 is concerned wholly with our own planet and its very local heavens. Some interpreters of Genesis find quite impossible the thesis that the creation account refers only to our own planet, since both Gen. 1:16 and the fact of light before the sun (Gen. 1:3) in distinction from Gen. 1:14) seem to them to imply other galaxies and the vast universe that science now recognizes. Dr. Boyd's essay contemplates the staggering immensity of this enormous universe, whose origin and all whose events, in conformity with the New Testament, he considers by implication to be the work of God. No one can miss the awe with which he meditates on the vast galaxies and on life that inhabits what some would now dismiss as a humdrum planet on the outskirts of a quite ordinary galaxy.

But I shall forego further comment about this and other essays. What is of supreme significance about this symposium is that men of devout evangelical commitment insist that the world of modern scientific learning is by no means the entire or even the most decisive realm of reality, critically important as it is. And for no generation more than for ours, they all agree, has the dialogue over Christian values and scientific commitments become so urgent.

CARL F. H. HENRY

HORIZONS
OF SCIENCE

1

The Space Sciences

R. L. F. BOYD

"He made the stars also." The final clause of Gen. 1:16 plants on the first page of the Bible an ensign of glory and crisis. This almost throwaway line establishes the anthropocentric perspective of all that follows. The sun and moon get five verses. They have a job to do for the *imago dei* so soon to appear. They will mark his seasons, days and years. They will "declare the glory of God" (Ps. 19:1, KJV). The sun will rule by day and the moon by night, as they clearly do, but not the stars. They are just there, each called forth nightly by name "and because He is strong in power not one is missing" (Isa. 40:26, RSV). So much for astrology.

Robert L. F. Boyd, an internationally known space scientist, has been Professor of Physics in the University of London since 1962 and director of Mullard Space Science Laboratory of the Department of Physics and Astronomy at University College, London, since 1965. He was created Order of the British Empire in 1972. He is co-editor (with Seaton and Massey) of *Rocket Exploration of the Upper Atmosphere* (1954, Russian translation 1957) and (with H. S. W. Massey) of *The Upper Atmosphere* (1958), and author of *Space Research by Rocket and Satellite* (1960, Spanish and Swedish translations 1962), *Can God Be Known?* (1967), and *Space Physics* (1975, Japanese translation 1976). He is a Fellow of the Royal Society, Fellow of the Institute of Physics, Fellow (and sometime Vice President) of the Royal Astronomical Society and former president of the Victoria Institute. He is a member of the Science Consultative Group of British Broadcasting Corporation and frequently broadcasts on science and religion.

INTRODUCTION

Even if we limit the scriptural use of *kokab* (Heb. star) or *aster* (Gk. star) to celestial points of light visible to the unaided eye, there are about 10^4 (or ten thousand) of them and the distance to the nearest is 2×10^{18} (or two million million million) times the stature of a man. Among them, our sun is third rate, and if we extend the use of the Hebrew and Greek words to objects of the same kind detectable only with instrumental aids or, where obscured, deducible indirectly from the nexus of observations, we find in our little galaxy alone two hundred-thousand-million (2×10^{11}). Light from the farthest of these takes a hundred millenia to reach us, yet on a cosmic scale all of this is so parochial as to be totally trivial. The universe contains whole galaxies in numbers as prodigal as their individual stellar content— a hundred-thousand-million at least—making the number of stars around 10^{22}—as many as there are atoms in a gram of iron.

Light from the farthest of these galaxies takes ten thousand million years or so to reach us, which is about twice the age of the earth and half the probable age of the universe.

"When I look at thy heavens, the work of thy fingers, the moon and the stars which thou hast established; what is man that thou art mindful of him?" (Ps. 8:3, RSV). Thus the Psalmist himself expresses astonishment, now multiplied beyond comprehension. The scale, age, history and character of the universe as we know it would surely have overwhelmed his spirit as it has many a person's since. To the Queen of Sheba, "The half was not told" (1 Kings 10:7, RSV), but less than one part in a billion billion was shown to the Psalmist. Never has the "scandal of particularity" been more apparent than it is today.

We can analyse our bewilderment by breaking it down in the following way:

- The size of the universe.
- The age of the universe.
- Relativity and the mysterious interrelationship between space and time.
- Sentience in the universe.
- God's relationship to the whole.
- Miracle and prayer.
- Eschatology.

Of course we cannot hope to deal with any of this adequately or, with that finite collection of neurones we call our minds, we cannot hope to comprehend the inscrutable mystery of being or to penetrate the *event horizon* before the primeval fireball, beyond the radius at which galactic recession velocities approach the speed of light or within the gravitational abyss of the Black Hole. But too easily the blazing glory of the Celestial Burning Bush unshoes us in a pantheistic adoration. A religious worshiping attitude is far from uncommon in the higher echelons of physical science, but how shall they and we avoid Christ's tender criticism of the Samaritans, "You worship what you do not know" (John 4:22, RSV)?

Even if they cannot be solved—and no explanation is ever ultimate —the problems must be faced squarely and the *Weltanshauung* must embrace—not violate—them, though they be more mysterious than a woman. What follows is an effort to glimpse the mystery; the embrace is a personal matter.

THE SIZE OF THE UNIVERSE

The immensity of the cosmos implies for the ordinary Christian's concept of God, not to mention for the abysmal caricature of that concept which circulates among non-Christians, a God of inconceivable greatness. The aptness of the title of J. B. Phillips's little book, *Your God Is Too Small,*[1] is apparent from any serious contemplation of the few figures quoted above. "Behold," said Solomon, "heaven and the highest heaven cannot contain thee" (1 Kings 8:27, RSV). "Whither," said the Psalmist, "shall I flee from thy presence? If I ascend to heaven thou art there! If I make my bed in Sheol, thou art there!" (Ps. 139:7–8, RSV).

The theism of the Bible considers a God who is the continual Giver of the whole, "upholding the Universe by his word of power" (Heb. 1:3, RSV). "In Him all things hold together" (Col. 1:17, RSV). He is not like Baal, a denizen of his world who may be "gone aside" or "on a journey" or "asleep" (1 Kings 18:27, RSV). The sunrise, the rain, the stellar procession, the grass, the animals are His doing: "Thou sendest forth thy Spirit; they are created" (Ps. 104:30, RSV). (Hebrew *Bara* as in chapters 1 and 2 of Genesis and frequently in Isaiah.) Yet God is not portrayed as "out there" or beyond some spatial boundary, as

Psalm 139 makes clear: "If I take the wings of the morning and dwell in the uttermost parts of the sea, even there thy hand shall lead me and thy right hand shall hold me" (Ps. 139:9–10, RSV).

Whatever else is implied by so incomparable and eternal a "weight of glory" (2 Cor. 4:17, KJV), it means that God is quite unlimited by physical law. Rather, He is the Giver of it. It is the description of His activity, the insight into the reliability of His actions, the consistency of His character. Whatever else is, however vast, God is, and that which is not God is His creation, not of necessity but contingent upon His will.

A second implication for the Christian of the vastness of the Universe would seem to be that God, at any rate, is not impressed by sheer size. Remember the sparrows (Matt. 10:29, RSV). "How unsearchable are His judgements and how inscrutable his ways . . . for from him and through him and to him are all things" (Rom. 11:33, 36, RSV). It may well be that it required a universe as vast as this for God to have a workshop in which He could make man and transform him into the "image of his Son" (Rom. 8:29, RSV). The process of evolution by which over a period of half the age of the earth man has, it would seem probable, been formed from the dust, is a process dependent upon mutations. That process may have been largely brought about by a flux of cosmic rays sufficient to yield this development within the life of a star and its planets but not so large as to fatally disrupt the genetic helix. What size of universe is needed to yield that flux we do not know, but at least it has been pointed out that we are only here to speculate like this because the flux is right, and it has been seriously suggested that there may even exist a whole spectrum of universes, with ours alone subject to study because it alone is the right size to evolve the student. In saying this I must emphasize that I mean universe not galaxy, the whole gamut of 10^{22} stars. Should it turn out that another factor of 10^{11} (say) is needed, the acclamation "How great Thou art!" would be still more imperiously demanded.

It need hardly be said, and yet perhaps it must, that in the context of a universe the proportions of ours, space travel is nothing. It is like walking around one's house and imagining one is exploring distant lands and meeting primitive tribes. The chance of unexpectedly encountering an aborigine in one's home is incomparably higher than that of meeting a creature from another world. That is not to say that such creatures (note the word) do not exist. I cannot doubt that among 10^{22} stars, God has some other populated systems, though populated by what I have no idea. Even in Scripture no doubt is left that there are celestial beings that serve Him. There may be reason to think that a relatively small fraction of stars can retain stable and suitable planetary systems long enough for extensive biological evolution to take place, while certainly some whole galaxies may be inhospitable. Even if the fraction is one in a billion, a billion stars remain potential life spawners. But if space encounter is practically inconceivable, space communication, though still in my view improbable for our species, remains a slim possibility.

THE AGE OF THE UNIVERSE

It is impossible to divorce the age of the universe from considerations of its size. The discovery of an all-pervasive thermal flux corresponding to a temperature of about 3 K (3 degrees above absolute zero) has found no convincing explanation other than that the history of the universe, as we know it at present, started some twenty billion years ago in what is called the Big Bang or Primeval Fire Ball. If this is the case, the most distant galaxies cannot be more than about 20 billion light years away and the universe, at least as far as its content is concerned, is finite in size and age. Of course, all this implies certain eminently reasonable beliefs (belief is reasonable when it is the appropriate response to the weight of evidence) about the uniformity of nature. In particular, it implies that natural laws known here and now apply equally to distant epochs, and cosmologists by no means agree on how valid this assumption is. It is not unreasonable to suppose that some of the fundamental constants of nature may be linked to the (changing) size of the universe. Mach's principle, which relates the inertial properties of each piece of matter to the matter in the universe as a whole and which played a significant part in Einstein's thinking, points to the importance of at least examining a possible temporal variation of the gravitational constant. We shall see later that time and space are related to a degree beyond that obviously necessitated by a finite velocity of light. They are so inextricably bound, in fact, that they must be considered as one entity.

Although the start of the universe begins to look like a datable event, I do not think it need be thought to have special theological significance. For one thing, it may have been preceded (though the term itself is not wholly unambiguous) by an infinite succession of expansions and contractions and may be succeeded by the same movements. The theistic assertion that the cosmos is contingent upon God, that He created (creates) it (even in its chaotic characteristics), is not a temporal priority but one of status. What it is at any moment, it is by His word of power, and if in its own derivative time scale that word has created from $t = -\infty$ to $t = +\infty$, neither deism nor dualism nor pantheism is here implied.

A good deal of nonsense has been written about the tendency of entropy (disorder) to increase in the universe and the implication that this must have for a creative (in the theistic sense) event. Two things must be said about this. First, the universe is, by definition, but one, as far as we observers are concerned. Thus, any extrapolation from the thermodynamics of closed systems in the laboratory to the thermodynamics of a possibly oscillatory universe must be treated with great caution. Second, and more importantly, theistic creation is, as we have seen, a continuing relationship between God and His world, not a mere event at $t = 0$. A continuous increase in entropy is as much God given as would be an initial minimum entropy condition. In any case, the main lessons to be learned from the age of the universe are the same as those from its extent. Our concept of God must be large enough to see Him as the eternal Giver of space–time. I use the word *eternal* here not to imply that space–time has always been given in the sense that $t \to -\infty$, but that God's being is always other, beyond, prior. We have no reason (of course) to suppose that these riches mean more to Him than "one sinner that repents" (Luke 15:7, RSV), "for as the heavens are higher than the Earth, so are my ways than your ways and my thoughts than your thoughts" (Isa. 55:9, RSV).

RELATIVITY

A discussion of space and time on a cosmic scale leads inevitably to the insights of Einstein. It is not, of course, that Special Relativity places any constraint upon God. (General Relativity, being a replacement of dynamics by geometry, though revolutionary enough and a better model of nature than Newtonian mechanics, does not, I think, have the same dramatic impact on our understanding of the world.) Any constraint must be of His own making and voluntary acceptance. But Special Relativity provides a warning against making meaningless statements or entering into meaningless theological debate. Perhaps the most common error of this kind is natural enough to our minds, linked as our consciousness is to the stream of time. Having recognized that biblical theism requires that God be, not localized in space, but other than, and in some nonspatial sense beyond, it, the Christian readily falls into the trap of thinking that somehow God's relationship to time is different. Space and all that it contains is His doing, His making, but what of time? Surely for Him, too, time passes, though a thousand years be as a day. But this will not do. God inhabits no otherwise given time but Eternity—a characteristic of Himself, the *I am*. If this means that God is unimaginable, should that surprise us? The imaginable turns out all too often to be the familiar or even banal. It is not our main concern to imagine God but to hear his Word and so to live (Matt. 4:4, RSV).

The relativity of simultaneity is perhaps the most startling and significant insight of relevance. Put simply, this aspect of relativity refers to the fact that two events which to one observer occur one before the other but separated in space, to another observer moving with respect to the first may occur in the reverse order and be separated by a different distance. It is a special and particularly dramatic case of the fact that time and space have some degree of interchangeability, though the exchange rate does involve the imaginary number $(-1)^{1/2}$.

Now, this aspect of relativity requires that we approach such doctrines as "Before they call, I will answer" (Isa. 65:24, RSV) and Predestination with a reverent humility. To say that God hears my prayer at the instant I utter it, is true to the Bible (but notice "Before" in the foregoing reference) and theologically valid, but to base any argument upon whether He hears my prayer before that of a friend on the other side of the world, who only prayed after he heard by telephone that I had done so, might well be found on analysis to involve an implicit statement about God's velocity with respect to the earth—clearly impious nonsense.

SENTIENCE IN THE UNIVERSE

I have known the question, Is there intelligent life on other planets? to be parried by the substitution of the words "this planet" for "other planets." Certainly the Bible gives us no encouragement as a species to pride ourselves on our wisdom. The importance of the question depends a good deal on what we mean by intelligence. To discover life of any kind elsewhere would be the scientific achievement of the epoch. To discover intelligence, though improbable because of sheer distance, would be even more exciting, awesome and perhaps even dangerous. But for the Christian, the important questions arise in connection with the possible existence in the past, present or future, here or elsewhere, of other self-recognizing creatures who can also relate to God in a conscious, free manner. Perhaps the experiments on teaching monkeys language may soon include Sunday school for them! If so, the results will be interesting, possibly even challenging. But at the moment we can only speculate on the implications and theological significance of any contact with extraterrestrial beings.

I have introduced the work on monkeys and language (I might also have cited studies on the ability of porpoises to grasp abstract ideas such as the rewardability of their inventing a *new* trick) because I think it brings a rather hypothetical situation, that of the existence of mental capacities not utterly incommensurate with our own, literally down to earth. Encountering travelers from space or visiting other such beings is highly improbable, as we have seen, not because we do not expect them to be there, but because getting from here to there or there to here is almost unimaginably difficult, especially when we do not know where "there" is. But of course the real shock to our thinking comes with the idea that "they" too might be religious and that religious conciousness might even be acquired by "purely natu-ral" processes, as in my hypothetical Sunday school for monkeys. But the problem here is, at least in part, that "purely natural" is a deistic or even dualistic idea, or at worst a radically secular notion that natural events and processes are autonomous. It implies that pro-cesses occur which are not ultimately contingent upon God.

Most Christians, I imagine, would claim that man is a "special creation" of God; indeed, that is the way I interpret the Genesis account. But the noun *creation* and the adjective *special* both need very careful consideration. There is no doubt that a wide variety of meanings is given to the Genesis creation account by Christians equally devout and equally devoted to Holy Scripture as God's word.

It seems to me that even at so early a time as the book of Job recounts, the uniqueness of man was not thought to be in a once-and-for-all quickening of dust, for Elihu says to Job, "I too was formed from a piece of clay" (Job 33:6, RSV). Indeed, the whole tenor of Scripture in referring to man as a creature of dust is to emphasize his humble origin, frail substance and mortal corruption. In Ecclesiastes, the "Preacher" therefore expresses half the truth when he writes that "the fate of the sons of men and the fate of the beasts is the same; as one dies, so dies the other. They all have the same breath, and man has no advantage over the beasts. . . . all go to one place; all are from the dust, and all turn to dust again" (Eccles. 3:19–20, RSV). In spite of the apparent differences in the expression used for the creation of man and the animals in some translations of the first two chapters of Genesis, the Hebrew words are the same for each and the message is brutally (if the expression may be forgiven) clear. Man is consubstantial with the beasts, though made in the image of God. It is evocative to read that Christ was "born in the likeness of men" (Phil. 2:7, RSV), though we confess him as "of one substance with the Father."[2]

In what then shall we say the *imago dei* consists? Creativity may be relevant, but hominds (pre-*sapiens* species of the genus *homo*) made tools, and porpoises can invent tricks and monkeys sentences (even if only in sign language). It is tempting to see the likeness to God in some aspect of self-expression and communication in harmony with the beginning of St. John's gospel. Mere communication with others of the same species is an inadequate criterion. Many creatures do that. It may be that the ability to recognize one's self in the sense of the Cartesian *cogito ergo sum* and to recognize other selves in a way that makes for an intercourse of ideas is some characterizing part of the image. I am inclined, however, with Derek Kidner[3] to see the *most* characteristic aspect of the likeness as *that* most distinctive attribute of God—Love *(agape)*, self-creating, self-giving love of another being whose autonomy is recognized. *That* aspect of God's image was surely lost and is slowly and often painfully regained "from the Lord who is the Spirit" as "we all with unveiled face, reflecting (margin) the glory of the Lord, are being changed into his likeness. . . ." (2 Cor. 3:18, RSV).

Now if I were to meet someone from outer space who loved like that, I would recognize a special creation in the same sense as I recognize one in Adam; a creature in God's image, no matter how many eyes or legs he or she had. Such love cannot be intransitive. It must flow in order to be. (Perhaps this can illuminate a little the ineffable mystery of the Trinity.) I would humbly expect such a creature to have a conscious relationship to the Eternal Love and probably to other creatures, since, presumably, it is not good for a creature in God's image to be alone.

It is usual at this point in the discussion of hypothetical, other-worldly denizens, if not before, for someone to raise questions relating to the Fall, Incarnation, Redemption and so on. The questions are often not well articulated, but there can be no doubt that, given the plausibility of other God-knowing creatures, many Christians feel uneasy, or at least curious, about the possible or likely history of such creatures, both as a species and as individuals. Though the possibility of extraterrestrial life brings the problem home to us, we should also recognize that, as in the case of educating monkeys, it could be a terrestrial problem at a different epoch. If we set aside for the moment eschatological considerations, the possibility of life in the solar system a million years hence, whether genetically related to us or not, raises the same kind of speculation as does life now in another galaxy megaparsecs away. (One parsec = 3.3 light years.) It would, of course, be immensely intriguing to learn of or encounter such creatures and it might well dispel some agnosticism. But my own attitude is to suppress speculation as futile for much the same reason as Hamlet's famous advice: "There are more things in Heaven and Earth Horatio than are dreamt of in your philosophy."[4] One may sketch an artist's impression of a Martian sparrow with eyes on the end of stalks, but in fact we have not the faintest idea what physical form life might take elsewhere in the universe, much less what spiritual nature.

Implicit in all I have said is the idea, consistent with our admittedly very incomplete and quite inadequate understanding of the history of life on this planet, that life will arise and evolve wherever conditions are "suitable." That statement is almost tautological, but it implies for the theist a recognition implied also by the scientist's belief in the uniformity of nature, namely, that God acts elsewhere as He does here; a fact that is well established when it comes to the behavior of (say) iron atoms on earth and in (say) a star in another galaxy where their varying characteristics are identical. We have already noted that "suitable" conditions may be expected on a copious scale.

Science fiction and the lunatic, or merely dishonest, fringes of science journalism commonly portray celestial creatures as having reached a high degree of civilization and as possessing a wide variety of moral, amoral or, to us, immoral attitudes. The same kind of idea can, as we have said, be applied to the future of our own planet, with bioengineering generating nightmares or, much more rarely, utopias, on a scale limited only by the ingenuity or sickness of the author's mind. My own attitude to the possibility of this kind of thing either here or elsewhere is strongly qualified by the theistic conviction that all that is, all that happens, all that ever will be, is God's making, God's doing. Not only is God still on the throne but unless he was, nothing would continue to be. Any creaturely rebellion is only possible because of a derivative freedom and can only persist as long as that creature with his freedom exists. Moreover, it is all too evident that we ourselves may make this planet uninhabitable.

GOD'S RELATIONSHIP TO THE WHOLE

We have outlined some of the extraordinary facts and related ideas that arise in space science, astronomy and cosmology which affect our Christian view of the universe in one way or another. The prevailing impression of most of us must be, now more than ever, that our concept of God is too small. To recognize that God must be great enough to be the eternal and continuous giver of space–time, of every subatomic entity and of every event in which any entity takes part, poses awesome questions of which the most insistent is probably, Why do I claim that He is and, if He is, that He is concerned with man and with me?

Formally, the answer to perplexity about the immensity of the universe and the associated task of creating and sustaining it is first, that God has to be big enough for the task. The evidence that He is big enough is, in part, that the task is performed. No real relief can come to any but the naïve by accepting the universe without a gasp of astonishment and then refusing a God big enough to be responsible. If it is true, and I think it is, that the universe (it begs the question to say the Creation) does not logically demand a Creator, in spite of Paley and all the other apostles of the argument from design, it is equally true that the breathtaking wonder of being, that anything is, that so vast (in time and space) and complex a universe exists, is no less mind boggling, if no more, than that the Creator exists. In fact the theistic idea stands or falls on quite other evidence than the nature and existence of the universe. For me, at any rate, that evidence is Jesus. I would not expect the existence of a Supreme Personality to be derivable by any kind of scientific study any more than a scientific study of an uncommunicating human being could show that he thinks of himself in the *cogito ergo sum* way, or has any of the other characteristics that I tacitly take to be associated with my selfhood and evidence for my personal existence. If Christian theism is true, it has to be a God-revealed truth.

The central question is have we this revelation? Has God spoken? Now I am, of course, well aware of the objections the logical positivists raise when they claim that such questions are meaningless. But I am not too worried because, taken to its logical conclusion, their method undermines their own falsifiability presupposition. I believe that other self-knowing personalities exist and so (I believe!) does nearly everyone. But I doubt whether it can be proved to the satisfaction of some philosophers; indeed, to hear some behaviorists talk, my recognition of myself is some sort of irrelevant delusion.

The arguments in support of divine revelation have been set out endlessly, sometimes avoiding, sometimes embracing, the perils of subjectivism. I will not attempt to summarize them here. I note however that part of the business of science is to make sense of nature, and my own acceptance of Christian theism is in part because it, though not logically demanded by empirical considerations, makes sense of human history, especially Jewish history. It makes sense of ethical imperatives, of self-sacrificing love of the unlovely, of unemotional, but all the more dramatic, personal conversion, and so forth, but above all it makes sense of Jesus from Nazareth. When all is said and done, when all the evidence of the enthralled lives, nobility, conviction and martyrdom of the first followers of Christ is weighed, I am forced to ask what was it that so biased them in favor of Him and to come to St. Paul's, no doubt at one time unwilling, conclusion: "God was in Christ reconciling the world to himself." (2 Cor. 5:19, RSV). In St. John's record of Jesus' reply to the perplexed Philip, "He who has seen me has seen the Father" (John 14:9, RSV), I hear the ring of truth.

I agree that for St. Paul God was an accepted fact and Christ was the holy title that, under the weight of evidence and the blinding light of experience, he had to ascribe to Jesus. I agree that for Philip God was an undebated *a priori* and Jesus an adored friend and the connection had but to be made. But for me the fact that God is, that He is concerned with me, that He makes His sun rise and sends rain—in short the theistic assertion—rests on the fact of Christ as the cornerstone, whatever superstructure may help to bear the load.

Probably both Paul's and Philip's personal conceptions of God as Creator and Sustainer of the physical world were as inadequate, myopic even, as their knowledge of that world. But no one can deny that the prophets from Isaiah to St. John the theologian stretched language as far as they could to express the supreme, transcendent, greatness of the self-revealed God. If our concept of God is too small, it is not the fault of the Bible.

If the first part of the answer to our perplexity over the immensity of the universe and our microscopic proportions is that our God is big enough to concern Himself with elementary particles and with men, the second part is, as I noted earlier, that God may be much less impressed with great distances, long times and huge numbers than we are. In fact the *imago dei* may well be supremely important to Him and may even be the occasion of the whole universe. We who "are like grasshoppers" may well feel overwhelmed by the unnumbered multitudes of humans, and we have no idea whether the "image" exists elsewhere in space–time. But "he who sits above the circle of the Earth . . . who stretches out the heavens like a curtain" (Isa. 40:22, RSV) may be expected to see things in another perspective and to have His own definitive values. The divine love for the world is indeed the message of the incarnation: "I will send my beloved son; it may be they will respect him." (Luke 20:13, RSV). Only *hubris* can make us think ourselves worthy of His consideration.

The enormous extent of space–time is perhaps the most widespread problem posed for Christian theism by our current understanding of the universe. Another, more insistent, difficulty, not to be resolved by a recognition that God is far greater than we think, is presented by the character of natural law. By law of nature we imply, not of course a prescriptive edict, but a verifiable formula that gives an adequate account of the behavior of nature as we observe it. Though the laws are of course far from complete, their rigorous application to our observations enables us to trace the geological history of the earth, the probable history of the moon, planets and solar system as a whole, the evolution of the sun and other main sequence (neither pathological nor geriatric) stars, some plausible outline of galactic evolution and the gross history of matter and energy in the universe back to within three quarters of a million years of its beginning. The 3 K isotropic microwave radiation referred to earlier appears to have arisen at this time when the temperature was about 3000 K and the whole thing a great deal smaller than it is at present. The microwave photons we observe made their last encounter with matter, hot electrons, at this time and in a sense it is these electrons we "see." The photons have been traveling ever since ($\sim 2 \times 10^{10}$ years) and have been doppler shifted by the expansion of the universe by a factor of 1000 in wavelength. Even before the end of the 700,000 year infancy of the cosmos we can distinguish evidences of its history from the relative amounts of hydrogen and helium and relative paucity of heavier elements which (on the thereby strengthened presupposition that the laws of physics then were much as they are today) enables us to get a good idea of the first twenty minutes of the life of the cosmos and which points to an initial "Hot Big Bang" having a density around 10^{14} gm cm^{-3} (not very different from the density of the nuclei of atoms) and a temperature of over 10^{12} K.

The overwhelming majority of reasonably mature scientists see this history as consistent with a wholly law-abiding nature. Newton, who was something of a deist in thinking of nature as a rather autonomous artefact of God, still introduced God during cosmic history to keep the system in adjustment. It was the success of Laplace in his more advanced mathematical model of the solar system which led to his famous remark to Napoleon about the absence of God from his book: "I had no need of that hypothesis." Laplace was not thereby adopting an atheistic stance. He was taking the attitude we almost all take today. I have hinted several times that biblical theism knows nothing of deistically autonomous matter, recalcitrant, chaotic, even evil until subdued, ordered and sanctified by God. That is a Greek idea and if St. Paul's doctrine of the "flesh" seems sometimes to reflect it, that misinterpretation is given the lie by his (and the other New Testament writers') declaration of the Incarnation: sinful flesh yes; evil matter no.

I have neither the task of nor the competence to carry this common scientific thinking on through biology to the appearance of mind, self-consciousness, society and ethical responsibility. Here more people, perhaps particularly in America rather than in Europe, will differ from me. I can only in honesty assert that I see the whole process from Big Bang (or even from an endless succession of expansions and contractions) to the occurrence of *homo religiensis* as wholly natural and as, in principle, a proper realm for humble scientific study. But equally, more importantly and, I believe, biblically, I see the whole process from beginning to end as the Act of God. To the insurance companies an Act of God may be the unpredictable, but to the Old Testament writers and to the Christian today it is the very reliability and constancy of nature—the procession of the stars, the recurrence of the seasons, the sins of the fathers visited upon the children, those things that we see as the natural outcome of events, that declare the glory, trustworthiness, unchangeable character of *Jahweh,* that mark him off from the capricious gods of the nations.

Now, as I see it, the difficulty in this emphasis on God's universal involvement arises from the problem of pain and evil. The Bible is pretty uncompromising here. "Does evil befall a city unless the Lord has done it" (Amos 3:6, RSV), cries Amos. "I form light and create darkness, I make weal and create woe, I am the Lord, who do all these things," teaches Isaiah (45:7, RSV). (Note the use of *Bara,* create, for the negative qualities darkness and woe.) St. Paul's and the Old Testament prophets' doctrine on the right of the divine Potter (Isa. 64:8; Jer. 18; Rom. 9:21, RSV) has something of the same tension. Whatever may be the correct translation of Bildad's remark, "His hand hath formed the crooked serpent" (Job 26:13, KJV), Gen. 3:1 makes clear that nothing is gained by denying that the ultimate responsibility for evil is God's except an unbiblical and terrifying dualism. Satan is a creature and his and our evil is only possible because in incomprehendable humility (and dare I say, love?) God creates and sustains us free to choose rebellion, holds the iron rigid and the cross upright as we impale and hang His Son.

I sometimes think that the Christian faith is easier for scientists. They know they do not really understand but merely picture to themselves the behavior of God's world by insubstantial images of an ever elusive reality. I draw attention to the problem of evil in the universe and to that of pain, and to that of waste, which is not evidently the result of creaturely wrong choosing, because our faith can only be weakened by not facing it. I am well aware that the reddened tooth and claw and the quivering flesh are a more insistent problem for the zoologist. To me it seems that there are some problems which are resolved not solely by explanation but also by sympathy, in the literal sense of "suffering together with." Elsewhere I have put it like this with reference to the cross:

> . . . I see unconquered love,
> Stretched in the awful tension of the tree,
> Refuse the scornful challenge to remove,
> And choose to stay transfixed there for me . . .
> Your love has won. . . .[5]

If you believe that God's choice was unconquerable love, it may not help you to understand why there is pain and evil, but it may do far more to help you accept it than any number of arguments about the existence of good requiring the possibility of evil. It always seems strange to me that it is the atheist who curses God most.

In what I have just said I have implied that the freedom to play with the stuff of God's world (incidentally an argument against pantheism) for good or ill is part of God's creative giving. I will not pursue this important idea further as it is more relevant to other essays, I will remark, however, that those who concern themselves with the potentiality of extraterrestrial civilizations, while sometimes considering automatons, for the most part tacitly assume that the creatures of space will experience the same sense of free will and will exercise it as creatively as we do.

Our discussion of the history of the universe and the existence of pain and evil demands some reference to the opening chapters of the Bible. The ideas of some students of so-called creation research are not so much unscientific as they are untheistic (some of them indeed are unscientific in the sense that they will not stand up to a detailed quantitative analysis of their implications. The hypothesis of "a great vapour canopy surrounding the Earth"[6] as the cause of the deluge would be a case in point, since the dynamical stability of the envisaged quantity of matter poses insoluble problems for the hypothesis. We have already seen that the Bible claims that God's creative activity is continuous and certainly no *ex nihilo* situation is necessarily implied, for not infrequently the source is given.

Moreover as we saw at the start the creation narrative is thoroughly anthropocentric. I take it, therefore, that the account in the first chapter of Genesis is intended, not to discuss the primeval fireball or the solar nebula, but to address itself to this little earth and its local heavens—the habitat prepared for man. It is a history which was full of meaning to those who first received it and which is still quite undated by the advance of science, the story of the preparation of the world from the point of view of a hypothetical observer here.

We start with a flooded and featureless globe in darkness. The fog thins and light penetrates. The humidity falls and the waters of the seas and of the clouds are separated. The lands appear and with them, vegetation. The skies clear to reveal the celestial bodies. The waters swarm with reptiles and birds and eventually the cattle arrive (from the ground, as calves and sheep assuredly and obviously still do). The same is true for man and his mate.

Sublime, eternally valid, gloriously free from pantheism or paganism; here is an account which seems rightly to demand the acclamation Herod usurped: "The voice of . . . God, and not of man!" (Acts 12:22, RSV).

The story of the ensuing chapters is not strictly a matter within the scope of this essay except in so far as the doctrine of the Fall of man impinges on creation, especially in St. Paul's teaching. We will return to this briefly under eschatology but for the present I will content myself with the recognition that whatever degree of literality or symbolism we ascribe to the account (and the style clearly changes at the end of the first chapter of Genesis). I take the Fall of man to be taught as a fact in the history of the species. This does not necessarily mean a drop in intellectual capacity (indeed, some aspects of the story would suggest the reverse), but it surely implies a changed relationship, a destroyed confidence, a broken bridge only to be rebuilt in

Christ. The particularity implied by events of such significance in the very recent life of a species perhaps a million years old is a fact that must be faced in its relevance to the future of the species and in the context of the likelihood of extraterrestial creatures such as we have already considered.

MIRACLE AND PRAYER

Two strands of our discussion converge here to require some consideration of the above topics. They are the relationship of God to His world which I have depicted as a continuous creative activity seen as natural and described by natural law, and the particularity of *homo sapiens* as being the *imago dei* though now defaced and as now the object of redemptive activity and love involving so great a mystery as the Incarnation.

The questions raised by the idea of miracle and divine response to human prayer, though not identical, are clearly related. While a materialist may be scandalized by both ideas, no full-blooded theist can reasonably doubt the possibility of either, even if his direct experience takes in neither. To the Christian, who sees God's relationship to the world in terms of biblical theism, there has never been any question as to *whether* God can work miracle or respond to prayer: The whole issue has been would he? Yet even that question is to bring the Eternal to the bar of human valuing and to ask does it seem fitting to me with my knowledge and understanding that God would depart from His normal activity as described in natural law and act differently in an interaction with our microscopic species? That He could is implied by the theistic belief in the contingency of nature. To doubt whether He would under any circumstances at all seems strange if we are prepared to concede, as our empirical response to the phenomenon of Christ, so great a wonder as that He loves the world. If our belief approximates even remotely to orthodox Christianity as enshrined (say) in John 3:16. we have already taken on board the whole crisis of particularity. If God stoops to consider this planet at all then I am already so overwhelmed with worship and wonder that the details of His interaction pose no further problem of fitness but only evoke further adoration. There is no point in straining at a gnat when one has found it imperative to swallow a camel.

Now, of course, none of this implies that God sets aside His normal procedures frivolously or frequently. I think the evidence strongly favors very rare departures from normality for very exceptional reasons such as very important encouragements of faith or authentication of servants or acts of mercy or judgment with a special message. The majority of miracles ('signs' St. John calls them), though as indubitably acts of God as the sunrise and the rain, are just as indubitably natural. I imagine too that the same is true of answers to prayer.

It seems to me also that God stoops to speak our language. He gives an empty tomb not because the resurrection of Christ (1 Cor. 15:20, RSV) is different in character from ours (in which it seems our bodies can play no essential part if only because of the famous problem of the converted cannibal who ate a missionary!) nor as if the "body celestial" incorporates the "body terrestrial" but (at least) in order that the disciples might believe. He gives an Ascension not because "the right hand of the Majesty on high" (Heb. 1:3, RSV) is above the clouds of Palestine but like the vision "on the holy mountain" and the "voice . . . borne to him by the Majestic Glory" in order that we should "have the prophetic word made more sure" (2 Pet. 1:19, RSV).

ESCHATOLOGY

The Christian doctrine of the end of human history presents us once again, as does almost every aspect of Christian teaching, with the "scandal of particularity." If God comes here in Incarnation, then answered prayer, miracle, consummated history, "heavens . . . kindled and dissolved . . . a new heavens and a new Earth" (2 Pet. 3:12–13, RSV) are all possible. Of course, we must not interpret apocalyptic language with the unimaginative literalness of naïve scientific realism. But we have here an issue that has to be faced.

Popular and often scholarly consideration conceives of our species, or extraterrestrial ones, evolving (or evolved) to an unrecognizable extent, usually with genetic engineering to speed and guide (not to say misguide) the process. Now we have already noted that our own species has not assured its own future all that well. War or pollution could end us in scenes that make the Apocalypse look pale by comparison. Or just as *homo sapiens* may well have become the *imago dei* after a million years of specific identity, so he might end eschatologically, leaving behind a mere animal (no matter how intelligent), not even a shadow of his former spiritual self.

St. Paul says, "We know that the whole creation has been groaning in travail together until now" (Rom. 8:22, RSV); and some have taught that the sin of man (or an earlier satanic Fall) marred the whole creation. Of course, there is a sense in which one blemish spoils the whole, and, in any case, the idea that physical death came in with Adam's sin is simply untenable in the light of geological evidence. God's word in Scripture and in nature complement, not contradict, each other. So the question of the corruption of myriads of extraterrestrial beings by our evil scarcely arises. However, I take the Scripture as having at least two other possible meanings for us. First, sin has spoiled the whole world for us and it can never be restored until our mortal bodies are redeemed. Second, the *imago dei* is perhaps, after all, the point of everything, no matter how many other beings there are or are not, and toward our rebirth, adoption and redemption the whole cosmos amazingly travails.

The future of this planet and the future of the universe is obscure. Whatever it is to be will be God-given, as it is now and always has been. In the meantime we "wait for a new heavens and a new Earth in which righteousness dwells" (2 Pet. 3:12–13, RSV). Whether that transpires here or elsewhere in the universe, or in some inconceivable sense "beyond," I do not greatly care, so long as I may only "be conformed to the image of His Son" (Rom. 8:29, RSV).

NOTES

1. J. B. Phillips, *Your God is Too Small* (London: Epworth Press, 1952).
2. Nicene Creed.
3. Derek Kidner, *Genesis* (London: Tyndale Press, 1967), p. 51.
4. Shakespeare, *Hamlet*, act 1, sc. 5, line 166.
5. From the writer's poem, "The Glory That Should Follow."
6. H. M. Morris, *The Bible and Modern Science* (Chicago: Moody Press, 1956), p. 75.

II

The Failure of the God-of-the-Gaps

RICHARD H. BUBE

In earlier days it was both possible and common to sustain a religious interpretation of the world by looking directly to God as the immediate Cause of those physical and biological events which man was then unable to describe or understand. In the historical context of growing scientific description of the world, this religious interpretation became known as a concern with a *God-of-the-Gaps*. The practical consequence of the view that God's existence could be proved by man's ignorance of certain key physical and biological mechanisms was that evidence for God's existence decreased as man's scientific

Richard H. Bube is Chairman of the Department of Materials Science and Engineering, and Professor of Materials Science and Electrical Engineering at Stanford University, Stanford, California. A graduate of Brown and Princeton with work in physics, Dr. Bube became associated with Stanford in 1962 after fourteen years as Senior Staff Scientist at the Radio Corporation of America laboratories in Princeton, New Jersey. He is the author of *Photoconductivity of Solids* (1960) and *Electronic Properties of Crystalline Solids* (1974), as well as of *The Encounter Between Christianity and Science* (1968) and *The Human Quest: A New Look at Science and Christian Faith* (1971). A Fellow of the American Physical Society, the American Association for the Advancement of Science, and the American Scientific Affiliation, he is editor of the *Journal ASA*, associate editor of *Annual Review of Materials Science*, on the editorial board of the Christian University Press, and a consulting editor for *Universitas*.

knowledge grew; the more man knew of the creation, the less reason he had to believe in the Creator.

It is a common belief that traditional Christianity had no alternative but to commit itself to a God-of-the-Gaps. Ralph W. Burhoe, for example, writes: "The mainstream of Christian theology properly avoided that solution [the Deist position], but, to do so, it had to separate its realm of spiritual and moral values from the scientific world view and thus remove itself to a 'God of the gaps' position in which it has been withering as the scientific world view proceeds to fill the gaps."[1]

Although they may not have actually represented the mainstream of Christian theology, enough influential Christian apologists have espoused a God-of-the-Gaps to require a careful appraisal of their position. Such consideration involves both a re-evaluation of God's relationship to the physical world in the light of biblical insights, and an understanding of the nature of scientific and alternative descriptions. Earlier in this century the choice seemed to be between God-as-an-Exile and God-of-the-Gaps; this essay claims that biblical Christianity affirms instead that God-at-the-Center best correlates with the totality of life and experience.

HISTORICAL BACKGROUND

A defense of a God-of-the-Gaps developed over many years in a series of events in which each stage seemed to follow in a direct way from the preceding. Before the sixteenth century a comfortable relationship could be maintained between contemporary religious and scientific descriptions of the world. In the Aristotelian heritage, "how" questions and "why" questions were answered in much the same way. Purpose was inherent in descriptions of events in the natural world. An acorn fell to the earth so that a new oak might arise. Rain came so that crops might grow and people might be fed. A moving wagon came to rest because a state of rest was the normal condition for a body on earth. In this context the direct participation of God in the daily affairs of life was easy to accept. God was the Good, the One who made all things to function in such a way that His purpose might be fulfilled. God's revelation was the ultimate source of wisdom, and the role of man's reason was to interpret that revelation and to apply it to daily life.

But Christian thought profoundly influenced human thinking in other ways as well. Through emphasis on the world as the creation of God the Creator, earthly things were effectively desacralized. What had been worshiped, or at least regarded with awe as representing the immediate presence of a god in the world, was now understood instead to be a created thing, event or process. The spirits of animism were exorcised; the familiar spirits of rocks, trees and rivers were stripped of reality. It was right and proper for man to find out for himself how the world functioned. Instead of attempting to settle scientific questions on the basis of conjectural reasoning or tradition alone, it now became appropriate to "think God's thoughts after Him" by attempting to understand the natural mechanisms that control the created universe.

As a consequence, Galileo, Newton and other devout scientists contributed to the development of a new scientific approach to descriptions of natural events and processes. The ranks of seventeenth and eighteenth century scientists are replete with men who were driven to understand the natural mechanisms of the world as a way of glorifying the God they served.

But as they developed the experimental method and mathematical models of the world, they introduced radical changes in the way questions about the world were answered. Now an acorn fell because of the force of gravity. Rain came because of the interaction of warm and cold air fronts, high and low pressure areas. A moving wagon with no force acting on it came to rest because of the friction of its axle. Teleological "explanations" gave way to mechanistic descriptions. Recognition of God's immediate activity in the world began to fade. The view in which evidence for the existence and activity of God depended upon His direct intervention in the world was increasingly threatened.

This threat was accentuated by philosophical conclusions that seemed to be demanded by a growing scientific understanding. Initially a special creature made in God's image to rule over the very center of the universe, man found himself displaced to a small planet somewhere in a vast machinelike universe. The concept of God was altered from that of God the Good to God the Mechanic, the Master Architect, the Clockmaker *par excellence*. If it could no longer be maintained that God was directly active in the events of this world, then it could still be maintained that God had made the clockwork that scientists were describing. But once God is relegated to the position of First Cause, His significance for the present is swallowed up by His activity in the distant past. Despite the firm intention of many theistic scientists to defend God's significance, the way they did so seemed inevitably to lead to a perspective in which God played little role in contemporary life. It was argued that what once could be found only in revelation, could now at least be duplicated by human reasoning. And if thus duplicated, why could not human reasoning finally replace revelation altogether? While revelation may have been necessary in a time of man's intellectual infancy, now that man was growing up, why could he not take over and work out his own system, without dependence on ancient mysticism?

The final blow in this sequence of events seemed to occur with the appearance of Darwin's *Origin of Species* in 1859. Although now demoted positionally in the universe and deprived of a teleological perspective on the physical world, man could still gain religious comfort from the fact that he alone was made directly in the image of God and hence in complete discontinuity with the rest of the creation. But the theory of evolution toppled this final refuge; man was, so it now appeared, nothing more than a highly developed animal. He existed without ultimate significance or enduring purpose, being presumably the end product of impersonal chance operating throughout time. In the words of Bertrand Russell, "That Man is the product of causes which had no prevision of the end they were achieving; that his origin, his growth, his hopes and fears, his loves and his beliefs, are but the outcome of accidental collocations of atoms . . . if not quite beyond dispute, are yet so nearly certain, that no philosophy which rejects them can hope to stand."[2] Born without choice, man was destined to die without choice, with no more meaning in the sequences of human history than in the dropping of a leaf in autumn.

Our concern now is to ask whether the philosophical and religious conclusions drawn from these scientific developments were actually the appropriate ones. Must one conclude that only in the shrinking areas of our persisting ignorance can modern man still hope to find evidence of God and His work in the world, and that He has been decisively squeezed out everywhere else? Are we forced to invent dichotomies in order to maintain that, although we have apparently lost our evidence for God in the physical dimension, that evidence can still be found in the spiritual, where science cannot penetrate and religion has safe anchorage? Or have these philosophical and religious conclusions no necessary connection at all with our increased scientific understanding, finding their origin, rather, in presuppositions that have always been alienated from historic Christian thought and have been simply waiting for opportunities to find suitable arguments? Can we argue that, after all, the God-of-the-Gaps is the result of a faulty understanding of the biblical revelation, and that those Christians who have fallen into this trap have failed to distinguish cultural influences from a truly biblical theology?

RESPONSES TO MAN'S INCREASING KNOWLEDGE

The application of science has staggeringly increased man's knowledge of the universe in the last few centuries. At least three basic responses have been made to this vast growth of knowledge. Two of them, one commonly made by non-Christians and one commonly made by Christians, agree in accepting a God-of-the-Gaps. Only the third view is able to integrate modern scientific understanding with a biblical perspective on the relationship between God and the universe.

The first response to man's increasing scientific knowledge of the world and of himself is to hail this knowledge as the foundation of man's liberation from the chains of ignorance. When man was ignorant of what *really* was happening in the world, he readily fell victim to myths and superstitions. Instead of exercising his reason, he was subjected to the ritual of priests. As a result, he had a false perception of reality. He fell easy prey to exploiters who made use of his weakness for religion to control him for their own benefit, and he could not develop his full potential. Our understanding of scientific mechanisms has liberated mankind from the anthropomorphic projection of a cosmic deity. Instead of being led astray and handicapped by subjective illusions, man is now able autonomously to face the reality of the world and to develop his own future.

Such a response to the growth in man's knowledge is common to many non-Christian interpreters who find a God-of-the-Gaps increasingly expendable as those gaps are closed by an extension of scientific understanding. For them, the circumstance that modern knowledge banishes a God-of-the-Gaps is a cause for rejoicing.

The second response is to regard man's increasing scientific understanding as a threat to faith in God. It is argued that there are aspects of life where only God has the power and the right to act; human encroachment on these areas recreates a modern Babel where men seek to exalt themselves and to bring God down. Christian faith rests, so it is believed, upon the existence of areas of human ignorance and impotence, areas that can properly be described only as the direct activity of God in the world, without involving any phenomena capable of natural description. It is essential that man shrink from further encroachment of this kind and, wherever possible, combat the impression that increases in scientific understanding are indeed firmly established. God is accepted as a God-of-the-Gaps; evidence for His existence is to be found primarily in human limitations. Here, the recognition that a God-of-the-Gaps is being squeezed out by modern knowledge is a cause for lamentation.

The third response to man's increasing understanding rejects the idea that God is a God-of-the-Gaps. It is God who has brought man to his new level of understanding, and it is God who can bring man the ability to make responsible decisions thrust upon him by this understanding. It is possible for Christians to accept responsibly their new position of knowledge and choice—but only with trembling, and as sustained by a vision of God as the Lord of all reality. God is to be found at the center of life, as Dietrich Bonhoeffer declared:

Religious people speak of God when human knowledge . . . has come to an end, or when human resources fail—in fact it is always the *deus ex machina* that they bring on to the scene, either for the apparent solution of insoluble problems, or as strength in human failure. . . . It always seems to me that we are trying anxiously in this way to reserve some place for God; I should like to speak of God not on the boundaries but at the center, not in weakness but in strength; and therefore not in death and guilt but in man's life and goodness.[3]

It is therefore right and appropriate that the God-of-the-Gaps has been dislodged by man's increasing knowledge, for this "God" never was the God of the Bible. It is possible to rejoice, therefore, that the

God-of-the-Gaps has been squeezed out, to refrain from attempts to restore this God-of-the-Gaps, and to seek to glorify the Lord of all created reality by placing Him at the very center of life.

CHRISTIAN DEFENSE OF A GOD-OF-THE-GAPS

To characterize God as a God-of-the-Gaps is to attempt to prove or defend belief in the existence and activity of God by proposing that it is God alone who acts in areas in which man is ignorant of any scientific basis. There is a long history of Christian acceptance and use of this position. Such a choice ironically has allied the Christian with the non-Christian who also sees God as a God-of-the-Gaps, and has thus served to obscure the Christian witness to biblical theism.

The argument runs this way: Man may now know much about physics, chemistry, biology and the like, but certain key physical, chemical or biological mechanisms must forever elude him because such mechanisms do not in fact even exist. These gaps in the description of natural events and processes can be filled only by recognizing that God acts in these gaps above and beyond any physical, chemical or biological mechanism. In this interpretation God remains the Great Mechanic, and His very existence and activity forever rule out the possibility of a complete physical, chemical or biological description—even in principle.

Newton invoked the God-of-the-Gaps when certain irregularities in the motion of the planets could not be explained by his theory of gravitation. Since the mechanics of the theory of gravity could not explain the irregularities, Newton inferred that it was a direct manifestation of the intervention of God. Newton was wrong; subsequent analysis of the planetary system provided a natural explanation for these irregularities. Supposed evidence for the intervention of God was discredited.

The list of phenomena invoked by Christians to defend the God-of-the-Gaps is very long and still with us. The healing of physical sicknesses continues to be an area of special interest. Fifty years ago many diseases now curable had no known treatment; confronted with an incurable disease, doctors would tell the patient's relatives that nothing further could be done by medical science. The ill person was now completely in the hands of God, who could heal the sickness if He so willed. If the ill person recovered, the relatives thanked God for having intervened. Today if doctors are confronted with the same disease, they consider it wrong to withhold treatment and tell relatives that only prayer can meet the patient's needs. Instead they administer treatment. If the relatives have been influenced by the God-of-the-Gaps fallacy, they will now thank the doctor and forget God completely. Insofar as it has become possible to heal by natural methods what formerly could be healed only by supernatural means, another area of evidence for the existence and activity of the God-of-the-Gaps is lost. If the relatives have not been trapped by the God-of-the-Gaps fallacy, they will thank the doctor *and* they will thank God for the wisdom and skill of modern medicine. These remarks should not be construed to be an argument against the *possibility* of God healing by direct action nor against the historical *fact* of such action; rather, they are a warning that if supernatural action is our only, or even our primary, evidence for the existence and activity of God, we have committed ourselves to a God-of-the-Gaps.

The supernatural intervention of God was advanced as the direct cause of weather patterns; now that we know that such weather patterns are meteorological phenomena, this evidence for a God-of-the-Gaps is gone. A place was reserved for the God-of-the-Gaps by some Christians who objected to human space travel on the grounds that earth was man's proper domain, whereas the heavens were reserved for God. A large portion of the battle over evolution centered on the need to reserve the origin of life, or at least the origin of human life, for the domain of supernatural intervention; the theory of evolution that advanced natural mechanisms as the means by which life and human beings came into existence was an obvious threat to the God-of-the-Gaps. The possibility that laboratory scientists may construct a living creature from nonliving substances is seen as another threat to the God-of-the-Gaps, whose existence and activity demand that human beings be unable to accomplish this goal.

In many areas human beings today are called upon to confront responsibly a variety of dilemmas that our ancestors did not have to face and to exercise new capabilities. Those committed to a God-of-the-Gaps see these areas as ones in which God has the right of direct intervention, and they therefore contend that humans should leave these areas totally alone in order to give God His due. But may not

God rather be bringing us to the point where we have the ability and knowledge to respond to more and more human needs, as well as to situations where our previous efforts to improve life have only created new dilemmas? If this is the case, then it is not only possible for man today to make more informed decisions than ever before, but it also is wrong for him to shirk this responsibility. A retreat to making no choice is no longer possible; in many areas, not to make a choice is already to have made one.

Bernard Ramm has stressed the need to understand that God is active in all areas of life. Having indicated that man must supply some answer to a host of problems previously ignored or left "in the hands of God"—for example, genetic engineering, the definition of death, and the electrical, chemical and surgical alterations of human behavior—Ramm continues:

> In the light of developments in behavioral sciences and psychiatry we need to take a second look at our doctrine of the Holy Spirit. Put in simplest and most direct terms, many of the things we now claim *only* the Holy Spirit can do with man supernaturally, man will do for himself. We see no ceiling to the control, shaping and modulation of human behavior in the future.[4]

Ramm argues that we must reflect on what it means to speak of the immanence of the Holy Spirit in every dimension of the universe. While maintaining clearly the uniqueness and discontinuity of the work of the Holy Spirit in the appropriate context, we must also be careful to maintain the continuity between the Holy Spirit's work and the natural mechanisms of man's increased technological control over the world. It is in this direction that a response to the God-of-the-Gaps must be found.

RETHINKING THE GOD-OF-THE-GAPS

Two quotations are helpful in setting the stage for what it means to rethink the God-of-the-Gaps and replace this concept with the biblical emphasis. The first is a statement by Malcolm Jeeves: "God, to the theist, while being the cause of everything, is scientifically the explanation of nothing."[5] The second, somewhat enigmatic, statement is by Bonhoeffer: "Before God, and with God, we live without God."[6]

The thrust of Jeeves' remark is that God is to be conceived as the underlying cause of *all* created reality. One way to describe the world is in terms of natural science; in such a description God does not systematically enter at places where natural mechanisms are absent in order to provide a supernatural explanation. The God-of-the-Gaps is therefore avoided, not by giving up the witness for the activity of God in the world, but by seeing this activity in the context of all of created reality—not simply in those aspects where we presently lack a scientific description.

Bonhoeffer's statement can best be understood by focusing on the meaning of the three prepositions he uses with respect to God: (1) *Before*— our life is lived in the created universe that God has called into being and sustains in being; we are constantly in the presence of God. (2) *With*— our lives are joined to God in constant fellowship in Jesus Christ, so that we are never alone but rest wholly in the arms of God. (3) *Without*—while not denying the possibility of God's activity in the world without us, we do not use this possibility as an excuse or stopgap for our own ignorance or apathy; instead we seek to serve God fully in all of life without constantly invoking Him to deliver us from the need to serve Him.

Bonhoeffer draws a sharp distinction between religion in general and Christian commitment. He argues that human beings are intrinsically and incurably religious. Without a Christian commitment and the personal relationship of faith in Christ, humans will use religion to answer to insoluable problems when they are in trouble, or they will exalt and deify religion itself when they are successful. Both responses are God-of-the-Gaps responses. Only commitment to Christ permits man to escape from what amounts to a religious denial of God's reality in the world in order fully to participate in the world as a servant of Christ.

Any perspective, therefore, that limits the evidence for the existence and activity of God to a particular sphere of experience—the peripheral, the miraculous, the unique, the spiritual, the sacred—is a perspective built on a God-of-the-Gaps. If there is evidence for God in the rare events known as miracles, there is as great evidence for Him in the constant normal events known as natural. Unless a person's commitment to God embraces the ordinary as well as the special aspects of life, the physical as well as the spiritual, and the secular as well as the sacred—unless, indeed, he sees that distinction within these pairs is not a distinction of kind but of convenience—he will be under the limitations of belief in a God-of-the-Gaps.

THE RELATIONSHIP BETWEEN GOD AND THE WORLD

The uneasiness engendered when Christians are called upon to give up the God-of-the-Gaps is typified by remarks such as, "If the development of man can be described in terms of natural categories according to the theory of evolution, then what becomes of the biblical picture of God as Creator?" Or, "If human beings can put together nonliving matter and produce living creatures, then what becomes of the biblical picture of God as the Giver of life?"

Such uneasiness can be dissipated only by realizing that the concept of God giving rise to these questions is too limited and nonbiblical. What is involved is our fundamental concept of the way in which God and the world are related. This is a theological question, and our answer must come from the biblical revelation that God Himself has provided.

By faith we understand that the world was created by the word of God, so that what is seen was made out of things which do not appear (Heb. 11:3 RSV).

He [Jesus] reflects the glory of God and bears the very stamp of his nature, upholding the universe by his word of power (Heb. 1:3, RSV).

He [Jesus] is before all things, and in him all things hold together (Col. 1:17, RSV).

In his hand is the life of every living thing and the breath of all mankind (Job 12:10, RSV).

In him we live and move and have our being (Acts 17:28, RSV).

There is one God, the Father, from whom are all things and for whom we exist, and one Lord, Jesus Christ, through whom are all things and through whom we exist (1 Cor. 8:6, RSV).

From these and many other passages it is clear that the Bible teaches that we depend moment by moment upon God for our very existence. There is nothing *natural* that can happen without God's free activity. To describe events in terms of natural categories is not to explain

God's activity *away;* it is rather a fuller exposition of the ways in which we perceive this activity.

It is true that the world has an existence *separate* from God—it is not a part of God, as pantheism would maintain—but it has no existence *independent* of God. Only because the continuing free activity of God maintains it in being does the totality of our universe remain in existence at all. It is not just the order of the universe, or the design of the universe, or the stability or moral character of the universe that depends on God's own existence and activity. He sustains the very *existence* of the universe on a moment-by-moment basis. There is no event, either natural or supernatural, either physical or spiritual, either secular or sacred, which does not depend ultimately and completely upon the sustaining power of God. Every particle of created matter is as instantaneously in relationship to God as is every point on a two-dimensional circle to a three-dimensional creature.

The God-of-the-Gaps is a god who intervenes in the world in order to effect his purpose. But the God of the Bible does not *intervene in* the world. There is no world for Him to intervene in except for that world whose being and character is constantly maintained by His free activity. We describe what God does in terms of processes and laws, but these are modes of our description of God's activity. Neither does the God of the Bible "use natural processes" or "work through natural law." Again, natural processes and natural laws are *our* descriptions of God's activity, not independent tools that God makes use of. To perform a miracle, God needs only to act in a manner different from His "regular" or "normal" action; He does not need to suspend natural law to do something "unnatural." The God of the Bible is not a Master Craftsman who adjusts a former creation that exists independently of Him; the God of the Bible is the Creator and Sustainer who holds all things "in the palm of His hand."

The existence of the God-of-the-Gaps can be debated. If he were not there, the gaps would be empty, but the rest of the universe would continue as before. The God of the Bible is the very foundation of creaturely existence itself. The Bible accepts His reality but does not debate His existence, if indeed that term can be properly applied to God.

The God-of-the-Gaps makes his presence known primarily through the performance of miracles; it is departure from the natural that provides the evidence for his existence. But the God of the Bible is attested as well by every aspect of the created order. The natural cries out to the Psalmist as loudly as the supernatural; in fact, this distinction, so often sharply drawn, turns out to be a good deal less sharp than commonly believed. A natural event presupposes God's activity, no less than a supernatural act. If, for example, the development of a human being could be consistently described in terms of a set of evolutionary natural mechanisms, such a possibility would pose no necessary threat to the Christian. The uniqueness of man as a creature made in the image of God does not necessarily *demand* a nonevolutionary development. What we describe as evolutionary natural mechanisms in the created world are themselves, if valid, the evidence of God's activity. The normal mode of God's free activity in sustaining the world is what we term *natural process.* Unusual modes of God's free activity in sustaining the world, undertaken for the purposes of special revelation, are what we term *miracles.*

DIFFERENT LEVELS OF DESCRIPTION

A second response to the God-of-the-Gaps is the realization that a scientific description is only one of a number of possible types of descriptions of reality, each drawing on categories of experience different from the others. Even if we could give a complete description of the universe using the categories of physics and chemistry, for example (i.e., even if there were no gaps in our physical and chemical descriptions), we would still need other descriptions for dimensions of life not encompassed by the physical and chemical. We either accept the need for such other kinds of description, or we deny the need to symbolize experience in categories other than the physical and chemical; in the latter case, we choose to reduce man to an organic machine.

Reflection on this question shows that it is both possible and necessary to describe reality on several levels corresponding, for example, to the physical sciences, to biology, psychology, sociology and to theology. Every phenomenon that occurs in the world can, at least in principle, be described on every one of these levels. Furthermore, to be able to provide even an exhaustive description on one level (i.e., with no gaps *on that level*) does not rule out the necessity or utility of descriptions on other levels. Complete knowledge would require exhaustive descriptions on every level simultaneously.

The understanding of this rule of multilevel descriptions rescues one from many of the dilemmas that give rise to a defense of the God-of-the-Gaps. The theologian, seeking to describe reality in terms of a relationship between man and God, need not reject scientific descriptions of the same aspects of reality in order to "reserve room for God." Similarly, the scientist, seeking to describe reality in terms of natural categories, need not reject theological descriptions of the same aspects of reality in order to preserve intellectual integrity from supernatural mythology; having found a scientific description of a phenomenon or event, the scientist has neither the need nor the grounds to claim that this discovery in itself does away with evidence for the existence and activity of God.

An understanding of the possibility and the necessity of multilevel descriptions of reality removes many kinds of false dichotomies that frequently give rise to arguments involving a God-of-the-Gaps. It is no longer necessary to debate whether Christian conversion, for example, is a psychological or a theological phenomenon. A significant contribution to understanding the totality of phenomena involved in conversion can be made by providing descriptions on a variety of levels, including the sociological, psychological and even the physical, along with the theological.

Multilevel descriptions make it possible to admit that man is a highly developed animal and a complex organic machine—as those terms are commonly used. Such descriptions, however, do not exhaust the nature of man and must be supplemented with other types of description, including, of course, that of man as a creature made in the image of God. As Vernon Grounds has pointed out,[7] man can truly be described as garbage, machine or animal, depending on whether we focus our attention on chemical, mechanical or biological descriptions, but that a full description of man must include the fact that he is also a unique creature of God, made in His image, with the possibility of fellowship with God shared by no other creature.

NOTES

1. Ralph Wendell Burhoe, "The Human Prospect and the 'Lord of History,' " *Zygon* 10, No. 3 (1975): 333.
2. Bertrand Russell, "A Free Man's Worship," in *Mysticism and Logic and Other Essays* (New York: Norton, 1929).
3. Dietrich Bonhoeffer, *Letters and Papers from Prison,* rev. ed., ed. Eberhard Bethge (New York: Macmillan Co., 1968), p. 142.
4. Bernard Ramm, "Evangelical Theology and Technological Shock," *Journal of the American Scientific Affiliation* 23, No. 2 (1971): 52.
5. Malcolm A. Jeeves, *The Scientific Enterprise and Christian Faith* (London: Tyndale Press, 1969), p. 103.
6. Bonhoeffer, *loc. cit.*, p. 188.
7. Vernon C. Grounds, "God's Perspective on Man," *Journal of the American Scientific Affiliation* 28, No. 4 (1976): 145.

III

Man in the Context of Evolutionary Theory

D. GARETH JONES

Much has been written over the past 120 years about evolutionary ideas, and in particular about the mechanisms responsible for evolutionary processes. In spite of this, however, and in spite of the strides made at the level of mechanism, many gaps remain to be filled.

Unfortunately, confusion has reigned concerning even the most fundamental questions about evolution. For example, the level of scientific theories about origins has not always been distinguished from the level of philosophical representations of the ultimate character of existence;[1] these two issues have often been interlaced. General ideas have frequently occupied a position of paramount importance

D. Gareth Jones was born in South Wales in 1940 and was educated at University College, London, and University College Hospital Medical School. After five years on the staff of the Anatomy Department at University College, London, he was drawn by academic opportunities to Perth, Western Australia, where he is currently Senior Lecturer in Anatomy and Human Biology at the University of Western Australia. Dr. Jones's research interests center on the brain, in particular, on the synaptic junctions between nerve cells. He is the author of a research monograph, *Synapses and Synaptosomes: Morphological Aspects* (1975). He has also written widely on the interrelationship of science and the Christian faith, with particular emphasis on biological issues, including evolutionary topics, psychosurgery, and genetic engineering. He is author of *Teilhard de Chardin: An Analysis and Assessment* (1970).

in the evolutionary debate, and concepts such as chance and purpose-lessness have been viewed as the guiding principles behind evolution-ary mechanisms. Man has then been interpreted according to these principles, with the result that he has emerged as a product of chance and blind flux.

Consequently, what began as a search for the mechanism behind change now engenders intense anxiety concerning man's under-standing of himself. The tools of scientific inquiry have been trans-formed into the philosopher's touchstone, and man the dispassionate scientist has become man the dispossessed. Man himself has been brought under the rubric of purposeless change, and all too readily moderns conclude that man is simply the product of a vast lottery, existing only because his number has come up in a cosmic Monte Carlo game.[2]

It is hardly surprising therefore that views of man's very essence are transormed by evolutionary prejudices. No longer is he considered a being set apart from nature, because within the evolutionary context man is declared its product, an integral part of nature and wholly one with it. No longer is he then viewed as possessing a unique status. Man's moral sense and every other faculty that appears to be uniquely and distinctively human are regarded as wholly explicable by mech-anisms operating within the natural world. Once man is declared to be the product of an all-encompassing evolutionary process, this re-ductive overview becomes not simply a possible but an inevitable interpretation of man's status.

Yet the emphasis placed by different people on biological continuity between man and other living creatures differs widely, and the conse-quences for the biological and social sciences vary accordingly. It is important to identify the principles that govern these divergent inter-pretations of the same data, and to note their significance for the understanding of man.

PHILOSOPHICAL NATURALISM

The first outlook with which we must contend is *philosophical naturalism.* Here, the scientific description of man's past and present nature dispenses with any necessity for theological explanation. This view is of course, not new nor is it confined to evolutionary explanations of man. Nevertheless, in the modern evolutionary context it has exerted an unduly powerful influence.

The simple transposition of a scientific understanding of man's origins from a nontheological status to an antitheological one lies at the heart of naturalistic evolutionary affirmation. While this transposition could be illustrated by quotations from innumerable biologists, it is perhaps most starkly shown by the writings of Julian Huxley. On many occasions Huxley contended that the advance of knowledge makes supernaturalism and the very idea of God untenable. The rationale behind this claim lay in an appeal to the discoveries of biology, which, for Huxley, generally implied evolutionary concepts that necessitated a naturalistic explanation.[3] In other words, explanations predicated on natural processes invalidate supernatural referents. Huxley regarded evolution as a comprehensively natural, all-embracing process. From this view it appears to follow that nothing whatever in this world exists specifically for man's benefit.[4] Man's detachment from a supernatural realm releases him from abject servitude to a divine dictator and elevates him instead to the forefront of the procession of earthly living things.

I do not wish to trace Huxley's reasoning any further. Enough has been written to demonstrate the ease with which he, and many like him, read their own antitheological premises into tentative scientific findings. In this way, evolutionary theories and findings were readily converted into various forms of *evolutionism* and a philosophical, and very frequently, expressly anti-Christian, face was grafted onto scientific investigations.

Philosophical naturalism is not at all indispensable to evolutionary concepts, but it is unfortunately an all-too-frequent accompaniment of evolutionary theorizing and is one of the main forces revolutionizing contemporary views of the nature of man and, indirectly, of the relevance of God.

The contemporary form of philosophical naturalism is *evolutionary humanism,* which seeks its rationale and dynamic in a view of man wholly grounded in evolution. In attempting to understand the way man works, or even more fundamentally, what makes him the being he is, evolutionary humanism is in fact tackling one of the profoundest issues. It ventures to do this with no reference at all to God. Its aim is to answer every question about man and his goals by a reference to man's place within the evolutionary process; this framework alone supplies the background through which man is to be understood. Whatever meaning and worth man acquires is to be measured solely by an evolutionary yardstick.

The conclusions evolutionary humanism reaches are therefore diametrically opposed to the Christian view, and this is inevitably so because the fulcrum of the universe has been shifted. God has been replaced by a process at first allegedly independent of God and then directly opposed to Him. The concept of evolution here takes on not only an anti-Christian cast in defining the nature and role of man, but it acquires also a religious authority of its own.

The significance of this movement away from God and toward nature as the center of reality cannot be stressed too heavily. Whenever this transition is incomplete and doesn't alter the inherited view of man, the consequences remain limited, because man is temporarily thought to continue much as before. But once the view of man has been altered, revolutionary changes are inescapable. This helps us to understand the stark dilemma of modern man. Existing in a supposedly purposeless universe with no assurance that humankind is of enduring value and facing a highly problematical future, both as individuals and as a species, he is torn by the apparent necessity of dismissing all the cherished beliefs and hopes of his theistic religious inheritance as sheer myth. Philosophical naturalism has radically changed our view of man and his role in the world through its conversion of the scientific enterprise into a scientifically based philosophy of evolutionism.

Reactions to this transformation of man's nature and role vary greatly, from casual acceptance to deep perplexity to express repudiation. Jacques Monod, for instance, stoically accepts as a fact that "man at last knows he is alone in the unfeeling immensity of the universe, out of which he emerged only by chance." Man's destiny and duty are held to be unknown; it is therefore up to man to chart his own future course.[5] This mood also typifies that of many contemporary biologists, although as much as anything else it merely reflects their antitheological presuppositions.

Those who, on the other hand, seek to accommodate evolutionism within a God-oriented world view find themselves sooner or later overtaken by the dilemma of modern man. Perhaps the supreme exponent of this position was Teilhard de Chardin, who felt at one with contemporary man in experiencing the world's hostility, yet considered it his supreme goal in life to find a "way out," that is, a purpose for man. The futility and anguish of puny man in a vast, evolving cosmos haunted Teilhard, and it motivated him to construct an all-embracing synthesis aimed at integrating the evolving cosmos and the cosmic Christ. In so doing, he satisfied a deeply felt personal need to reconcile his own love of the world with his deep love for God.[6] Interesting as this synthesis may be, it fails to cope with the fundamental confusion of scientific and philosophical categories, quite apart from the fact that Teilhard's synthesis creates a host of theological problems since his comprehensive evolutionism threatens to engulf his undergirding Christian position.

MAN'S ORIGIN AND DESTINY

Another issue central to understanding man's nature within an evolving world concerns the belief that man's origins determine his present significance. This implies that man's ancestry determines his nature, a premise the validity of which both advocates and opponents of evolutionary theory appear to have assumed. As Ian Barbour has commented, for many involved in evolutionary controversies, "a sub-human past somehow came to imply a less than fully human present."[7] At this juncture, our concern is not with the validity or invalidity of evolutionary theory, but with the use of these concepts as a basis for assessing the status of present-day man.

Taken for granted as the transposition of the themes of origin and of nature has been in virtually all evolutionary approaches to man's status, it has received remarkably little attention. Among evolutionary humanists, the views of Monod, Huxley and G. G. Simpson are illustrative of the point. The need such biologists have to bestow a nonreligious meaning upon man's existence restricts the choices open to them. For many scholars, an exclusively evolutionary context for man's development has become of crucial importance for any biological approach to contemporary man.

The belief that an understanding of man's origins is essential for an understanding of man's nature is not confined to evolutionary systems of thought. It appears to be held by many Christian antievolutionists.

For instance, Henry M. Morris writes: "Probably the most important single issue confronting Biblical Christianity in these days is the question of origins. . . . What a man believes about ultimate origins and about God's revelation concerning creation will inevitably affect his beliefs concerning destinies and purposes. . . . If evolution can explain the origin and development of this universe and its inhabitants, then there is no need for any kind of personal God at all."[8] In a similar vein, Philip E. Hughes contends that "it is axiomatic that if we are in error about the origins of things, whether of the universe, or life, or religion, or salvation, we shall be in error about all that follows."[9]

As with the issue of philosophical naturalism, the surreptitious interplay of scientific and philosophical data complicates matters. The origins of any biological or physical system lie in the past, often in the remote past. As a result, they are not subject to conventional scientific investigation. The events constituting the beginnings of such a system are neither observable nor, in a narrow sense, repeatable. In short, they cannot be scrutinized at will in the laboratory, all attempts at reproducing analogous events being tinged with a profound element of uncertainty.

The further an event lies in the past, the greater is the uncertainty that attaches to it and the greater is the role played by presuppositions. Thus, questions of origins are largely questions of philosophy or, perhaps more accurately, "the problem of origins has its roots in philosophy."[10] Morris and Hughes are therefore quite justified in so far as their views are confined to philosophical issues. It is important to determine whether God or some other agency lies behind this world, and whether man is the epitome of God's creation or simply a chance product of an impersonal cosmic force. On the other hand, it is questionable whether this same argument applies to the mechanisms of development. In principle, there are many ways by which God *could* have created man, the preferred mechanism lying largely outside the confines of the philosopher's or theologian's spheres of concern. The argument that the *mechanism* of man's development necessarily has consequences for the *nature* of man involves a confusion of scientific and philosophical approaches.

Also relevant to any discussion of the problem of origins are the various built-in limitations of science. Besides the time limitation, to which we have already alluded, there is the fact that science is a human activity. In the words of Max Planck: "Science cannot solve the ultimate mystery of nature. And that is because, in the last analysis, we ourselves are part of nature and therefore part of the mystery that we are trying to solve."[11] When confronted by the task of constructing hypotheses about origins and development, therefore, the balance between scientific data and philosophical presuppositions becomes a tenuous one, particularly so when man's own origins are in question. Unfortunately, scientific theories are all too readily converted into materialistic philosophy. The claim that "man has risen, not fallen"[12] is the outcome of converting a scientific hypothesis about origins into an antitheological statement with ethical overtones. The ethical judgment in this instance has been injected into evolutionary thinking, with the result that it is no longer a statement about biological origins. In a similar manner, the discarding of an external purpose in evolution and the belief that man's destiny is to be the agent of the world process of evolution[13] reflect philosophical premises about the human condition rather than scientific data about human origins.

The issue of origins is central, therefore, to any view of man, with the proviso that what is determinative are philosophical premises. But the manner in which man's development has occurred is an issue to be considered on its own terms, according to principles relevant to any historical scientific inquiry.

ALTERNATIVE APPROACHES TO MAN

Of crucial importance in this debate is the type of approach one adopts in the study of man. Naturalistic approaches demand that man be viewed within a closed system, with man as part of the natural order and explicable solely in terms of this order. Principles for understanding man's present structural and behavioral make-up assertedly originate within the natural order, and can be elucidated only by a study of their rudiments in other animals. This is the "naked ape" type of approach, with its total dependence upon evolutionary and ethological concepts and with its implicit (and sometimes explicit) rejection of the validity of supernatural relationships.

Over against the naturalistic approaches stand those based on an open system, in which man is considered in relation to a larger reality than the purely natural realm. While these approaches do not of necessity incorporate supernatural vistas, they leave the way open for them, as well as for greater emphasis upon the perception and aspirations of the human person. Accordingly, while these approaches take serious account of man's relationships with the rest of the natural order, they also seek to incorporate other forms of evidence relating to his condition, whether these belong to revelatory, meditative or social categories. Man requires a more comprehensive assessment than that provided by the hard sciences alone, and this is where the usual objectivity of naturalistic theorists gives way to arbitrarily restrictive assumptions.

It would be easy to see this distinction between closed and open systems as a distinction between scientific and nonscientific approaches, but this would be very misleading. Although a scientific approach may lend itself to a closed system, it does not predicate it. Moreover, an open system has within it considerable scope for scientific investigation. At base, the differences between the two systems are philosophically determined, the characteristics of the systems being derived from their initial premises.

Quite apart from differences of experimental emphasis, there is no one evolutionary approach to man. An evolutionary context does not, by itself, predetermine whether man is part of a closed or open system, although it is frequently interpreted in closed system terms. In a Christian context, an open system is the only acceptable one in which to consider man. This is because the Christian approaches man as a being whose primary relationship is to God, a relationship governing all others, which consequently assume secondary places. Man in an evolutionary context is also man in a God context, the former requiring elucidation within the latter.

EVOLUTION AS THEORY

Without going into details, we can distinguish broadly between the *special* and the *general* theories of evolution. The special theory refers to the relatively small changes including the production of new species that can be *observed* to occur in living species of animals and plants. The general theory, by contrast, asserts that all the living forms in the world today have arisen from a single source which itself arose from a nonliving form.

Simplistic as is this distinction, it draws our attention to two important points. The special theory operates within a strictly experimental context, with the result that its scope is limited and its generalizations few. The general theory, however, is far more speculative, making vast assumptions and suggesting far-reaching hypotheses. The one is science in its narrow, disciplined sense; the other is science in its broad, predictive sense. The one is capable of rigorous scientific testing; the other is not and never will be.[14]

The dividing line between the general theory of evolution and philosophical evolutionism is a fine one, on some occasions difficult to determine and on others blatantly ignored. The principal distinction between them lies in the reliance that is placed on the underlying assumptions and speculations. In the scientific arena, speculations are regarded quite openly as speculations. They have a purpose in holding together a scientific idea long enough for it to be tested. Subsequently they are discarded if found wanting, or modified and strengthened if shown to be useful. In the philosophical arena, speculations are readily transformed into essential concepts. Their conjectural nature is soon forgotten and they emerge as indispensable principles.

The reliance placed upon the assumptions and speculations of the general theory of evolution depends upon the philosophical presuppositions of those making them. For humanists, these assumptions and speculations are essential if they are to acquire a coherent and unified picture of the world. Hence evolutionary theory within a humanist framework almost invariably undergoes a mutation to become evolutionism. Christians, holding a more supernaturalistic view of the world, are free to accept or reject such assumptions.[15] They possess a degree of freedom unknown to humanists, whose philosophical premises drive them toward an unbending evolutionistic position. This freedom enables Christians to take a far less restrictive view of the scientific evidence. This indeed is a precious liberty in such a difficult area, and it behooves them to value this freedom highly and to use it wisely.

It is in such an area as evolutionary theory that, as Reijer Hooykaas has pointed out,[16] our commitment to the worth of the scientific enterprise as a fully Christian activity must make itself felt. Whenever strong philosophical pressure favors the scientific position, an attitude of complacency is likely to develop in scientific circles towards the reigning theory. This presently applies to evolutionary ideas, which seem to many to lend support to humanistic concepts. There is an urgent need for the existence of a nonconforming, questioning minority whenever supposed scientific probabilities are declared to be certainties. The corollary of this principle is that care also needs to be exercised in accepting the apparent support of a scientific viewpoint for a philosophical or theological position. For example, there can be little doubt that the prevalance of a preevolutionary cosmology, which seemed to favor Christian attitudes, lulled eighteenth and early nineteenth century Christians into a sense of complacency with regard to the natural sciences.[17]

Christians today are in a position to either accept or reject the current assumptions underlying scientific theories of evolution. There is however, one proviso: as long as they are thinking scientifically, their governing criteria must be scientific ones. The possibility of rejecting evolutionary ideas is open to them, as it should be to all scientists. Nevertheless, in scientific terms, the rejection of one hypothesis follows from its inadequacy to account for available evidence and, in turn, hopefully leads to the emergence of a more satisfactory one. Both old and new hypotheses are continually subject to the same scientific principles of verification through experimental testing. From this it follows that evolutionary theories, as long as they remain within the domain of science, can be regarded as neither permanent nor impregnable. This does not mean, however, that their demise is imminent. The question is a scientific one, to be settled as far as possible in scientific terms.

Christians are free to view scientific validity and usefulness in as objective a manner as possible. They have, therefore, the potential for retaining a distinction between scientific and philosophical aspects of evolution, although this is no easy task. Nevertheless, it is a task to be pursued because, in so far as these aspects can be distinguished, the detailed mechanism of evolution will be of no concern to Christians *in their standing as Christians.*

This point calls for further comment because it is central to evolution-creation debates in general and because it is particularly relevant to the way in which evolutionary concepts are applied to man. It is also open to misinterpretation. On the negative side, this principle does not allow just *any* view to be held about either evolution in general or man in particular. The limitations noted in the previous section on approaches to man still hold, although Scriptural revelation may at times convey information bearing on mechanisms. Furthermore, this principle does not imply that man could have originated in any manner whatsoever, and it certainly does not imply that descriptions about the origins of man are irrelevant. What it does specify is that there are different categories of descriptions detailing man's origins, each of which may be legitimate, although operating on different levels and serving different purposes. Of these descriptive categories, the one concerned with the mechanism by which man came into being is not of essential theological concern to Christians, although man's status and relationship to God are of vital theological importance. The mechanism of man's development may well be of scientific concern to *some* Christians, as it will be to many other people, but this is a different matter.

Once again, the scientific, philosophical and theological aspects of man's origins require separate investigation. All too easily, they may be confused with each other, and it may be difficult to prevent this. What is essential is that such confusion needs to be realized and brought to the surface. Only in this way can a better appreciation of man's origins be reached within a framework allowing for both theological and scientific components.

Rejection of this principle that different aspects of man's origins require separate investigation opens the way, on the Christian front, to the traditional arguments of antievolutionists. These arguments rely heavily on alleged difficulties in evolutionary theories, including the deleterious nature of macromutations, the lack of intermediate forms in the fossil record, the apparent contradiction within a closed system between the entropy of the second law of thermodynamics and evolution, and the inconsistencies of certain forms of radioactive dating. Some of these criticisms, such as the lack of intermediate forms, are valid considerations and are generally recognized as such within the scientific community, while others, such as the inconsistency of radioactive dating, are frequently grossly exaggerated.

These criticisms require several general comments. It cannot be denied, and no scientist should wish to do so, that there are weaknesses in current biological theories of evolution. Nevertheless, as much should be expected of these theories as is expected of other scientific theories—neither more (because of fervent antievolutionary tendencies), nor less (because of an ardent proevolutionary view). The rejection, as unscientific, of anything not directly observable entails a view of science in which facts alone are valid. Such a science, devoid of imagination and hypothesis, would be sterile and would hardly constitute science in the modern sense. And yet the "science-equals-facts" argument is still met today in some antievolutionist circles. Although this view should be rejected, it is nonetheless salutary to remember science's comparative lack of certainty about events in the remote past. This does not necessarily deny their validity, although it does bring to the fore the reliance placed by exponents of these sciences on a variety of presuppositions (both scientific and philosophical, and in some instances, theological as well).

It should also be pointed out that merely exposing the weaknesses of evolutionary theory in no way provides a workable scientific alternative to evolution. Neither Christians nor non-Christians can live in a scientific vacuum. Rejection in principle of currently held evolutionary concepts should usher in some positive scientific alternatives to evolution. These alternatives, by their very nature, must be capable of passing tests no less rigorous than those applied to evolutionary ideas. While so-called creationist alternatives to evolution take a number of forms, the dominant schemes proposed to date are based on the universality of Noah's Flood, with considerable reliance on catastrophism.[18] My intention here is not to criticize such schemes suggested by way of complete contrast to geological uniformitarianism and gradual evolutionary development—this has been done elsewhere[19]—but simply to insist that all such schemes stand or fall on their scientific credibility. This is the only criterion acknowledged by the world of science and, even if it is not always as resolutely upheld by some scientists as it might be, Christians should accept it too.

ALTERNATIVES TO EVOLUTIONARY THEORY

If these points are accepted, a number of consequences follow for Christian thought. For a start, evolution must be seen in precise terms, thereby clearly indicating where alternatives are required and the nature of such alternatives. For instance, in rejecting the anti-Christian stance of evolutionary humanism, Christians will recognize which emphases are of a metaphysical nature and which are scientific in character.[20]

The importance of this distinction between science and metaphysics is paramount. Although it is honoring to God to reject a false theological position, it is far from honoring to Him to reject experimental findings in the name of Christ. This distinction also bears on the nature of the suggested alternatives to evolution. Simply because it is believed that evolutionism, with its humanistic presuppositions, must be replaced with a God-centered view of the created universe, it does not logically follow that evolutionary theory must be replaced by catastrophic creationism. The former is essentially a religious-philosophical issue; the latter should be more expressly a scientific one. In practice, however, both are frequently treated as religious–philosophical issues, thereby confusing categories and blurring the scientific challenges to Christian thought.

The confusion of categories that may arise can be illustrated by asking, What are the biblical alternatives to evolution? The biblical writers knew this world to be dominated by God, not by an evolutionary process nor by autonomous man nor even by an emerging Christ-like consciousness. God created, sustains and directs all that exists. From this it follows that, in the religious-philosophical sphere, the activity of God is the Christian alternative to evolution—the two are mutually exclusive. It behooves Christians, therefore, to think constructively about the cosmic role of Christ in the universe, a realm too often left by evangelicals in the past to liberal theologians.

Far more controversial perhaps are the possible alternatives to evolutionism at the mechanistic-scientific explanatory level. From my earlier argument it follows that Christians, as such, have no need to find "Christian" alternatives, although, as I have also mentioned, Christians (and others) should not be complacent about the alleged adequacy and validity of currently accepted evolutionary ideas. (In saying this, I am not denying the possibility of miracles, or any of the miraculous aspects of the earthly life of Jesus. These are not encompassed by the evolutionary context of the present discussion).

I do not believe there are specifically Christian alternatives at the mechanistic level. This brings me back to a question which is perhaps the crux of the creation-evolution controversy. Should Christians view as their chief task in this controversy the erection of systems of thought designed to combat evolutionary thinking at the level of mechanism? My view is that, in striving to provide such systems, they are misguided. First, whatever the biblical writers do or do not tell us about the mechanisms of creation, it is in the form of very general principles. Second, even if we today are able to discern the direction in which these principles point, the task of applying them concretely using current scientific concepts would involve an enormous amount of speculation, in the same way that evolutionism incorporates a major speculative element. This, in turn, would inevitably depend upon a whole host of extra-biblical principles and data. Third, any system based upon general biblical principles, however valid it may be in theological terms, is not, by its very nature, experimental and hence is not scientific. This is because the principles, if they are truly biblical ones, are immutable. They are independent of experimental evidence for their validity, and so are not subject to the testing–retesting, proof–disproof approach of scientific experimentation. Therefore, although biblical principles present us with the revealed Word of God, and are absolute in a sense in which empirical science can never be, they do not provide us with the sort of knowledge appropriate for scientific endeavor.

THE PROBLEM OF MAN

When we turn to the status of man, our fundamental presuppositions starkly confront us. We are back at the variety of roads by which man can be approached. In terms of the principles already covered, the question of the precursors of modern man is no longer of supreme importance. This follows, first, because, in scientific terms, only limited reliance can be placed on distant origins, and second, because the mechanisms by which modern man came into existence are not of crucial significance in the theological domain. My emphasis here is on the anthropological mechanisms by which modern man came about, not on the nature of Adam. Knowledge of the former is principally derived from scientific studies, while knowledge of the latter is dependent upon scriptural revelation. The study of both the primate forerunners of man and early man himself is an interesting and, in some respects, an enlightning area of anthropology. It may help clarify certain features of the life of contemporary man. The simple fact that implements and skeletal remains have been found is itself adequate reason to study the possible relationships between ancestral and contemporary man.

From a Christian perspective, there appears to be no good reason to reject the data linking modern humans with such skeletal forms as *Ramapithecus, Paranthropus, Australopithecus, Homo habilis, Homo erectus,* and *Homo (sapiens) neanderthalensis.* Their importance, however, is less certain,[21] although here again most of the debate needs to be scientific, rather than theological, in character.

Of far greater significance than attempts to argue either the pros or cons of our links with these ancestral forms is the issue of man's uniqueness. Even this discussion, however, involves a presupposition —either to emphasize the differences or the similarities between man and other primates (and even nonprimates). Although this dialogue, of necessity, involves evolutionary assumptions and touches also on other philosophical premises, it is largely a scientific issue, and I shall deal with it as such.

For many years it was fashionable to stress the similarities between man and other primates, until man was considered truly indistinguishable from other animals.[22] The resultant loss of human distinctiveness had an unforeseen consequence: in losing his lofty status in the animal world, man also lost his meaning. The ethical nature of man was clouded, along with all hope of establishing a humanistically structured society. Consequently, the basis of optimistic evolutionary humanism vanished, along with any fixed purpose or meaning to human life.

The contrary approach emphasizes the distinctive features of man. While acknowledging indispensable respects in which man resembles other primates, it elaborates what specifically characterizes man. This is the approach I wish to take here. I speak as a biologist, seeking to discover how much can be learned about man within a biological framework which, in the nature of contemporary biology, is essentially founded on evolutionary concepts. Yet I hope to show that the picture of man that emerges from this analysis does not necessarily diverge from a Christian view; the two perspectives are compatible and together constitute a potential unity.

MAN AS A BIOLOGICAL PHENOMENON

Whatever else man is, he is a biological phenomenon. He is part and parcel of the biological world, possessing all the attributes of a living species and subject to many of the environmental constraints imposed upon other living things. But of course he appears to be more than this. He is not completely dominated by the environment; he exercises a degree of control over it and over himself that marks him off from the rest of living things. And this is where the limitations of a purely biological approach to man become evident.

By way of a beginning, we might consider the range of definitions of man given by human biologists. According to T. Dobzhansky, "Man is the sole product of evolution who has achieved the knowledge that he came into this universe out of animality by means of evolution."[23] In a similar vein, Teilhard de Chardin asserted that "man is nothing else than evolution becoming conscious of itself."[24] For anthropologists in general, man is a tool-making animal; stated in more elevated terms, "Man is aware or conscious of his self; he has a mind, an ego and a superego; he is capable of insight, abstraction, symbol formation, symbolic thinking, and of using symbolic language."[25] Another commentator remarks: "Man is the animal who relinquishes nothing. He simply adds to what he already is and has."[26]

These and comparable definitions of man can be classified under two main headings: those based on evolutionary data and emphasizing man's distinctiveness from other primates, and those stressing the attributes of man's brain and his consequent capacity for conceptual thought, culture and a search for meaning and purpose. (In this discussion I use the term *man* to include both early man, of which the best known example is Neanderthal man, and present-day man. Both types are encompassed within the species *Homo sapiens,* although present-day man is sometimes concentrated in the subspecies *Homo sapiens sapiens*).

The first area I shall discuss is the realm of the physical anthropologist, whose primary concern is man's osteological characteristics, that is, his bone structure. Among these features, man's hand and forelimb are perhaps of foremost interest, because they have been relieved of their locomotive functions and have instead become specialized in manipulating small objects. The human hand is superbly adapted for fine movements, enabling man to use either a precision or a power grip when manipulating small artifacts. In evolutionary terms, possession of hands with this range of functional potential opened the way to the use and, later, to the construction of tools. This was the first sign that man was breaking free of the bondage of his environment; it also signaled the beginning of human inventiveness.

Important as tools were to the development of modern man it would be misleading to consider their use in isolation from other, closely related, factors. The early stone tools implied hunting, which itself involved cooperation between individuals and the emergence of a nascent form of social life. Integral to both these developments was man's upright posture and system of language, the latter presupposing a brain capable of nurturing speech. Toolmaking assumes significance only within the context of these interrelated developments because, "from this point on, hominids were cultural animals, imposing arbitrariness on the environment, thereby making it more complex" and hence opening the way to the further development of humans characterized by speech.[27]

The brain of man underlies all facets of man's uniqueness. At this juncture, it is sufficient to point out that the branching of the nerve cells within the human brain and the connections between them contribute to a level of internal organization that result in uniquely human features. This is, however, but one intriguing aspect of the complex organization of man's brain. Other features include the increased volume and the expansion and deep infolding of the cerebral hemispheres compared with other primates and mammals. Certain areas of the superficially situated cerebral cortex are particularly well developed, while the expansion of the frontal, parietal and occipital lobes are noteworthy when taken in conjunction with one another. These are important structural substrates for the organization of certain higher intellectual functions, for motivation and social control, for the development of language and conceptualization, and for associated visual skills.

Other distinguishing features of man include numerous facets of his dental apparatus, a slow rate of development during childhood, relative lack of body hair, reproductive variability and the length of postmaturity. Interesting as these characteristics may be, they tell us little about just what makes man the sort of being he is. In order to advance in this direction we need to look further at the human brain, particularly at two of its products—language and thought.

Man can be described as having two language systems: a *thinking* language for manipulating concepts inside his brain and a *speaking* language for communicating with others. Man is man in part because he can communicate with other men by way of a genuinely linguistic signaling system. Human language provides a means whereby a very large number of signals can be combined to produce new words and combinations of words, and because it is not programed in the brain, it is capable of modification at will.[28] Language is also important because it enables individuals to learn from a variety of other individuals and not solely from their parents. In consequence, the richness and diversity of human life is immeasurably enhanced. By contrast, the signaling systems of other animals are closed ones, lacking the potential of a linguistic mode of communication. It has also been postulated that the communication systems of nonhumans are concerned with motivational state, whereas humans experience no comparable limitations.[29]

In the realm of thought, humans have the capacity to form abstract concepts. One of the glories of the human intellect is that it allows man time to ponder and to meditate, with the result that he is capable of indulging in activities lacking any immediate goal.[30] At the intellectual level this means he can use abstract concepts and ultimately identify new possibilities. This calls forth imagination, from which poetic language and scientific concepts arise.

Before concept formation can be adequately utilized, however, another trait is essential. This is generalization, a capacity which lies at the basis of all human systems of explanation and forecasting. Man is capable of going far beyond either the given or the experienced. He can integrate the present with the past and, to a limited extent, with the future as well. Thus being capable of thinking in these abstract and general terms, man is in a position to attempt to understand himself and his world.

But how does man see himself? What of his conceptual world and his culture? Man possesses a degree of self-knowledge and is continually confronted by a demand to understand himself as a human being.[31] Through encounters with others he becomes aware of who he is. This is his self-consciousness, which helps remind him of the limits of his person. To identify our bodies with ourselves is indeed one of the supreme achievements of the human brain.[32]

Self-consciousness carries with it, therefore, the implication that those who possess it know that they know.[33] Man is a *self*-knowing being, whereas the most highly developed nonhuman primates are restricted to simply knowing. Self-consciousness ensures that man is continually asking questions—about himself, his existence, his destiny and about any and every aspect of his world. Man is also an answering being, because without answers, self-consciousness is self-limiting.[34]

Man's conceptual attributes have placed him in a position where he can imagine new solutions to problems and even question his own existence. In short, they have bestowed upon him inventiveness. Man, therefore, and man alone, can plan for the future, devising new methods of accomplishing goals and, in the end, live as much in a world of his own making as in the physical world inhabited by his body.

From here it is but a short step to the idea of culture, a concept which is generally used to cover all those skills and ways of life that are transmitted nongenetically. The basis of culture lies in the ability of man to communicate linguistically and, in more advanced cultures, to communicate also by such means as art, writing, and music.

Today it is clear that man's ever-increasing technological prowess has made many aspects of the environment subject to his manipulation, and it has made man himself more subject to his own control, whether it be in the spheres of reproduction, genetics or the brain. Man's own body is therefore increasingly being encompassed by the constraints of human culture. Man is making himself increasingly unique, if we can use such a term, because he is producing for himself an increasingly different world, not only man-constructed but also man centered.[35] This largely materialistic notion presents a major challenge to Christian apologists, who demand that man be viewed as God's creature.

In spite of all I have written so far, the human person as such has still been bypassed. Each individual has a sense of his own personal uniqueness, he is aware of his transience and he knows that one day he will cease to exist in his present form. And alongside such thoughts go specific questions: What is my destiny? Where am I going? What is life all about? Questions such as these make explicit the overtly religious dimensions of man's thinking.

According to Bronislaw Malinowski: "Religion . . . can be shown to be intrinsically although indirectly connected with man's fundamental, that is, biological, needs. Like magic it comes from the curse of forethought and imagination, which fall on man once he rises above brute animal nature."[36] Underlying these ideas is man's transience and the knowledge that he is transient. In these terms, religion can be viewed as man's attempt to be included in some domain larger and more pertinent than mere existence.[37] This is illustrated by the emphasis placed on the recognition of death, an emphasis that has a long history, being well known even among such nonhuman primates as baboons. Burial of the dead, however, signifies more than mere recognition of death, it involves some idea of an afterlife. It is generally accepted that Neanderthal man buried his dead in a ceremonial manner. In spite of this and other evidence for burial of the dead in prehistoric times, obviously recognizable shrines and temples become commonplace beginning only about ten thousand years ago. Their appearance is evidence of the establishment in human life of a firmly based religious dimension.

Closely related to these ideas is man's death-awareness. This, in turn, is a prelude to what Dobzhansky[38] terms man's ultimate concern. By this he means man's concern with things beyond himself and his present life; it is concern with the infinite and may reflect a violated relationship with God.

This biological perspective has highlighted numerous features of man's being and has brought us a remarkable distance. Man can be described fairly completely in purely biological terms, but man also insists on presenting himself as a being of value, as a person continually asking questions and continually searching for meaning in life. These are not mutually contradictory sides to man; they are different levels, each essential for a unitary view of the whole man. He is unique in his search for truth, his concern for moral values, and his acknowledgment of universal obligations. He is rooted not merely in his biological connections but also in his ethical aspirations. He is a creature of this world but is not limited to its immediate, material dimension. He is explicable in biological terms only as long as the human and ethical side of his nature is not overlooked. And it is this side of man which is exciting and forbidding.

SEARCHING FOR PARAMETERS

What is interesting about this account of man as a biological phenomenon is that it reveals his aspirations for something greater than himself. Man's religious dimensions appear integral to his biological make-up. Man's yearning for that which is beyond him reflects a biological need. He is not the rank materialist he is sometimes made out to be. Rather, a study of man in his biological—and this includes his evolutionary—connections reveals a deep longing that can only be realized in religious terms.

This is, of course, a far cry from acknowledging the God of Christianity or recognizing that the universe inhabited by man is the creation of a personal God. Nevertheless, it allows for a Christian interpretation, and in this regard it is consonant with some of the presuppositions basic to the Christian position. For instance, it can be argued that the reality of human personality demands "that the ultimate origin and ground of being for the universe is personal."[39] A personally derived universe, in its turn, is one manifestation of an "open universe," open to God, who is its Creator as well as the Creator of man himself. This personal-infinite God has, according to Christians, created man in his own image, with personality, with the ability to respond to and communicate with God and with other humans, and with a deeply felt need for meaning, significance and purpose in his life.

A Christian view of man does not repudiate the biological perspective. Rather, it provides a perspective which is logically necessary and which transforms the biological one. In doing so, it provides a means by which man's yearning for that which is beyond him can be met. The Christian view that man is at least partly rooted in nature and formed in the image of God embraces the biological position within its compass, setting it in a dynamic, God–man, Creator–creature context. The Christian knows that man stands in a meaningful relationship to his Creator and thus is capable of a level of experience and existence essentially different from all other living things. Man is made with the intention of responding to God's gracious word in personal love and trust, and only in this response can he be what he truly is intended to be.

Although much more could be written about a Christian view of man, the preceding discussion has highlighted the intimate relationship between the biological and the Christian perspectives. The significance of this discussion is that this relationship has emerged from a study of *Homo sapiens*. By concentrating on what is known of him in his present form, we have been able to make considerable progress in analyzing man from both biological and theological standpoints. Although I have paid little attention to general revelation, facets of this, such as conscience, answerability to God and to coming judgment, strengthen the case I have made from scientific analysis.

In adopting this approach, I have made use of the most reliable scientific sources available. The bulk of the evidence has been gleaned from contemporary, and hence readily examinable, sources. The view of man that emerges from this approach is a relatively holistic one, unfettered by the usual methodological stringencies which confine man to physical dimensions.

As illustrated in the diagram on page 58, man is taken as the starting point of my approach, with the result that he can then be viewed in relationship to God and in the dimensions we have loosely termed biological. This approach does not demand that all these dimensions be taken into consideration, but allows for their validity and even encourages their integration into a holistic view of man. It highlights the unity of man, emphasizing his grounding in the purposes of God and his thoroughly biological nature. For the sake of convenience, I will refer to this as a *man-based approach*.

The principal alternative approach is, as we have seen, that of the evolutionary humanist which, as indicated in the diagram, starts with evolutionary concepts and fits man entirely within their compass. This *origins approach* suffers from difficulties that are virtually implicit within evolutionary theorizing. As discussed above, the fine distinction between general evolutionary ideas and philosophical evolutionism is frequently ignored in order to foster particular philosophical presuppositions. Not surprisingly, an evolution-based, origins approach interprets the nature of man in areligious terms; it minimizes man's distinctive characteristics and leaves little or no room for God. Although features such as these are more or less typical of the approach, they are not demanded by it. This is amply illustrated by the existence of reputable theistic evolutionary viewpoints. Nevertheless, in the intellectual climate of the late twentieth century, an evolution-

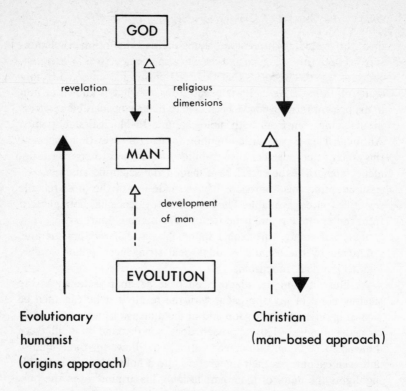

Evolutionary
humanist
(origins approach)

Christian
(man-based approach)

This diagram shows the essential differences between a man-based and an origins approach to the nature of man. In the *center* are indicated the basic data obtained from biblical revelation (solid arrow) and biological investigation (broken arrows); this signifies that God's revelation provides definite knowledge about man while scientific analysis supplies hints of some aspects of man's existence (his religious awareness and possibly the mechanisms of his development). On the *left,* an origins approach utilizes only evolutionary concepts (solid arrow) for its picture of man; God's revelation is ignored. On the *right,* a man-based approach starts with man as we know him, viewing him primarily in terms of God's revelation (upper solid arrow). Revelation also throws light on the general theological principles governing man's origins (lower solid arrow). Biological investigation (broken arrow) also plays a part by casting light on the mechanisms of man's development. This approach, therefore, it seems to the writer, holds the potential for integrating revelation and scientific analysis.

ary, origins approach lends itself to an atheistic interpretation of man.

According to such an origins approach, man is part of a naturalistic, closed universe. He has no "way out" to God or to any supernatural realm; neither is there a "way in" from God. Man's relationship is solely with the world of nature, from within which he achieves whatever significance he can find. Such significance arises only from the philosophical presuppositions of those investigating him, with the result that man becomes the hostage of current scientific evolutionary concepts which, as we have already seen, become more nebulous and tentative as they delve further back in time.

The origins approach, therefore, is bedeviled by imprecise scientific data and by a plethora of speculation. This, although not invalidating it as an adjunct to other approaches, makes it a hazardous exercise in its own right. Far too much emphasis has been placed on this approach, to the detriment both of a unitary view and of a biologically substantiated view of man. On these grounds alone I hold that this approach is inferior to a man-based approach.

From a Christian viewpoint there is another urgent need for such a transition. The majority of Christian apologists have adopted an origins approach to man and, when confronted by its evolutionistic context and frequent atheistic overtones, have felt obliged to do battle with biologists over their view of both evolution and man. This has led some Christians into a general hostility toward science. Their fear that the Christian view of man is being engulfted by philosophical evolutionism propels them into a concerted attack on the validity of all evolutionary ideas. On both fronts an enormous amount of impoverishment has resulted, whereby some Christians lack appreciation of the scientific enterprise and neglect biological aspects of man as a consequence of a largely negative approach to evolution.

In some Christian circles these trends are manifested in the equation of antievolutionary with orthodox Christian ideas. This, in turn, is often matched by an equation of antievolutionary ideas with creationism, the latter being restricted to static concepts on the assumption that there is a biblical mandate for this interpretation. Christian apologetics in consequence is largely devoted to disputing the validity of all evolutionary concepts because of their anti-Christian overtones. This disputation, however, can only be carried out by challenging the data of special evolutionary theory because the distinction between the mechanism of evolution and the philosophical stance of evolutionism has been ignored. To the exponents of this type of Christian apologetics there is no escape from this impasse, because the status of man and even the existence of God have been made wholly dependent on the question of origins.

The other side of this dilemma is that, for this type of apologetics, biological investigation can add little of value to the appreciation of man because it is hamstrung by its anti-evolutionary emphasis. Consequently, the biological status of man is inadequately stressed, so that our knowledge of him is limited to our theological knowledge which, although essential, cannot provide total insight into man's condition.

A CHRISTIAN ASSESSMENT OF MAN

On all these counts, a man-based approach is preferable to an origins approach. In addition to providing the possibility of a unitary view of man, it is also more consistent with biblical data. A scientifically based origins approach insists on seeing man in terms of his ancestry, with the result that it is never able to build up anything resembling an adequate picture of his wholeness. The man to emerge from this approach is less than man, lacking the "mannishness of man"[40] demanded by Christian thought.

By contrast, a man-based approach is able to start with man as he is and, for the Christian, this means starting with the revelation of man's creation in the image of God, his knowledge of God and of the world as God's handiwork, his responsibility to God and his fellowman, and his failure to live up to God's expectations in the moral and intellectual realms. A man-based approach holds man's origin and nature together in a comprehensive unity unknown to evolutionary science (see diagram).

In other words, man can know God and must take this knowledge and its consequences into consideration when assessing the biological evidence relevant to man's status. These are necessary elements of a biblical approach to man, and they in turn remind us of another all-important truth, namely, that God knows man. The man-based approach to man I am advocating is not a man-centered or a man-confined approach. It takes contemporary man as the starting point and recognizes his place in an open universe, one open to God who is the Creator and Upholder of all that man holds dear.

The man-based approach offers at least some guidelines on man and his relation to evolutionary theory. At a scientific level, we may have much to learn from evolutionary approaches to man. These however should not be confused with secular philosophical principles invoked to delineate the nature of man and indicate future directions he should take. For the Christian, man's nature is clearly outlined in the Bible, although its general principles require specific applications which may, in some instances, be enlightened by our biological understanding of man. The tension between biblical revelation and biological understanding is a real one. Nevertheless, together they provide the way for increasing man's knowledge and supplying him with the necessary tools to come to terms with his natural environment, with himself and with God.

NOTES

1. Langdon Gilkey, "Evolution and the Doctrine of Creation," in *Science and Religion*, ed. I. G. Barbour (London: SCM Press Ltd., 1968), pp. 159–181.
2. Jacques Monod, *Chance and Necessity* (Glasgow: Collins/Fontana Books, 1974), p. 137.
3. Julian Huxley, *Religion without Revelation* (London: Watts, 1967), pp. 156 f.
4. George Gaylord Simpson, *This View of Life* (New York; Harcourt Brace Jovanovich, 1964), p. 12.
5. Jacques Monod, *op. cit.,* p. 167.
6. D. Gareth Jones, *Teilhard de Chardin: An Analysis and Assessment* (London; Tyndale Press, 1969), pp. 11–13.
7. Ian G. Barbour, *Issues in Science and Religion* (London: SCM Press Ltd., 1966), p. 93.
8. Henry M. Morris, *The Twilight of Evolution* (Grand Rapids, Michigan: Baker Book House, 1963), preface.
9. Plu E. Hughes, *Christianity and the Problems of Origins* (Philadelphia: Presbyterian and Reformed Publishing Co., 1964), p. 37.
10. D. England, *A Christian View of Origins* (Grand Rapids, Michigan: Baker Book House, 1972), p. 13.
11. Max Planck, quoted in Hughes, *op. cit.,* p. 21.
12. George Gaylord Simpson, *The Meaning of Evolution* (New Haven: Yale University Press, 1960), p. 310.
13. Julian Huxley, *Essays of a Humanist* (Harmondsworth: Penguin, 1966), p. 37.
14. D. Gareth Jones, "Evolution—A Personal Dilemma," *Journal of the American Scientific Affiliation,* in press.

15. Jan Lever, *Creation and Evolution* (Grand Rapids, Michigan: William B. Eerdmans Publishing Co., 1958), p. 58.

16. Reijer Hooykaas, quoted in M. A. Jeeves, *The Scientific Enterprise and Christian Faith* (London, Tyndale Press, 1969), pp. 99 f.

17. D. Gareth Jones, "Some Byways of Creation," *Faith and Thought* 96 (1967): 13–26.

18. Henry M. Morris and John C. Whitcomb, *The Genesis Flood* (Philadelphia: Presbyterian and Reformed Publishing Co., 1961).

19. D. Gareth Jones, "Does 'The Genesis Flood' Solve All Our Problems?," *Eternity* 24 (1973): 48 f.

20. D. Gareth Jones, "Evolution—A Personal Dilemma."

21. C. E. Stipe, "An Anthropological Perspective on Man," *Journal of the American Scientific Affiliation* 28 (1976): 173–180.

22. Ian G. Barbour, *Issues in Science and Religion*, p. 91.

23. Theodorius Dobzhansky, "Genetic Control and the Future of Man," Barbour, *Issues in Science and Religion*, p. 315.

24. Pierre Teilhard de Chardin, *The Phenomenon of Man* (London: Collins/Fontana Books, 1965), p. 243.

25. Theodorius Dobzhansky, *The Biology of Ultimate Concern* (London: Collins/Fontana Books, 1971), p. 64.

26. Victor C. Ferkiss, *Technological Man: The Myth and the Reality* (New York: Mentor, 1969), p. 33.

27. David Pilbeam, *The Ascent of Man* (New York: Macmillan Co., 1972), pp. 12, 14.

28. E. McMullin, "Man's Effort to Understand the Universe," in *The Uniqueness of Man*, ed. J. D. Roslansky (Amsterdam: North-Holland, 1969), p. 14.

29. Pilbeam, *op. cit.*, p. 79.

30. J. Bronowski, *The Ascent of Man* (London: British Broadcasting Corporation, 1973), p. 432.

31. A. J. Heschel, *Who is Man?* (Stanford: Stanford University Press, 1965), pp. 6, 11.

32. D. Gareth Jones, "What is Man?—A Biological Perspective and Christian Assessment," *Journal of the American Scientific Affiliation* 28 (1976): 165–173.

33. John Carew Eccles, *The Understanding of the Brain* (New York: McGraw-Hill, 1973), p. 220.

34. D. Gareth Jones, "What Is Man?"

35. *Ibid.*

36. Quoted in Dobzhansky, *The Biology of Ultimate Concern*, pp. 77 ff.

37. Quoted in *ibid.*, p. 78.

38. *Ibid.*, pp. 68–69.

39. T. V. Morris, *Francis Schaeffer's Apologetics: a Critique* (Chicago: Moody Press, 1967), p. 30.

40. Francis Schaeffer, *The God Who Is There* (London: Hodder and Stoughton, 1968).

IV

Environmental Problems and the Christian Ethic

ROWLAND P. MOSS

Environmental problems are of great contemporary concern. The present interest has been growing for the past twenty years, although twentieth century precursors date from earlier decades, at least back to the publication of Aldo Leopold's *A Sand County Almanack* (1949)[1] and to Jacks and Whyte's *The Rape of the Earth* (1939).[2] Contemporary concern, however, is marked by at least three new dimensions: first, the urgency with which present problems are popularly presented; second, the rapidly widening awareness of the importance of

Rowland P. Moss is Professor of Biogeography and Coordinator of Environmental Studies at the University of Birmingham, Birmingham, England, having become lecturer in geography there in 1962. From 1957–1962 he was a senior lecturer in the College of Technology in Ibadan, Nigeria, where he had earlier served as a soil scientist with the Department of Agriculture of the Nigerian Ministry of Natural Resources. A member of the British Ecological Society and the International Society of Soil Science, and a past president of African Studies Association, he was editor of and contributor to the volume *The Soil Resources of Tropical Africa* (1968) and *The Population Factor in African Studies* (1975). These volumes reflect his special interest in the planning of agricultural land use in the tropics on an ecological basis. He also contributed a two-part essay on "Responsibility in the Use of Nature" to the *Christian Graduate* (Vol. 28, No. 3 [Autumn, 1975]; Vol. 29, No. 1 [Spring, 1976]).

environmental issues to a wide range of political and planning decisions; and, third, an urgent realization of the need for an overtly
ethical approach to most current problems.

The purpose of this essay is to demonstrate that environmental
problems are, in fact, as old as civilization itself, to suggest what
elements are new in the present concern, and to outline an ethical
approach to current problems based on biblical foundations.

THE ANTIQUITY OF ENVIRONMENTAL PROBLEMS

The prior question concerns the antiquity of environmental problems. It is clear that man has been destroying his environment almost
since the beginnings of organized society. The discovery of the use of
fire for clearing land or for driving game animals into the open initiated a process of forest clearance and damage. It has been plausibly
argued that many of the world's grasslands have been the result of fire
damage in the more remote past. Mediterranean landscapes, now
considered so attractive, with their bare rock interspersed with scrub
vegetation, resulted from erosion of the soil cover initiated by forest
clearance and overgrazing. In Western Europe too, large areas were
cleared and depleted. The characteristic moorland landscape of High-
land Britain, with poor agricultural land, rough grazing and grouse
moor, has replaced areas once covered by deciduous woodland.
Reforestation in such areas is merely replacing lost resources, not
creating new ones.

Comparison of the Nile Valley with Mesopotamia serves as a striking example of the antiquity of environmental problems. The Nile
Valley has remained agriculturally productive for more than six thousand years, whereas the Euphrates and Tigris valleys now support a
small fraction of their former population. Land use in the floodwater
areas of the respective rivers is the critical factor. The silt load of the
Nile has always been relatively light and manageable because of low
population density in Ethiopia and Uganda. As a result, much of the
natural vegetation has been preserved, and a hydrological and ero-
sional balance has continued to exist, producing a silt load in the river
heavy enough to maintain fertility in the irrigation basins, but light
enough to preclude the possibility of silting up.

The source areas of the Tigris and Euphrates, however, have been the homeland for large populations of men, of sheep and of goats from remotest antiquity, and for thousands of years a highway for nomadic herdsmen from Central Asia. Overgrazing, intensive hill farming and deforestation have therefore characterized these areas for millennia. The major rivers transport the material from the eroding hillsides to the Persian Gulf, depositing a substantial proportion of their load along the way. The mouths of the Euphrates and Tigris are now 180 miles farther out to sea than in Sumerian times. During the period of ancient Mesopotamian civilization only a skilled and considerable effort by the population could manage the heavy silt load in the irrigation works. This coordinated effort depended in turn on a stable social and political organization; when this collapsed under the pressure of Tartar and Mongol invaders, the once prosperous civilization was rapidly buried under a layer of river silt. Only in modern times has an attempt been made to rebuild the canal system.

The demise of the cedar forests of Lebanon affords another example of ancient environmental degradation. The Phoenicians became the leading maritime power of their age by building ships from Lebanese cedars. Although cedars readily regenerate where adequate soil remains, this was prevented by the overgrazing of sheep and goats. Exploitation increased when timber was exported to Egypt for building cities, and to Jerusalem for Solomon's temple, palace, and other edifices. Cedar groves remain now only in a few favored locations, the erosion following deforestation and grazing having left many hills barren.

Nor can pollution be considered essentially a modern problem. For example, schistosomiasis, which is perpetuated by faecal and urinary contamination of the water supply, is a debilitating disease of great antiquity. Its symptoms have been noted in descriptions on Egyptian papyri and in Babylonian inscriptions at least three thousand years old. Furthermore, ova of the schistosome parasite that causes the disease have been recovered from mummies of the Egyptian Twentieth Dynasty, dating from 1200 B.C. Many other diseases are of course spread by similarly contaminated water. The use of chemicals in pest control is also very old, and there is evidence that the ancient Greeks used sulphur to control plant diseases.

THE CONTEMPORARY SITUATION

If environmental problems are not in themselves new, then what elements of the contemporary situation are in fact different? Three factors immediately come to mind: first, the sophistication of modern technology; second, the exponential effect of population growth; and, finally, the efficiency of modern journalism and the communication media.

Modern technology is sophisticated in two main senses. It is extremely efficient in achieving immediate and precisely defined aims, and, moreover, it is complex in the ways in which it uses natural resources. For instance, technology has synthesized highly effective pesticides which are precise and lethal in their effects and which come from the employment on an industrial scale of complicated chemical reactions rather than from naturally occurring substances. The use of atomic reactions in effect taps the energy inherent in matter itself, rather than energy derived from the molecules of chemical compounds, such as those which constitute our main fossil fuels—coal and oil. As such sophistication increases, so do the dangers inherent in the new processes, thus requiring ever more careful scrutiny of potential side effects. Indeed, some contend that absolute safety is the *sine qua non* for the development of atomic energy as a commercial fuel because the dangers inherent in even one major accident are predictably so great as to make the investment quite unacceptable. In the case of pesticides, misuse may affect large numbers of harmless, if not beneficial, organisms. But the prevalent technology of agricultural production demands their use on a large scale to achieve highly efficient yields; this massive use is thus, arguably, fully justified by the food needs of the modern world. In sum, the very sophistication of modern industrial and agricultural technology carries with it the correlative dangers of misuse and of undesirable side effects.

These dangers and side effects are themselves exacerbated by the growth in world population. As populations multiply, demands increase, which, coupled with desires for higher standards of living, exert pressure to continually develop ever more sophisticated technologies to meet those demands. This fact has an unavoidable corollary, namely, that an individual in a developed country makes a much greater—perhaps fifty times greater—demand on the environment than an individual in the Third World. Thus population growth is also an important element in current environmental problems. Population numbers have now reached a level where such demands with increasing frequency exacerbate tensions in world economics, and cause regional or local deficiencies of essential commodities.

Also significant in the present situation is the effect of the modern communication media. In the first place, innovations are rapidly diffused and their acceptance accelerated by modern advertising and sales techniques. Along with the technology the problems are also diffused. Then, second, modern advertising and sales techniques help to perpetuate the demand by which technological innovation is itself sustained and developed. Finally, environmental pressures generated by burgeoning technology increasingly impinge on individual experience, particularly in developed countries. In these lands highly articulate environmentalist pressure groups can readily capitalize on particular examples of accelerating "environmental damage," by using the media to feed and foster current concern.

Thus, in a real sense, modern problems result from the unrestrained and self-centered desire to "subdue" nature, a desire which can be traced back to the beginnings of urbanization and civilization. But this lack of restraint is in no sense an "obedience" to a biblical command, as some eager environmentalists would assert. For, as we shall see, the biblical command, taken in the context of the Genesis narrative, imposes unequivocal moral constraints on created and fallen man.

SOME MODERN PROBLEMS

Modern environmental problems may be conveniently grouped into five categories. The first four groups concern man's relationships with nature, while the fifth involves diverse relationships with his own products. The first four groups pertain to the conservation of resources, to the preservation of nature, to the prevention of pollution, and to the growth of population; the final group embraces problems of the constructed environment and, to a greater or lesser degree, impinges on the first four.

Resource problems are the first group we shall consider. In order to live and to sustain his culture, man needs certain environmental resources. Some, principally food, fibers and wood, come from natural biological systems which are manipulated to produce the required resources. Others, like coal, oil and metals, come from the earth, the products of past geological processes. Water is obtained by using another natural, self-renewing system, the hydrological cycle. Furthermore, each of these groups of resources can be provided only by using particular areas for specific purposes, so that land itself constitutes a space resource.

In an unsophisticated economic situation resource needs are met by the direct activities of individuals in their immediate environment. As technology and economic relations become more complex, technical requirements are met by natural resources geographically removed from the process. Because demands become more precise and selective, more processing is required before the natural resource is suitable as material for the technical process. Such increasing sophistication is associated with the development of transport facilities, and natural resources remote in location from the technological processes soon become suitable sources of the required materials.

Furthermore, technological advance is always bought at the price of an increased energy demand. Thus farming done using only a hoe as a cultivation tool requires only crude iron and cut wood as material inputs and the energy of one man to use the hoe. On the other hand, modern commercial agriculture, with its increased yields per hectare and its more efficient use of labor power, is bought at the cost of vastly greater inputs of energy in terms of electricity and fuel oil, fertilizers, herbicides and pesticides, and hidden inputs such as the energy required to manufacture complex farm machinery and maintain the complex transport and marketing system upon which economic success depends.

Thus, even without an increase in population, developing technology exerts increasing demands upon those natural resources it requires to turn out its products. When these demands are exacerbated by those consequent upon a growing population, particularly in the developed countries, it is easy to see the persuasiveness of the case made by many environmentalists regarding the exponential growth of resource demands. There can be little doubt that at least some natural resources will become quite scarce in the not too distant future.

Two contrary points, however, need to be made. First, the precision of the resource demand made by a modern technological process means that the demand can frequently be met from a diverse set of natural sources. The dominant factor is not the direct one of resource availability, but the economic one of the cost of extraction and processing, cost which itself varies with technological advance and general economic conditions. Second, the natural sources of the necessary primary materials are usually so diverse and widely distributed that it becomes extremely difficult to assess their actual availability with any reliability.

Thus it is extremely difficult to make an unassailable case for cutting back resource demands simply on the grounds that raw materials may someday be exhausted. There are certainly reasonable arguments for the conservation of resources, but man's technological ingenuity in the face of past challenges makes it plausible to expect that these new challenges will produce similar responses in the present situation.

The argument is sometimes put forward that we need to conserve resources for posterity. This, as John Passmore points out in his perceptive analysis,[3] is merely an emotional appeal unless we can predict with confidence what the needs will be, what resources will be required to meet them, and what sources will be available for the provision of the resources. None of these can be predicted with reasonable confidence even for ten years ahead, and certainly not for a generation or more. The best argument for resource conservation is that from the notion of *stewardship,* but this requires an ethical and moral, even a religious base, rather than a scientific one. (We shall turn to this shortly).

What then of the *preservation of nature*—the conserving of individual species of plants and animals, and of "natural" ecosystems, for their own sakes? The conservation lobby is very vocal, and Max Nicholson's book[4] affords an example of the powerful advocacy devoted to preservation. Significant scientific arguments for preservation may be legitimately advanced, such as the assertion that it is necessary to sustain the genetic diversity of nature itself in order to conserve the flexibility of adaptation upon which the continuance of nature depends and, incidentally, to maintain the gene pools upon which future plant propagation and animal breeding may depend. It is also argued that "natural" ecosystems are so complex and so little understood that we must preserve them for study, since scientific study of such complex entities may yield important information to man concerning the ways in which biological resources can most effectively be managed. It is further argued that man needs the experience of "wild" nature in a deep psychological sense and that "natural" ecosystems are necessary to provide this.

Most frequently, however, these basic scientific appeals to human self-interest are supplemented by a moral appeal, and it is asserted that man has some kind of *responsibility* to preserve nature. For example, it is suggested that what has been produced over millions of years by evolution has a natural right to preservation, and that therefore man *ought* to preserve nature as it is. Others, like Fraser Darling,[5] argue for a new ethic based on elements of nature mysticism, often explicitly oriental, or on mystical holism. But on the one hand, the appeal to evolution almost inevitably leads to its personification, which becomes a purposive, sacred, driving force, instead of the mere description of an historical process; and on the other, the metaphysical basis for the moral arguments is provided by the superimposition of a philosophical system on the scientific study of ecology. In either case a moral element is clearly involved, distinct from an equally necessary scientific component.

It might be thought that the third group of contemporary environmental problems, the *prevention of pollution,* would be independent of moral dilemmas. "Pollution is simply the process of putting matter in the wrong place in quantities that are too large."[6] But we are concerned not only with matter, but also with less tangible realities, like noise and radiation, that may have very serious effects on the human organism. Some pollutants are dangerous only if their quantity is too large at one time and place, so that natural processes of decomposition become clogged; others are dangerous because they are not degradable at all by natural processes. Some pollutants, like plastic containers, are simply a nuisance; others, like many modern pesticides, are potentially lethal. It is immediately clear, and often taken to be self-evident, that individuals should not engage in activities which harm other individuals, and clearly some pollution problems can be subsumed, from a moral viewpoint, under such a blanket principle. But what about pollutants that do not harm humans, but only other organisms? Here we return to the moral problem related to the preservation of nature. And what about the problem of pollutants such as radioactive wastes that do not affect us directly today, but may in the future? Here we return to the problem of responsibility to posterity. Thus, even if we do not ask the question, Why should I not harm my neighbor if I can do it without damage to myself?, we are still confronted with problems similar to those raised by conservation and preservation.

Control of population size has received a great deal of publicity in recent years. On the one hand the population problem is presented in neo-Malthusian terms, with the forecast of imminent disaster; and on the other, it is presented as a problem which will be solved by behavioral constraints as standards of living rise. The problem is, however, more intricate and complex than either view allows. First, population projections are themselves quite unreliable, owing to the dubious value of much of the data base from which they are compiled. Furthermore, mere extrapolation of a present trend is of doubtful methodological validity. Hence it is not surprising that many predictions of population numbers have proved to be grossly in error. Second, and perhaps more importantly, the significance and implications of the problem itself vary greatly from place to place according to the economic conditions and the cultural background. This is clearly illustrated by what has been achieved in China in the field of population stabilization, where conjoint economic and social methods have resulted in later marriage and consequently a lower birthrate. It is perhaps significant that the Chinese experiment has been associated with a new value system and new goals, leading to a new sense of purpose.

Three additional points need to be made. First, there are still some parts of the world where an increase in population is necessary if the available resources are to be adequately developed. Parts of Africa and South America fall into this category. *Second,* in terms of pressure on natural resources it is the developed nations that need to curb their population size.

Finally, the basic assumption behind birth control programs for the developing world is that large families and a high birthrate result because, like many Westerners, the people involved are unable to control their basic sex urges. This is an unjustified assumption. The real reasons for large families are more often found in social and economic pressures, such as the need for a son to continue the family line, for children to care for parents in old age, or for a large family labor force to extract the maximum from the resources available. Birth control programs ought not necessarily to be considered in global or continental terms. They need to be considered and implemented in the context of the total social and economic situation in which local groups and communities find themselves. It is dangerous and wrong for Western society to seek to improve methods of reducing the birthrate that are strongly conditioned by the prevalent mores of our culture—mores that Christians, at least, ought to judge by the standards of God's prescriptive moral principles. There is thus an ethical element in the control of population. The question of moral responsibility is again raised and basic assumptions are challenged.

Problems of the constructed environment impinge upon man as a result of the developments of modern urban society—factories, services, housing, transport networks, and so on. They embrace aspects of all the problems already considered—use of resources, destruction of wildlife and rural landscapes, pollution and the growth of population—but also include distinctive psychosocial, biosocial, and socioeconomic problems. They form a distinctive group of considerable importance to contemporary society, embracing as they do such individual questions as urban violence and vandalism, housing problems, traffic planning, and the location of industrial enterprises, electricity generating stations and motorways. Here we are concerned with the general environmental impact of the constructions and activities of man, and with the impact of those constructions on man himself, his behavior and his way of life.

It is clear that in this group we are concerned with a distinct set of problems relating directly to man, rather than with the general relations of man to his natural environment, which occupied our attention in the first four sets of problems. Because of the human focus, the ethical dimension of these problems is more obvious and direct. This directness of implication, however, does not mean that the ethical problems are less vital. The main principle involved is clearly my responsibility for my neighbor and his welfare, but the application is by no means clear, for it is inevitable that all human constructions have an impact on man directly or indirectly. The question therefore arises as to how much impact is tolerable. Sometimes such questions can be answered in terms of permissible levels medically defined on the basis of human tolerance to intrusion or pollution; often they cannot, because we are concerned with basic aesthetic values and so-called environmental quality. Here human preferences enter into the problem, and inevitably value judgments of an imprecise kind become vital elements in the problem. But even where permissible levels can be defined, the evaluation cannot be avoided, because generally lower levels than the permissible will need to be defined, including human preferences as a criterion. Furthermore, the problem may often be concerned not simply with one intrusion, but with several, and the question then arises as to the cumulative effect of several impacts. The problem thus is very complex and contains an ethical element bound up in the general questions. Therefore, the ethical element is highly significant and needs to be considered as an essential part of the discussion of any problem of the built environment. To this ethical dimension we now turn.

SOME BASIC QUESTIONS

In a perceptive discussion, John Passmore has shown that natural environmental problems embrace six elements, each of which requires a different approach to its solution.[7] Each element has its own distinctive contribution to make, and all six together usually form a solution to an environmental problem. These sets of questions relate to:

1. Understanding the functional relationships involved—that is, *scientific* questions;
2. What manipulations of the system of relationships are feasible within the terms of its own function—that is, *technological* questions;
3. What the relative benefits and costs of the feasible manipulations are—that is, *economic* and *social* questions;
4. Whether or not certain courses of action or goals are more right or wrong in relation to principles of conduct—that is, *moral* questions;
5. What means may be used to persuade or coerce the interested parties to take the action needed, and the allocation of the responsibility to decide on a particular course of action—that is, questions of *politics;* and,
6. How the course of action decided upon may be effected in the

situation in which the particular problem occurs—that is, *administrative* and *legal* questions.

In our paramount concern with the moral and ethical dimension of environmental problems we are not alone. Many environmentalist writings contain explicit appeals to moral principles, prescribing that man ought to behave in a certain way with respect to nature and environmental problems. Some, for example John Black[8] and Christopher Derrick,[9] are mainly concerned with these aspects. Furthermore, it has been common for environmentalists and others—among them Darling,[10] Nicholson,[11] and Toynbee,[12]—to lay the blame for ecological damage at the door of the Judeo-Christian ethic, though this is cogently refuted by Black[13] and Derrick,[14] and set in historical and philosophical perspective by Passmore.[15] Thus we shall be mainly concerned to outline the Biblical ethic of man and nature, and then to examine briefly its two main rivals in western Christendom.

THE JUDEO-CHRISTIAN ETHIC

The detailed biblical basis for a Judeo-Christian environmental ethic I have argued elsewhere.[16] Here we shall confine ourselves to outlining the basic principles there derived. These may be summarized as follows:

1. Fundamental assumptions:
    (a) The use of nature involves moral responsibility.
    (b) The use of nature fits into God's sovereign purpose.
    (c) Nature is unbalanced and imperfect owing to man's moral failure.
2. Practical implications:
    (a) "Creation" elements
        i. The satisfaction of need
        ii. The development of understanding
        iii. The conservation of nature
        iv. The enjoyment of nature
        v. Gratitude to God
    (b) "Redemption" elements
        i. The concern for posterity
        ii. The incorporation of ethical demands into a social code and a legal system

iii. The hope of a future full redemption of nature

These principles need to be examined one by one.

Fundamental Principles.   The intellectual framework with regard to man and nature that supports the Christian ethic has several main struts. Unique to Judeo-Christian thinking, they provide the underpinnings upon which practical action is based. Almost all other religions view nature either as irrelevant to spiritual issues, or as spiritual in itself—whether in a pantheistic sense or in a magical–fetish sense. In the biblical view nature is created and material, not eternal or essentially spiritual. God's purpose embraces nature as well as man, the material world as well as human history; God pronounced His creation "good" even before He fashioned man. Through man, who by creation is both material and linked to nature, and spiritual in that in responsible relation to God he is given authority over nature, nature is morally involved. God makes moral demands upon man in respect to nature; nature belongs to God, and man holds it in trust from Him. Man's disobedience and assertion of independence harm nature as well as man himself.

First, then, the use of nature implies real moral responsibility. The use of nature is no mere matter of mores or convention; it involves a responsibility to God similar in importance to man's relation to his kind. Failure to fulfill the divine requirements incurs real moral guilt. This is clear from the creation account in the early chapters of Genesis and from the requirements in the Jewish law which relate to nature and the land and its use. It is further borne out by the link in prophetic thought between the moral state of the people and the fate of the land and its fruits.

Man's misuses of nature in both past and present are therefore not an unfortunate result of ignorance or merely the sad consequence of human greed, as the contemporary mood often depicts them; they are morally blameworthy acts that imply a need for repentance. For the church, as the representative body of the new humanity, repentance must therefore be the foundation of positive action. Furthermore, contemporary decisions must be reached in the light of their moral import, and Christians should not be reluctant to confront the issues in ethical terms. They should not be content to accept arguments relating only to current consensus and mores, or to the projection of survival values, or to any other viewpoint that denies absolute moral responsibility. Furthermore, it may be argued that the only meaningful appeal to mankind as a whole must be made in terms of real moral responsibility, so that humans no longer err with impunity, or consider themselves blamelessly selfish.

Nevertheless the whole problem must be seen in the context of a continuing divine purpose which embraces creation, man's initial responsibility, man's self-assertion and failure, subsequent consequences in the natural world, and the recconciliation, redemption and consummation which focuses on Jesus Christ. Such a perspective ought to produce both realism and hope. The divine purpose is a moral one; it relates to values, to right and wrong, to human responsibility and to God's moral character. It impinges on and involves the natural and material. But God's purpose is not to be discerned primarily in terms of cause and effect within a mechanistic system that science may seek to elucidate. Its reality is known at a more fundamental level of knowledge, experience and understanding, a level apprehended by faith from which reason operates, one that requires a kind of knowing that transcends the limits of the strictly scientific frame of reference.

The assertion of such an important purpose provides a new perspective on events and problems and supplies a source of hope because of what God has revealed concerning His nature and the moral ends He has in view. But it is also a source of realism, because it make us look beyond the natural and the material to confront the inner moral dilemmas that haunt us. In this perspective, environmental problems are seen not simply as scientific and technological puzzles, but as expressions of inescapable moral conflicts that beset mankind. Thus the second main strut of the framework has important practical consequences reflected in distinctive attitudes toward environmental problems.

Man must realize, moreover, that nature is imperfect owing to man's moral failure. This is clear from the Genesis narratives, as well as implicit in much prophetic writing. Perfect and final solutions are therefore not possible in the present. While bending all their efforts to develop, propagate and apply a distinctive environmental ethic, Christians will always act in this awareness, looking forward to what God will consummate.

This is not to say that we should not seek present solutions or abandon attempts to improve the situation. We must pursue both. The Christian ethic supports both the search for solutions and the anticipation of the goal. But the quest for human utopias that dispenses with the relevance of God and His purposes is ruled out. This is especially salutary in the light of much writing that implies that greater knowledge will of itself ensure satisfactory progress toward a "better" world and an improved "quality of life." When coupled with the implication that such higher "quality" lies essentially in increasing affluence and material well-being, such commentary is especially to be deplored. This third principle asserts that environmental problems require the intimate intertwining of notions of moral responsibility and of scientific understanding. It is impossible to point to any merely human decision which subsequent events have proved an absolute good; conversely, of course, few decisions have proved a completely unmitigated evil. There seem no grounds for supposing that modern scientific understanding will produce any fundamental change in this respect. This principle enjoins us to constant vigilance in watching the outcomes of even the most apparently satisfactory solutions to environmental problems.

Practical Implications. Examination of the biblical evidence suggests eight major principles of conduct concerning nature that embrace the Christian ethic of environment. Five relate to the pristine state of man before the Fall, and the remaining three are added in the scriptural account after that event. The first five are to be construed as applying also after the Fall, since the biblical account affirms them both explicitly and implicitly, in the law and the prophets, as well as in the earliest chapters of Genesis. The distinctive contribution of New Testament thought is to be found in the last of the eight principles. Hence it is convenient to group the first five principles as creation elements and the last three as redemption elements.

The first creation principle relates nature as a divine gift to man by way of satisfaction of his need. The implication is that it is right for man to take from nature those resources that he needs to survive and to develop himself. The corollary is that all human beings ought to have the opportunity to satisfy their needs from nature, an emphasis that therefore supports efforts to distribute the resources of nature more fairly. It also condemns those excesses of Western or any other society that deprive others of the merest basic satisfaction of their needs.

On the other hand, this principle is not to be interpreted as an exhortation to asceticism. It implies that it is right for man to satisfy his needs from nature as a whole. Nature is made for man and not vice-versa, for to God, man is more important than nature, though nature is not on that account valueless. But the principle does not support the sanctity of all life. It does not prevent man from using nature, or from asserting himself against nature when conflict arises, as in the disposition of animals or crops or in the prevention and cure of human disease.

Yet the principle also implies constraints in relation to natural resources. Man has no licence to exploit resources merely to advance his own affluence and to pander to his own greed. Such exploitation has led in the past to striking desecrations of the environment.

The first creation principle raises two significant questions. The first is the extent to which it is possible for us to define human need, and the second concerns whether the principle's meaning can be extended to include entire nations. In the case of the individual the important point seems to be that the decision as to what I really need is to be made before God. It may be possible for me not only to readily convince myself, even others that I need something, but can I convince God, who knows and sees all? This can be answered only in the context of all the circumstances relating to the choice. Thus the fundamental principle of responsibility to God is of great practical significance, and gives a strength to the Christian ethic which is absent in a humanist or a pantheist approach.

More general questions arise at the level of society and nation. Recently, John Taylor has questioned the excess which is the present hallmark of the developed world.[17] Much that he writes is relevant and important, but must we necessarily shun economic growth and technological advance and attempt, in effect, to turn back the clock of development? Certainly excess is bad, and much in Western society is geared to multiplying that excess. To assert *need* as a basic standard is, however, neither neo-Arcadian nor necessarily ascetic. As Passmore has pointed out,[18] environmental problems will be solved, not by eliminating technology, but by developing it in the context of an appropriate value system.

At the national level, however, the principle of need poses two searching questions: Can we justify at a national level the way in which we spend our money?, and Ought the developed world to be committed to increasing standards of living and to economic growth, at the expense of the peoples of the underdeveloped nations of the world? In sum, Do we as a nation really *need* all we appear to *want?* The answers to these questions are not easy, but a realistic assessment of human need would be a realistic first step toward finding them.

The second creation element concerns the development of understanding. To develop an ethic based on the biblical revelation is not to deny the importance of knowledge and understanding, but rather to establish it. Knowledge is implicit in the responsibility given to man by God at the beginning. The Christian environmental ethic does not therefore merely tolerate scientific knowledge and understanding; it requires it. The important point is, however, that applications of the ethic are not to be based simply on comprehensive knowledge but made in the context of the other principles of conduct. Man should seek to increase knowledge in the environmental field and then use it in making moral decisions concerning the environment. This principle implies that Christians ought not merely to be neutral with respect to science and technology, but that they should be *pro-knowledge.* There is a middle way between the technomania criticized by Christopher Derrick[19] and the rejection of science and technology typical of the counter-culture, and the mystical–ecological subculture. The middle way is feasible, however, only if science and technology are incorporated into a rational scheme of responsible values like that provided by the biblical concept of moral responsibility and its associated system of binding ethical principles.

The conservation of nature is the third creation principle. Nature is to be valued for itself, and Christians should have an interest in its preservation. If nature was pronounced good by God before man was created, can Christians value it less? Part of the purpose of man's creation was to care for what God had provided. Thus there are real moral grounds for insisting upon the preservation of species, for the conservation of at least some wild regions, and for setting apart areas for the use of wild organisms. Although some management will undoubtedly be required, the aim of these preventative measures will be to benefit plants and animals not of direct use to man himself. Frequently this third principle interacts with the first, and certainly it depends upon the second, for effective preservation requires an understanding of those species and ecosystems that we are committed to preserve. It might even be argued that we devote not nearly enough money to research of this type compared with the staggering sums we spend for certain kinds of technology, such as the space program and nuclear science. Thus the principle provides a salutary counterbalance to anthropocentric tendencies characteristic of some interpretations of the Christian ethic.

The fourth creation element, the *enjoyment of nature,* forms a major practical principle for action. It appeals not simply to man's reason, but also to his emotions. The right use of nature ought to lead to the aesthetic enjoyment of nature. By creation, man is dependent upon nature, and he ought to enjoy that experience of dependence. The exercise of his responsibility to God for his use of nature ought also to be enjoyable. Such enjoyment is itself a constraint on exploitation, for the experience of enjoyment involves a desire to preserve what one is enjoying.

If man is ideally to enjoy nature, does it not follow that governments and planners ought to provide for that enjoyment and formulate legal constraints that prevent damage to and abuse of nature by those unwilling to accept their personal responsibility? It is perhaps a significant comment on the moral state of Western society that so often, as soon as virgin and unspoiled areas become accessible, they become spoiled by litter and vandalism. Such areas can also be spoiled by entertainment facilities that cater mainly to the leisure pursuits of visitors. Perhaps many moderns have lost the capacity to enjoy nature, a sad commentary on the state of humanity.

Thus we return to the fundamental point of human responsibility, and assert as a final principle gratitude to God for nature and its provisions. In his relationship to the world man is required to look beyond nature to God who made it, to whom it belongs, and who has committed it to man as a steward on God's behalf. If man thus acknowledges his real responsibility to God in a fundamental moral sense, he will seek to right the wrongs of the past. True repentance is acceptance of guilt coupled with an attempt to make amends by positive action, made on the basis of a real "ought" in accordance with the previously indicated principles.

Outside such a transcendently objective framework appeals for action can be made only on the basis of plausibility, or consensus, or at the most, self-interest. Even if the consequence of our present problems could be shown incontrovertibly to be disaster in twenty years time, then this would provide no basis for motivation except fear. Fear may sometimes supply strong motive, but it is not sufficient reason. If man is now in the position where his actions directly affect the survival of the species, as some would maintain, he still has no reason for deciding one way or the other; his decision is now often declared to be merely part of an essentially mechanistic biological process. If he decides one way then man will survive as merely an oddity among other animal species; if he decides another way, he will perish. Either way, the outcome is purely phenomenal, because in no sense can it be justified on typically modern premises as good or bad, nor indeed can it ultimately.

This final principle is therefore fundamental, because it implies that environmental problems are to be treated as involving real moral responsibility to a real God. The basis of any solution must then be repentance, not only from the mistakes of the past, but also from an attitude of mind which fails to live by transcendent moral claims. And this brings us to the redemptive purpose of God in Christ in relation both to man and to nature.

The redemptive principles are occasioned by man's alienation from God, being added after the Fall. The first is a concern for posterity; the second is the legal codification of ethical demands; and the third, the certainty of full redemption. Here man is provided with an added motive, an extra sanction and a safeguard against despair.

The concern for posterity is developed by the Old Testament and authenticated by the New. It forms an essential part of God's promises to the patriarchs. It underlies much of the teaching in Leviticus and Deuteronomy, and its neglect is reprimanded by the prophets. Thus it is fundamental to God's dealings with man in both mercy and judgment. The sins of the fathers do in fact affect subsequent generations for ill, and sound decisions do in fact benefit posterity. So we ought to be deeply concerned to make wise decisions in relation to the natural environment upon which we depend for sustenance and for survival.

It is important to notice that Black[20] and Passmore,[21] who have produced such balanced discussions of environmental problems, both arrive at this cardinal consideration in making environmental decisions. Both are aware of the impossibility of basing a moral vision of posterity upon merely scientific and technological projection, the implications of which for posterity are altogether too subtle. But the significant point is that the biblical ethic includes this vital principle as an essential structural element.

Social codes and legal sanctions form an important element in Old Testament thought. Numerous instructions, both practical and ritual, bear significantly on man's use of nature and his environment. Hebrew law was not solely concerned with God-to-man and man-to-man relationships, but also with those concerning man and animal life, man and plant life, man and the land and man and natural resources. The New Testament authenticates Old Testament emphasis. The Christian ethic thus embraces the necessity of including environmental ideas in appropriate educational programs, and in social codes and systems of law.

In my view, these ideas constitute an incentive to Christians as individuals and as communities to undertake a prophetic function in society in relation to environmental issues. They may suggest also the political involvement of Christians in public environmental action at all levels. The biblical ethic is not solely personal; it is also an ethic to which society as a whole is answerable. Christians should be determined and vocal in relation to environmental issues, and should support programs that enjoin or enforce a more responsible attitude to nature and to the natural environment. The Christian community should be the supreme model of environmental responsibility as part of its commitment to the gospel of God's grace revealed in Jesus Christ.

The Christian ethic, finally, holds out hope for the future. Environmental problems are not to be seen solely as issues in themselves, but in the context of God's continuing purpose that is moving forward to a final consummation that is both good and sure. Christians should see their own roles within this governing purpose. Since it is *God's* purpose they advance, they can pursue their own activities in the consciousness of authentic hope. They know not only that mistakes and wrongs will be forgiven, but also that right and wise decisions will reap their own good harvest for immediate posterity and for the long future. Christian ecologists, planners, agriculturalists or technologists can therefore pursue their callings in the context of its contribution to God's ongoing redemptive purpose. No other world view sustains this hope.

These eight elements, in their interdependence, provide a comprehensive, practical and realistic basis for an environmental ethic. I suggest that no other ethic or schema of social mores provides such a satisfactory structure, or such a persuasive basis for decision and action.

TWO ALTERNATIVE VIEWS

The Christian world view has already been implicitly compared with other views which purport to provide a basis for action in the environmental field. A review of current views of nature that are relevant to man's perception of his environment has been presented elsewhere.[22] Here we shall discuss only the two main views presently advocated in ecological circles, namely, evolutionary humanism and ecological mysticism.

Evolutionary humanism includes a wide range of broadly humanist and rationalist viewpoints, and provides the current intellectual background in the Western scientific world. It thus supplies the framework of assumptions on which much of the current debate is built. A number of problems, however, overarch the moral outworkings of this view.

In the first place, evolutionary humanism provides no real concept of responsibility. All affirmations are captive to the very system which is declared to be the object of study. But any attempt to evaluate the rightness or wrongness of a course of action must specify appropriate criteria outside the system in which the course of action takes place. In the view of scientific humanism, no system transcends what is accessible to scientific empiricism; hence no transcendent criteria are allowable or conceivable, and no concept of responsibility is possible. Ideas of rightness or wrongness often come back to consensus norms only. The problem comes when we have to decide between different sets of norms. The dilemma of secular moral philosophy—so far insoluble—of deriving an *ought* from an *is,* a moral prescription from a statement of fact, remains.

The result is that ultimately, in order to elevate certain principles to moral validity, a sheer leap of faith has to be made to principles and assumptions outside what is known. Thus the evolutionary humanist view does not rid itself of the need for an expression of belief; rather it substitutes faith in the abstract principles it postulates for faith in principles persuasively derived from a transcendent personal source. It is extremely difficult to think of responsibility merely to abstract principles, and much easier to weigh responsibility in personal terms.

In the second place, this need for a metaphysical dimension is revealed by the fact that in appearance, if not always in fact, evolution is personified and given a role in secular thought comparable to that which God occupies in Christian thought. Evolution is elevated from a general scientific theory relating to the historical sequence of development of organic life to an operative principle embracing all aspects of life—not only biological, but psychological, social, and moral as well. "Evolution" as a general philosophical system relating to human progress needs of course to be clearly distinguished from the theory of biological evolution. There is no necessary link between the two, and the latter could be valid and the former false. But it is with the basic assumptions of evolutionary philosophy that we are concerned. These are articles of faith. To include all of human life within biological mechanisms alone, moreover, is to destroy the whole basis of human choice, and thus also of human responsibility, so that ethical discussion becomes quite irrelevant and pointless.

Thus evolutionary humanism rests upon a leap of faith rather than upon rational demonstration. It is thus not necessarily more tenable than the Christian view, and is not so able to provide a reasonable ethic which human beings everywhere and always may be expected to fulfill.

Ecological mysticism is another viewpoint advocated or implied by numerous conservationists. Deriving its metaphysics from various Oriental philosophies, it maintains that humankind partakes of a common life with nature and must therefore respect life in all its forms. This bare view is often, indeed usually, augmented by an appeal to some mystical conception of "life," "life force," "sanctity of life," or "mystery of life."

One objection to this view is that it provides no real notion of responsibility. Its appeal is predicated on an intangible "mystical holism" that has no necessary logical connection with the general scientific approach of ecology, plausible though the analogy may seem. Its conception of an *ought* is spawned by an appeal to the mystical, which in itself involves a leap of faith.

While the mystical approach may provide sanctions *against* killing other organisms, it provides no reason *for* killing, which might seem to be a necessary action in the case of pathogens and other organisms dangerous to man. Most of those committed to the mystical view would, at this point, introduce other criteria, and see man as the high point of evolution so far, asserting some human superiority over other organisms on those grounds. But this merely brings the argument back to where it began.

Finally, this viewpoint is open to all the controversies which earlier surrounded the idea of *vitalism* in biology, because in effect it maintains that *life* is a distinctive something possessed by organisms, and that the possession of this something provides the ethical basis for action. In the Christian view already outlined, man shares biological life with other organisms, but man's life has special significance. This significance results, not from what life is "in itself," but from the special significance God gives it in terms of personality, intellect and reason, and, particularly, real moral responsibility. The Christian view is thus independent of differing biological views of life in a way that the ecological–mystical view is not.

CONCLUSION

An attempt has been made to summarize the character of environmental problems, and to set their ethical element in context. A conspectus of the biblical Christian ethic of man and nature has been presented, and it has been compared, both implicitly and explicitly, with some of its main rivals. The writer is persuaded that the Christian view offers a balanced, comprehensive and workable ethic of environment.

NOTES

1. Aldo Leopold, *A Sand County Almanack* (London: Oxford University Press, 1949).

2. G. V. Jacks and R. O. Whyte, *The Rape of the Earth* (London: Faber & Faber, Ltd., 1939).

3. John Passmore, *Man's Responsibility for Nature* (London: Duckworth, 1974).

4. Max Nicholson, *The Environmental Revolution: A Guide for the New Masters of the World* (London: Hodder and Stoughton, 1970).

5. F. Fraser Darling, "Man's Responsibility for the Environment," in *Biology and Ethics*, ed. F. J. Ebling (London: Academic Press, 1969).

6. Passmore, *op. cit.*, p. 45.

7. Passmore, *op. cit.*

8. John Black, *The Dominion of Man* (Edinburgh: Edinburgh University Press, 1970).

9. Christopher Derrick, *The Delicate Creation* (London: Tom Stacey, 1972).

10. Arnold Toynbee, "The Religious Background of the Present Environmental Crisis," *International Journal of Environmental Science* 3 (1972): 141–146.

11. R. P. Moss, "Responsibility in the Use of Nature (I)," *Christian Graduate* 28, No. 3 (1975): 69–80; "Responsibility in the Use of Nature (II)," *Christian Graduate* 29, No. 1 (1976): 5–14; "Nature, Man and God: a Biblical Perspective," in *God, Man and the Environment*, ed. I. Davis and B. Fewings, "God, Man and Nature: Contrasting Views in Christendom," *Countryside Perception Conference, Peak National Park Study Conference,*

12. John V. Taylor, *Enough is Enough* (London: SCM Press Ltd., 1975).

13. Moss, "God, Man and Nature: Contrasting Views in Christendom," *op. cit.*

V

The Ambiguities of Scientific Breakthrough

CARL F. H. HENRY

Is technology in our century a providential provision for the salvation of mankind? Or does it portend the self-devastation of the human race or even demolition of our planet? What attitude ought the religious man to have and to encourage toward the intrusion of genetic experimentation into the mystery of creation? What does Christian conscience require in regard to behavioral science—for example, toward experiments in genetic cloning and psychosurgery? What directive principles, if any, can revealed religion supply to guide frontier technology?

In the summer of 1975 evangelical scientists gathered at Wheaton

Carl F. H. Henry, theologian and writer currently serving World Vision International as lecturer-at-large, has taught on both American and Asian campuses. He was founding editor of *Christianity Today* magazine from 1956–1968, having previously served on the faculties of Northern Baptist Theological Seminary from 1940–1947 and Fuller Theological Seminary from 1947–1956. Crowning his twenty-two books is *God, Revelation and Authority,* the initial two volumes of which appeared in 1976. Among his many edited works are *Baker's Dictionary of Christian Ethics* (1973) and the Contemporary Evangelical Thought symposium series in which this present volume appears. He holds a Th.D. and a Ph.D. and maintains a keen interest in the reconciliation of theology, philosophy and science. He is a former vice president of the American Theological Society and a former president of the Evangelical Theological Society.

College in Illinois for the International Conference on Human Engineering and the Future of Man (ICHEFM) to hear presentations by
both secular and Christian scholars, to discuss some of the implications of recent scientific trends, and to contemplate the Christian
stance toward technology.[1] This volume widens that dialogue to include a more complete range of prestigious scholars working on different frontiers of science and is concerned with indicating moral issues
implicit in present scientific inquiry.

There is no doubt that technology has become for some persons the
utopian religion of the present generation. As Jacques Ellul has observed, in our time anything and everything except technology is a
ready target of criticism. We sometimes hear that technology is the
greatest single force for either good or evil in the modern world.
Because of its enormous inherent possibilities, some observers say, the
destiny of mankind now depends on what the twentieth century does
with pure and applied science. Speaking of its immense power to
change man's environment and even his body and mind and way of
life, social psychologist Kenneth Clark declared in his presidential
address to the American Psychological Association that "we might be
on the threshold of . . . scientific biochemical intervention which could
stabilize and make dominant the moral and ethical propensities of
man and subordinate, if not eliminate, his negative and primitive
behavioral tendencies." Clark even proposed that political leaders
"accept and use the earliest forms of psycho-technical, biochemical
intervention which would assure their positive use of power and reduce or block the possibility of using power destructively."[2]

Despite uncertainty over some future applications of technology,
man in this final quarter of the twentieth century is increasingly prone
to think that he has power to determine his own destiny. That human
ingenuity cancels out the need for God is of course a notion neither
modern nor specially grounded in technology; it antedates by many
centuries (cf. Ps. 14:1) the unlimited modern faith in applied science
and fully deserves the scorn that C. S. Lewis levels against the contemporary pride in technological genius. To be sure, some members of the
scientific community decry any unqualified adulation of science. But
they do not speak the universal mood. Social philosophers and scientific frontiersmen not infrequently voice exuberance over technology,
and many young people are once again eagerly pursuing vocations in

applied science. Whatever pessimism some scholars voice concerning science, ordinary people by and large still retain a practical idolatry of it.

Those who contend that runaway technology is a baneful development point to its impact on lifestyle and environment and, beyond that, to the misidentification of the real world in terms of merely impersonal processes and events. Others insist that technology is not intrinsically evil, yet nonetheless criticize its excessive diversion of human energies from ethicoreligious to material concerns, its support of a new moral permissiveness and accommodation of extensive revolt against a biblical ethic, not to speak of its special serviceability to totalitarian governments. As enormous possibilities of social misuse have become evident, more and more scientists are conceding that technology is not a one-way street to utopia. Informed scholars writing in respected technical journals discuss such doomsday possibilities as total environmental pollution of air, sea and land, or nuclear destruction of the human race and of our planet. Having now unraveled the genetic code, having discovered quasars and pulsars and placed men on the moon, our scientifically minded generation is calling for sober assessment of both long- and short-range technological involvements.

TECHNOLOGY AND THE POSSIBILITIES OF EVIL

The ways in which modern technology has already been used accelerates many fears about its long-term potential for evil. Among these are the scientific extermination of millions of adults and children and the forced sterilization of citizens in the interest of a supposedly master race. In Auschwitz alone, 4 million people were murdered in cold blood in less than five years. Such mockery of the worth and dignity of the human person may be highly exceptional among scientists. But universal limitations even on objectionable experimentation require not only strong international agreements but also genuine good will. Some social psychologists and social scientists who once counted on environmental improvement to upgrade humanity today give priority instead to the possibilities of biological intervention. Needless to say, the question of public control of scientific decision making in matters of frontier technology poses serious problems for freedom of research. But a society increasingly disturbed over secret, and potentially harmful, scientific experimentation on the citizenry increasingly insists that scientists consult with the larger public, not just with a few delegated representatives, in order to safeguard human dignity and freedom of choice.

Members of Congress have questioned the United States government's support of behavior technology programs that endanger basic human rights. Federally funded behavior control experiments in mental institutions and prisons, for example, have used brain-implanted radio transmitter–receivers to enable computers to monitor and determine behavior. Iowa prisoners who used vile language or smoked where prohibited were punished by doses of apomorphine, a drug that produces violent vomiting. In one California state hospital patients manifesting antisocial behavior or attempting suicide were punished by being given anectine, which produces respiratory seizures and muscular paralysis. One $3 million federal project in behavior modification involved perhaps ten thousand psychotherapy patients and more than thirty thousand institutionalized persons. The United States Army acknowledged that in 1956 and 1957 alone it administered LSD to nearly fifteen hundred military persons and simultaneously to nine hundred civilians in a testing program in which several universities participated. In one case, a civilian scientist unknowingly took LSD and subsequently committed suicide; the government withheld the facts from his family for many years. Disclosure of these and other behavior experiments conducted under the canopy of national security—often without the free consent of participating individuals or without awareness of the destructive potential of the drugs involved —has heightened public concern over research that might imperil human well-being.

The premature application of technology to human affairs in numerous instances has raised a cry for what is now called "preventive technology." Belated discovery revealed that Thalidomide causes harmful birth defects; that scientific techniques less accurate than believed actually imposed diets that could possibly lead to severe mental retardation upon newborn babies screened for metabolism defects; that the diagnostic tool itself may have somewhat increased the chances of women under age fifty-one having cancer when they were given mammograms (breast X-ray exams) as part of a breast cancer screening program; that claims made for thirty-five years that women can prevent breast cancer by regularly taking estrogen pills are questionable and that new medical findings indicate not only that the drug does not protect against breast cancer but also that "a definite possibility" exists that it may actually contribute to and perhaps even be a cause of this form of malignancy. The use two decades ago of heavy doses of radiation in treating childhood diseases like tonsilitis, adenoids and ear problems unwittingly made youngsters high cancer risks; several million are thought to have received such radiation as children, and seven in one hundred are now presumed to have thyroid cancer. After 50 million Americans were injected late in 1976 with swine flu shots, federal authorities temporarily suspended the immunization program when the risk of inducing paralytic Guillain-Barre disease seemed to outweigh the risk of a swine flu epidemic. What unforeseen adverse effects, some ask, may flow from the fact that American physicians now prescribe such vast quantities of tranquilizers that national addiction has become almost as widespread a problem as is alcoholism?

We now know that the pesticide DDT, despite its gratifying initial success in destroying insect pests, also destroys birds, animals and fish. All too tardily came warnings of cancer hazards related to use of chlordane as a pesticide and of vinyl chloride in plastics manufacture. More recently attention focuses on the unforeseen perils of nuclear radiation from power plants.

Christian Reformed scholar Allen Verhey has noted that by promoting literacy and developing new tools serviceable to the masses, technology contributed in earlier generations to the democratic ethos; today, however, it threatens that same ethos. By promoting mystification, Verhey contends, it creates a knowledge gap between the technological experts, with their analytic sophistication and technical vocabulary, and the masses.[3] Others note that much scientific research is mainly academic and of little interest to the masses; statistics indicate that despite the known menace of cigarettes to health, people continue to do whatever they choose. For much of the non-Western world, moreover, the fruit of most present-day research will necessarily be harvested in a distant future.

Strategic use of technology, in addition, sometimes requires a swiftness of decision less compatible with democratic processes (which rely

on public education and representative government) than with totalitarian procedures. During World War II, for example, the American
decision to drop the atomic bomb on two Japanese cities was made
—and necessarily so—by a small inner circle of leaders. Effective use
of the latest technology may therefore minimize representative processes. Yet delayed use may endanger a democratic power and perhaps yield victory unnecessarily to some predatory totalitarian nation.

The United States came into being in an age when diversity, manifested in the politics of individual freedom, in no way threatened the
homogeneity of the new nation. Now, global social and political differences are rampant, sometimes to the point of explosive conflict. Democratic political theory decries as the essence of tyranny the coercion
of behavior or even of consent. Today, however, according to Perry
London of the University of Southern California, the technology of
control makes possible an engineering of consent by governing both
behavior and desire.[4] We may presume to preserve personal liberty,
he says, while destroying personal liberty.

The additional fact that modern science and technology have facili-
tated hitherto unparalleled dimensions of ethical permissiveness is
well known. Contraceptives have little direct effect on sexual impulses, yet they immensely affect the motives and opportunities for
sexual intercourse; never before has any society experienced such
widespread disconnection of sexual intercourse from marriage. The
present controversy over abortion—"on demand" and not solely in
cases of rape, threat to the mother's life or hopeless genetic deformity
—indicates how deeply medical technology impinges upon moral
convictions; the number of reported abortions in the United States in
1974 alone totalled 763,476. Social critics ask whether abortion may
next be welcomed simply for purposes of sex preferences in human
progeny.

What particularly distresses some social critics is that astonishingly
few scientists have shown serious interest in ethical aspects of their
work. The academic training of most scientists and medical doctors
has been so narrowly focused that ethical concerns have remained
largely out of view. The recent swift technical advances in psychosurgery, genetic manipulation, molecular engineering, biomechan-
ics, prenatal screening and abortion nonetheless thrust upon these
leaders decisions that impinge upon the Judeo-Christian view of the

nature and sanctity of human life and that, in any event, involve moral determinations for which they are ill prepared.

Psychotherapy, for the most part, still caters to preoccupation with one's selfhood and encourages the exploration of behavioral alternatives. Often attracting those who rebel against the reigning social values, it offers an ethic of self-realization in which transcendent values are obscure. It therefore easily bends individual morality in hedonistic directions. The compatibility of this approach with yoga, transcendental meditation and mind-expanding approaches—over against the transcendently given ethics of Judeo-Christian revelation —is evident, since self-determination and self-reference become the only criteria of one's behavior. In their moral judgments about sexual freedom many practitioners in private offices or outpatient clinics engage in permissive counseling. Although not all psychotherapists, by any means, are morally permissive in private life, a formal survey shows them as a class to be among the most bohemian spirits in American society.

In view of these considerations, some would ask if any view is wise other than a very dim one of drugs that will shortly be available for improving memory and the intelligence quotient, of pleasure drugs that bring about aphrodisia, and of drugs that hold promise of a cheap and certain means of suicide. They are disconcerted by the prospect of "four-hour trip" pills that promise to "elevate the quality of life" of terminal patients not merely by easing pain but by additionally stimulating them "to see new things" and "to appreciate life more than before." Do not these developments, they ask, simply widen the potential for evil in a world where Christians are enjoined to promote desirable human survival by setting their hearts first on "the kingdom of God, and his righteousness" (Matt. 6:33, KJV).

After three decades of genetic and cellular biology research, medical specialists are increasingly able to influence human genetic structures. Genetic researchers do not yet fully understand the mechanisms of gene control, but they have presumably elucidated the chemical nature of the gene, the chemistry of mutation and the conditions of genetic diversity. Major genetic intervention will first be limited to simple organisms; in fact, the transfer of genes from plants or animals into microorganisms for propagation in laboratory cultures is already in progress, and chemically synthesized genes can already, in principle, be inserted into cells that serve as biological factories for desired combinations.

The creation in late 1976 of an artificial bacteria gene, considered the basic unit of heredity, was a major breakthrough in the study of genetics. The present inability to extend genetic technology to higher organisms, including human beings themselves, research specialists attribute only to the greater complexity of these genetic systems, and especially to the limited knowledge of human genetics. The bacteria gene has 126 nucleotides (minute bits of chemical), whereas a human gene contains millions of these. The recent precise identification of each of the human chromosomes, however, indicates that detailed manipulation of human genetics may not be far distant. Only under the most restrictive conditions can experiments involving the creation of DNA chimeras (test-tube fusions of the DNA of different organisms) between bacterial and mammalian genes be performed. To facilitate scientific inquiry while minimizing public hazards, such as unwitting spread of cancer or other diseases, the National Institutes of Health (NIH) have published guidelines for "recombinant DNA research," that is, the resplicing of genes in a test tube. The U. S. Commerce Department ruling that commercial companies may apply for accelerated patents on new forms of laboratory-created life stirred public controversy because it seemed to invert NIH guidelines.

Advances in recombinant DNA technology have now made the complex large genomes (overall genetic constitution) of man and animals more amenable to detailed study. The National Institute of General Medical Sciences (NIGMS) is probing the desirability of establishing a repository for mammalian DNA fragments and of reproducing and distributing replicated and characterized fragments of human and other mammalian genomes.

If sperm carrying a Y chromosome and those carrying an X chromosome can be isolated, then the control of the gender of offspring may be possible. Robert L. Sinsheimer, chairman of the Division of Biology, California Institute of Technology, notes that "the social consequences of a major change in the human sex ratio—or even of more subtle changes such as that a large majority of first children might be male—are difficult to imagine, but certainly they will be profound."[5] A marked change in the human sex ratio would have fully as much impact upon the social order as would a significant extension of the human life span. Can a world already beset by staggering problems of population, famine, energy, pollution and fear of nuclear annihilation cope with the strain of such a sudden additional complication? Would an extended human life span of ten, twenty or thirty years place intolerable stresses upon an already burdened social order? Will an expansion of human freedom to include intervention in the balances of nature lead ultimately to an unanticipated diminution or cancellation of that freedom?

The ability to identify genetic factors that determine human characteristics raises the further prospect of preventing the birth of fetuses with defective genes. We now know, and have the technological means to eliminate, genetic factors that contribute, for example, to Tay-Sachs disease or sickle cell anemia. Does such knowledge give us license to abort defective fetuses, or does it only add to the moral accountability of prospective parents? Should screening of potential parents be mandatory as a safeguard against possible defective offspring? Or has a parent the right to remain ignorant of such information if he or she is willing to risk the financial burden? Would we prefer to know that a given child is genetically likely to die of heart disease before he or she reaches age forty? If one knows that he or she has some particular genetic propensity for physical or mental disorder, is that very knowledge likely to become self-fulfilling? Before someone's presumed doomsday, may not presently unforeseen alternatives perhaps be discovered? And if biomedical techniques could keep man alive indefinitely without aging, and make perpetual youth the norm, would human beings then yearn for death rather than for survival? Are there intrinsic human limits of physical endurance—say eighty years or so—beyond which we are doomed to die of increasingly crippling diseases?

If genetic intervention has already aroused these and other momentous questions of ethical and social importance, nowhere does it more graphically raise issues of human individuality and dignity, freedom and responsibility than in the projected cloning of human beings. To be sure, the possibility of cloning a human being is at present remote. Because of the remarkable diversity of human genetic factors, identical twins provide the only existing examples of natural duplication. But the fact that all the genes of the human person are duplicated each time one of his or her cells divides makes cloning a possibility. One's entire genetic complement is believed to be present in the nuclei of any individual cell, despite the fact that different types of cells use different sets of genes. Laboratory specialists have already reproduced genetically identical insects and amphibians, notably frogs and salamanders. To be sure, the cloning of mammals—even mice—poses far greater difficulties. But Sinsheimer contends that the problems stem from disruptive aspects of nuclear injection into microscopic mammalian eggs rather than from fundamental differences that impose some kind of biological block.

If human cloning were to become biologically possible, it would raise a host of complex ethical questions and social issues. Here we mention but a few. For what purpose or reason shall we venture this reproductive procedure? What of the morality of using surrogate mothers? What effect will asexual propagation have upon clonees? What are the implications of this practice for the family and home, already severely threatened as the basic unit of society? Since the first human clones would obviously be subject to sustained scientific scrutiny and society would consider them oddities, how normal could and would their responses and behavior be? Is it inhumane to clone a person for a predetermined role in scientific experimentation? As Sinsheimer points out, "The first interveners will be experimenters and the first designed progeny will be guinea pigs. And not all the experiments will be successful. In plant genetics if some experiments yield a patch of weak crops of low yield, it is simply discarded. But what if these were human beings?" Thus we come to the ironic possibility that while promoting the destruction of genetically defective fetuses produced in the course of natural birth, scientists will nonetheless want to spare monstrous deformities of their own making.

Does seeking to clone a human being trespass on divine prerogatives? Some observers question whether man has, or can acquire, the wisdom to be entrusted with the programing of his own species and think that future generations may curse us for experimenting with the human psyche. They consider the unraveling of the genetic code an unjustifiable intrusion into the mystery of life; they see it as an illicit desire to know all that God knows, something that will be punished in turn by ethical dilemmas greater than those man can bear. "As our knowledge of human genetics grows," Sinsheimer comments, "our power to predict bids to outstrip our power to avert." Sinshimer answers the question whether it is inhuman to design a being with the characteristics of *homo sapiens* with a resounding yes: "Genetic self-design has never been a human prerogative. . . . To enter this new dimension would change the nature of humanity, both by act and consequence." He cautions against underestimating the significance of limitations that ethical problems pose for human experimentation: "The traits of greatest interest to those who seek to 'improve' mankind —psychological qualities such as intelligence, foresight, stability, compassion and altruism—are precisely the traits least understood in physiological terms." No persuasive evidence as yet exists, he adds, for thinking that such traits are multigenic, that is, due to the interactions of numerous genes. "We have no understanding at this time," he says, "of the physiological and biochemical processes involved whereby genetic elements express themselves in psychological terms . . . nor is it evident how we shall ever obtain such information save by the experiments with their obvious potentials for grievous failure."

Sinsheimer observes further that "we have long feared, and in the main rejected, human experimentation with human beings, lest once begun we know not where to leave off. This concern has been expressed in such basic principles as the liberty and dignity of the individual, and in medicine in the doctrine of informed consent. In what name, and by what principle, and to what end should one human being use another as his research object?"

The achievements of technology have at the same time bequeathed us enormous dilemmas. The rapid reduction of death rates and decrease of infant mortality around the world have not been matched by an equal decrease in birth rates. Doubling every thirty-seven years, global population threatens food supplies in those lands where the need is greatest and famine a common spectre. Efforts to control childbirth have altered sexual relationships and placed unprecedented stress on family and society. Increasing the human life span by drugs or mechanical means often poses the problem of whether to extend the miseries of terminally ill patients. Maintaining life artificially also brings up the vexing question of just when death itself occurs—when brain function ceases, when the heart stops, or when the whole body is beyond restoration? Can we, moreover, answer the question of the dignity of human life one way in respect to the rights of the fetus at procreation and another in respect to the rights of the aged at senility?

The overall question arises, therefore, whether scientific experimentation has already intruded so far into the ultimate issues of life and
death that, because of its intrinsic limitations, science itself may perhaps now threaten as much as it promotes the larger well-being of the
human species?

Yet Sinsheimer reminds us that "no man chooses his genes." He
speaks in this context, not of Elohim and creation, but of evolution
and chance. "To a biologist our uniquely human qualities, our capacities for speech, our abilities to learn and to reason are also an evolutionary gift, a part of our animal heritage. . . . The question really is
[whether] to trust design or to enthrone chance?" By thus framing the
question in the context of evolutionary naturalism, he sees technocratic imposition of design as the sole alternative to chance and contingency.

In the realms of natural catastrophe and of physical ailments, Sinsheimer argues, "we have not hesitated to intercept the tumbling dice
—to mitigate the role of chance and thereby to enlarge the domain
of human choice and freedom." "Could it even be," he asks, "that
genetic change offers the only true solution—the only way out of the
dilemma that increasingly arises . . . from our internal flaws and
imperfections?" Sinsheimer therefore sees human engineering as the
way to outwit both "evolution's genetic lottery" and man's sufferance
of " 'the slings and arrows' of outrageous chance."

The biblical view affirms, to the contrary, that the "the whole
disposing thereof is of the Lord" (Prov. 16:33, KJV); God displays his
providential purpose even in the life of the blind (Exod. 4:11). Donald
MacKay, the distinguished British brain psychologist, notes that,
whereas naturalistic scientists consider themselves face to face with
chance wherever they cannot humanly predict or foresee the turn of
things, the Bible sets both what science knows and what it does not
know in a significantly different context. The desire for technological
omniscience is usually predicated on the view that human knowledge
is the only knowledge there is and that the only alternative to such
knowledge is a universe left to caprice and chance. Fears that a
multiplied mankind may soon compete beastlike for food and shelter
reflect no confidence in the divine providence that stands at the center
of Scripture. For biblical warnings of the divine moral judgment
awaiting unrepentant mankind at the end of time, contemporary so-

cial critics readily substitute a secular "weeping and gnashing of teeth" that concentrates on physical and economic needs while it eclipses the demand for moral renewal to escape "the wrath to come." The Christian knows that in this fallen world not even finite misjudgment or sinful misuse of technology can separate the believer from the love of God. Even if all should perish in ecological pollution or nuclear destruction—a view for which the doctrine of the Lord's return leaves little room—God works all things "together for good to them that love him, to them that are the called according to his purpose" (Rom. 8:28, KJV), an assurance that gains more, rather than less, relevance in a technological era.

TECHNOLOGY AND THE POSSIBILITIES OF GOOD

So much has now been said about the temptations, miscalculations and even devastations of technology that the Christian might want to dismiss it as not only undesirable and useless, but as perhaps even intrinsically Satanic. But it would be a costly and tragic mistake to view technology as essentially wicked and to oppose it in the name of Christian ethics and biblical sensitivity. For technology is not by definition an adverse cultural development that the spiritual man or woman must oppose. Although it can be deployed to monstrous harm and destruction, technology *per se* is not evil. Its proper uses are to be defended and promoted. Technology has played a role in the rise of all civilizations (e.g., transportation, sanitation) and now as never before is essential to their survival (e.g., improving and distributing food supplies, developing new energy sources, such as solar, geothermal and nuclear fission). The fact that technology is praised less in religious than in scientific circles stems not from any fundamental pessimism toward the place of science, but rather from a strong sense of moral sensitivity. While technology is obviously not a means of salvation, it, too, is nonetheless God's gift and as such, is not to be neglected for what it can accomplish.

The use to which technology is put, of course, necessarily and always involves a certain view of values; indeed, the very development of technology itself reflects the value system of a particular society. While technology's availability doubtless encourages full exploration of its many potentialities, that availability does not of itself bestow upon any generation, society or nation a mandate to pursue each and every possibility. Some options technologically possible—for example, the nuclear destruction of the human race—are unthinkably wicked. Unfortunately, many scientists, like many nonscientists, tend to concentrate so exclusively on the positive achievements of their work that they fail to wrestle moral implications; indeed, some scientists aspire to be value free. Technology raises serious and urgent problems that it cannot resolve by itself; to say that it is self-rectifying has no basis either in fact or in experience. Amid its hitherto unparalleled insights into some of the secrets of the universe, scientific technology increases the need for integrity and good will amid pervasive human unregeneracy. It demands superhuman wisdom and moral guidance to weigh the decisions and options now open to a generation beset, like all others, by skewed values that flow from the infectious consequences of sin.

The prospects now advanced concerning the scientific modification of man's constitution and behavior clearly impose new obligations of ethical determination and decision beyond those specifically addressed to traditional ethics. But the notion held in some circles that modern technology—particularly the new possibilities of biomedicine—calls for moral standards and judgments other than those sponsored by the Judeo-Christian revelation reflects the prejudice of those for whom moral criteria are transient rather than transcendently given and for whom every spectacular scientific advance seems to call for a new era of experimental ethics. This emphasis on "new values" supposedly required by scientific technology not only echoes the naturalistic notion that value judgments, like all others, are always revisable but also fails to identify by what methods values are to be assuredly recognized.

Judeo-Christian revelation declares boldly that God is himself Creator of the universe, that the Logos of God is the source of all the substance and structures of created reality, that the eternal Christ as the divine agent in preservation upholds all things by his all-powerful Word, and that truth and the good are grounded in the nature and will of God. The biblical view of nature and history recognizes the universe as God's manual of universal revelation alongside Scripture as God's specially revealed redemptive news. God intends man to be his fellow worker, his co-worker, in developing creation for its divinely purposed goals. Contemporary science has unveiled remarkable new frontiers whereon man may exercise a divinely intended dominion. Many uses of technological power need not fall under the biblical condemnation of presumptive pride and can instead usefully serve the divine purpose for mankind. Scriptural perspectives of the orderliness of nature as a divine creation helped to stimulate the early beginnings of modern science, and much that technology can now contribute is consistent with a biblical view of man and the world.

The biblical view focuses at once on the importance of material–physical resources and the theological–ethical concerns that overarch them. Daniel Callahan, former editor of *Commonweal,* points out that even amid the modern ethical dilemmas Hebrew–Christian morality still serves us quite adequately, for it remains the heartbeat and life-blood of Western respect for individual rights and human dignity, sanctity of life and compassion for the sick and distressed; it has in fact shaped our abhorrence of totalitarianism, human cruelty and disregard for the weak and aged.[6] And he is patently right.

What one believes about God and man inescapably influences research and its applications. The principles governing human community inevitably govern also how we treat other persons. In behavior control, for example, both political ideology and moral imperatives can quickly outweigh medical factors. Crime and mental illness raise the question of how much social deviance society will, and should, tolerate; a decision on permissible irregular behavior will influence policies of rehabilitation and release. If therapeutic shock could alter patterns of homosexuality, crime and lawlessness, or social rebellion so that society could impose upon deviants a willing conformity, would such personality conditioning be permissible?

Christianity enjoins the dedication of all human activity to the glory of God as life's chief end. All achievements of civilization and culture, including the contributions of science and art, ideally advance, not the prideful glorification of a nation or the self-gratification of mankind, but the extension of spiritual and moral goals in human affairs to the Creator's glory. Technological prowess is not to evade or to belittle ethical responsibility, but must rather support and augment man's fulfillment of his moral duty. To channel human energies toward human magnification is idolatrous and inevitably self-defeating because moral issues left in limbo return to haunt us. Donald MacKay

has therefore proposed the following check list to help Christians—
scientists and technologists included—articulate what the Bible expects in human endeavor: determination to please God above all else;
conviction of the overall need for a projected activity; love and compassionate sensitivity; evaluation of foreseeable consequences for individuals, family and society; clarification of priorities in proposed
efforts; comprehensive awareness of human needs, including those
elucidated by Scripture.

Such concerns would underscore the important role of prayer in
scientific endeavor, since the practice of prayer acknowledges God's
glory as the supreme purpose and goal of scientific and other enterprise. Whether Christian or non-Christian, the pure scientist is not
exempt from the obligation to decide whether he is opening up the
universe in a God-approved way. Science itself advances by creative
hypotheses more than by inferences from particular experiences. Interaction with the supernatural widens appreciation for the possibility of divine alternatives to the rigid schemata man imposes on nature. Prayer serves as a reminder that God, not nature, is ultimately
the source of all blessing and that science is but an instrument. It
enlivens the conviction, moreover, that God's concern extends even
to the powerless and defenseless—that He cares for the fallen sparrow.

The biblical revelation honors God as Himself, the Truth and
ultimate source of all truth. The Christian therefore welcomes truth
wherever it exists and fears nothing from it; only against untruth need
we be on guard. The reliability of any and all affirmations of science
ultimately derives, not from limited experimental evidence, but from
God's ongoing plan and preservation of the universe. Scientific experimentation can at best only eliminate patently false hypotheses; it
cannot identify permanently valid propositions. While its affirmations
are necessarily tentative and revisable, scientific observation is highly
useful. Christian confidence in Scripture as the revelational norm of
truth does not require us to reject the utility of science.

In honoring God as the source of all truth and wisdom the Christian affirms the limited understanding and wisdom of humanity. Man
is to walk humbly amid God's creation, recognizing that he can speak
with finality only where God has spoken in His Word. Even man's
inferences from Scripture are not beyond the possibility of error. Such

admission in no way relativizes the Bible, but points up man's creatureliness and fallibility. It is better even for theologians to admit mistakes than to hide them for others to uncover and then perhaps to attribute their misconceptions to Scripture rather than to themselves. But Scripture unerringly identifies the good, whereas empirical science cannot do so. And if we do not know the good, the value even of our scientific insights is unsure.

Confident that we can do nothing against the truth, Christians have every reason to welcome, rather than to oppose, scientific inquiry and research. Sinsheimer is surely right that "there would be a terrible damage to the human spirit if we should decide that we do not wish to know more, if we came to believe that we must forever accept certain ills because we do not trust ourselves with the responsibility to mitigate them."

The question of the extent to which we are obliged to do good has a ready Christian answer: "To him that knoweth to do good, and doeth it not, to him it is sin" (James 4:17, KJV). Simply to deflect harm from others does not discharge our full moral duty; there is no license for sins of omission. To resist technological progress because misuse may be harmful to some persons is no more defensible as a comprehensive moral stance than to oppose involvement in politics because government is so often corrupt. It is an unfortunate part of man's predicament in sin that the greater his power to do good—whether through technology, politics or whatever else—the greater also is his power to do evil. But to withold the doing of good because of hostility to wrong is an unacceptable commitment.

It is folly to demean the technological feats that gave us electricity, automobiles and airplanes, radio and television, and countless mechanical conveniences that have both benefited and plagued us and our environment. Medicine has conquered an impressive list of once debilitating diseases; cardiac patients now live with capabilities unimaginable a half century ago; the human life span has been impressively extended, in some instances by organ transplants and in others by sophisticated mechanical devices. More than seventy special centers in the United States now function to detect prenatal abnormalities.

While one may be apprehensive over the possible adverse consequences of laboratory procedures that transfer genes or insert chemi-

cally synthesized genes into microorganisms, one must not overlook
the fact that insulin, growth hormones, clotting factor VIII and specific antibodies may soon be available in quantity for significant
human benefit. Genetically reprogramed microorganisms for agricultural and industrial use may also serve mankind beneficially. Applying genetic technology to higher organisms is at present a rather
remote prospect, and modification of the human gene line even more
so. But medical progress in conquering infectious disease has already
done much to reveal the connection between genetic factors and
numerous specific illnesses; more than two thousand ailments have
already been correlated with genetic influences. Moreover, should it
become biochemically simple to identify latent genetic defects in prospective parents, perhaps through mass screening, then the range of
doomed or vulnerable fetuses could be notably reduced by a more
informed choice of marital partners. Mass screening could identify,
for example, carriers of defective genes that can lead to sickle cell
anemia, Tay-Sachs disease, and perhaps even cystic fibrosis. Genetic
information greatly increases the moral responsibility of prospective
marital partners and of parents, both in begetting and in rearing
children. Somatic gene therapy, a far from remote possibility, could
remove the social stigma from some parents of being genetically defective, and it could spare many children the tragic consequences of
defective genes.

Few people would refuse the higher quality of physical life that
biomedical technology might offer their children. Even philosophical
naturalists, whose world view disallows transcendent and changeless
moral principles, speak, however inconsistently, as does Sinsheimer,
of "a cancer upon our conscience" if we do not repair or prevent the
genetic misfortunes that burden so many humans. Yet when we speak
of "quality" of physical life we seem to imply not only physical
efficiency but normative ethical values, which empirical science is
impotent to identify or to guarantee.

The mass media bear a special responsibility not only to publicize
the abuses of technology but also to avoid needlessly fueling public
anxiety, fear and even paranoia through exaggerating its potential
misuse. To their credit, the media have raised pertinent questions over
debatable experiments in behavior control, and science editors have
provided informed commentary. But sensational journalism and sci-

ence fiction television programs are sometimes alarmist and irresponsible, especially the horror movie presentations of electrical and chemical brain manipulation. Some psychiatric patients have come to believe, possibly in the context of such programs, that during their sleep someone implants brain control devices to influence their thoughts and behavior.

TECHNOLOGY AND THE CLASH OF VALUES

The Christian researcher knows that in doing good the rights of individuals are not to be ignored. Taking away human liberties (including those of prisoners) in order to augment scientific information is questionable; indeed, it is unethical to offer the institutionally confined "irresistably attractive rewards and no alternatives." Every responsible community, of course, imposes some restrictions on individual freedom. The current clamor for reducing environmental pollution and preserving natural resources for the general welfare, for example, rests upon this principle. But the question arises whether either science or government has any moral mandate to cure people of mental and physical ailments against their will, to deal with deforming genetic defects or even to screen people involuntarily. Does not moral judgment, moreover, sometimes dictate a moratorium on certain scientific research until the consequences and implications of certain experiments are clear and convincing, as in the case of the American swine flu innoculations in 1976? Even where informed consent of those involved in hazardous experiments is a precondition for proceeding and is guaranteed, the irreversability of some experiments is an important consideration.

The clash of Judeo-Christian with so-called humanistic morality is evident from the ready utilitarian advocacy of "the greatest good for the greatest number." This approach often leaves the weak and underprivileged and powerless to die, subordinating the rights of a miserable minority to the choices of the majority, or of their presumed spokesmen. If the aggregate is what really counts and the distribution of individual benefits is a matter of indifference, compassion for the powerless is readily traded for majority concerns, and the dignity of the weak and the sanctity of their human existence are easily sacrificed to the whole. But if love for the needy and powerless is a fundamental virtue, the poor, the retarded and the disabled will be in view from the outset.

While Christianity does not consider the defective child a special blessing, it nonetheless looks upon the physically or mentally disadvantaged as a special entrustment. Those who have experienced in themselves God's compassionate love for spiritually deformed and morally monstrous sinners, moreover, see in the care of the helpless a humbling paradigm of divine sympathy and patience with sinners. Is human life valueless and dispensable simply because by majority standards it seems undesirable and unfit? Suppose an elitist cadre should some day consider the quality of life we ourselves now prize as inferior and dispensable? Will planned destruction of unwanted fetuses, whether normal or abnormal, slowly evaporate the spirit of compassion? Are normality and abnormality to be defined solely in terms of universally measurable physical criteria? Can we at one and the same time destroy defective fetuses and avoid compromising the sense of human dignity? Does one in principle destroy part of one's own worth if, alongside a commitment to the equal value of all human life, one is ready to forfeit fetal life that is judged inferior or unwanted? Does such destruction become a symbol of dehumanization and contribute to the view that the image of God is not universally significant?

The Christian seeks identity as one who cares for the defenseless and the powerless. Present fetal research is largely unable to determine the extent of prospective retardation. What may represent a crushing tragedy to one family in the matter of a defective child, moreover, may be acceptable to another. As Dr. Sara Finley comments, "Self-dignity, self-esteem and self-contribution may reside in the handicapped individual as well as in the perfectly formed."[7] Because the Christian knows the way of repentance and forgiveness and has the support of fellow believers, he or she seems more able and better prepared to risk what might be considered an unfortunate decision. Invoking the Holy Spirit for guidance, the Church as a praying and counseling community willingly shares with parents responsibility for the needy. Christian parents have the opportunity to show the world the Church's disposition toward the underprivileged and retarded and to demonstrate that neither disability nor genetic deformity can separate a believer from the love of God. Surrounded by the devotion of the Christian community, a Christian mother with a retarded child can manifest to the world the New Society's care for the defenseless and, in concert with the Church, can stimulate compassionate ministries and share them with society at large.

To relieve human suffering nonetheless remains a clear Christian duty. Donald MacKay therefore challenges opponents of technological assistance or interference to show that brain surgery to relieve anxiety is in all instances unethical. Even apart from the debatable naturalistic or materialistic explanations of mental phenomena to which it frequently lends itself, psychosurgery is a controversial as well as a relatively young and not yet fully developed science. All medical science is a balancing of risks and benefits. One of psychosurgery's awesome aspects is its irreversibility. Because of its uncertain long-term consequences, the medical profession is divided over when and if to use it for modifying human behavior and emotions. Present guidelines in neurosurgery are disturbingly vague. Its experimental procedures require both medical and legislative controls to safeguard patients. But while it has resulted in some unfortunate mental and personality distortions, psychosurgery already successfully uses many psychotropic drugs without hazardous side effects to achieve specific objectives significantly beneficial to some persons. In Michigan the use of such drugs is credited with reducing the hospital confinement of some mental patients from an indeterminate number of years to an average of seventeen days. Should we then view only with apprehension the medications being developed to combat depression and anxiety, elevate mood, increase mental alertness and perhaps quicken memory? One in eight Americans today suffers from serious depression, and many have deep psychic problems with which psychologists and psychiatrists can scarcely cope. Doubtless it is easy for a secular society to minimize the toll of moral and spiritual rebellion and of the suppression of conscience and to concentrate instead upon economic, physical and interpersonal stresses. But God is able to distinguish the consequences that flow from responsible personal decision, environment and heredity, and it becomes us not to hurriedly attribute chronic depression only to personal vice.

The present stage of brain control does not, however, confirm the idea that a particular stimulus will reliably produce the same human behavior or motivational state in all persons. Just the opposite seems to be the case. Similar stimuli apparently occasion different feelings and experiences in different persons. Causal relationships are unclear. Elliot S. Valenstein emphasizes, moreover, that no correspondence exists between distinct, separate brain areas and our social concerns. Aggression, for example, he considers a human abstraction, since it is not regulated by one specific area of the brain or biochemical substratum.[8] Valenstein stresses that we ought not consider electrical stimulation a reliable technique for determining the brain locus responsible for violence, nor ought we to look to drugs or brain surgery to control thought processes or mood alteration with the hope of solving psychiatric or social problems. "For the foreseeable future," he argues, "we should increase, rather than decrease, attempts to find social solutions for what are primarily social problems."[9]

As far as proposals to restore violent criminals to normalcy by brain surgery is concerned, Donald MacKay thinks it noteworthy that Jesus' cure of the Gararene demoniac (Luke 8:38) involved not an alteration of individual identity but rather a casting out of "unclean spirits." He stresses the high importance of distinguishing between surgical techniques or chemical treatments that involve destroying and those that involve preserving brain structures essential to maintaining human identity. MacKay questions the moral legitimacy of so altering individual identity that an alien personality is imported, as it were, into the same body. If, he adds, a lifelong Christian through brain surgery were to lose all apparent spiritual interest, he would not thereby be damned because one who has in the present already participated in eternal life (John 5:24, 6:54) will no more be separated from God's love by destructive brain manipulation than he would be by death. When the Christian moves at last toward terminal care, the believer knows—even if sometimes doctors and nurses may not—that he or she has not suddenly become a "nobody."

The apostle Paul emphasizes in his letter to the Colossians that Jesus Christ explicates God's purpose in creation and redemption. In Jesus Christ Christians have the decisive norm for what is "human." Ideal humanity involves an inescapable reference to Christ-likeness. There is, however, no Christian basis for encouraging human engineering in order to make people "more Christ-like." We have no way of knowing Jesus' genetic balances, all the less so in the absence of a human father, and the history of Christian art makes apparent how little we know of his actual features. If physical duplication were the divine intention, the New Testament would not have focused upon ethical and spiritual obedience as it does in its call for conformity to the image of Christ. The biblical invitation to Christ-likeness is addressed to every human being regardless of genetic balances and physical features. While this appeal is unmistakably moral, it pledges also that in the future resurrection we shall be completely like Him (I John 3:2). But it should surprise no one that a physically oriented age should think of the improvement of man mainly in physical terms. A generation preoccupied with cosmetics will sooner or later turn even the present interest in internal genetic defects to external enhancement. Yet one of the facts of history is that those most concerned with outward attractiveness and beauty are among humanity's least happy persons; inevitably, moreover, they are set on a course of artificiality and disillusion.

Improvement of the human species is one objective often cited by those specially interested in cloning or in genetic intervention. The biblical emphasis on man's fallen condition in sin in no way precludes the use of physiological or psychological means to ameliorate certain human imperfections. The Christian surely will not disparage the importance of seeking to combat disease and deformity. At the same time, he or she cannot disregard such basic issues as what truly constitutes human betterment, who will decide the ideal nature of man, and whether the preservation and multiplication of superior genotypes will guarantee the desired results. To say that technology does not tell us either what behavior needs changing or in what direction, but does tell us how to change human behavior, is naive. The New Testament adversely judges merely human gnosis and science indifferent to the truth of god and the claims of righteousness (Rom. 1:22; I Cor. 1:17–29, 2:4 ., 13).

In some respects, genes do indeed "furnish the capacity for humanity" and "set the stage for the act of civilization" and influence one's potential for social and cultural interaction, as Sinsheimer notes. But one arbitrarily imposes purely naturalistic presuppositions upon empirical experience if these considerations are thought to exclude man's divinely created dignity, his rational and moral aptitudes as aspects of the divine image, and his responsible creaturely decision and action in expectation of final judgment. Sinsheimer, for example, considers man "half a creature of Nature and half a creature of culture. . . .

There are no rights in Nature. Nature uses the individual; each is expendable. . . . Rights . . . exist only within human societies." Such analysis fails to deal seriously with the truth of revelation unveiling the true dignity and moral predicament of man, and with man's need for spiritual salvation to mitigate human depravity. Adam in the Edenic garden was devoid of physical deformity but fell voluntarily into moral disgrace. In a prescientific era Jesus of Nazareth lived a life of perfect moral sonship to the Father and quite obviously identified the enduring significance of human life with something other than longevity. If the cloning of human individuals should become an actuality, such sired creatures will not be exempt either from Adamic guilt or from the stricture that without spiritual rebirth humans remain alien to the Kingdom of God. The changes which technology brings cannot and do not in any way assure a better life or even happiness; not all the achievements of biomedical surgery in the world carry a guarantee of felicity. At best, they only alleviate or cancel certain distresses. Sinsheimer fails to see that the age-long battle between humility and pride is not settled by man's remarkable rise from "the evolutionary cocoon" but is increased, rather, by confidence that "we are emerging . . . to a new level of self-mastery." "Having conquered much of Nature," Sinsheimer writes, "we become impatient with human nature." The impatience he cites is not that of which the Bible speaks—man restless in his sins and haunted by a guilty conscience pointing him to God—but simply that of earthbound restiveness: "We grow impatient with the throws of the genetic lottery and invent genetic engineering. We grow impatient with our finitude. . . . We would be gods. . . ."

While, as Daniel Callahan observes, "our generation is perhaps faced with the most critical decision human beings have had to make" — the decision about "man's own nature,"[10] we must not be misled into thinking that this decision has a specially contemporary locus and character. The basic question concerning man's nature is ultimately the enduring one of spiritual and moral renewal (cf. John 3:3–5); the issues of freedom, individuality and dignity posed by modern genetics are but parts of a profounder problem. Human biological life affords no adequate definition of what it means to be authentically human, nor can it fully explain human unregeneracy or precipitate spiritual restoration. When Sinsheimer writes of "lifting the unsought curse" by genetic manipulation he clearly bypasses the deeper issues of man's predicament in respect to the transcendent supernatural world. What does Sinsheimer's verdict, "it will come to seem increasingly irrational to tolerate genetic inability of any sort if we can prevent it," say to a generation that is equally heedless of the scriptural warning, "How shall we escape, if we neglect so great salvation?" (Heb. 2:3 KJV).

Long before the age of genetic manipulation the New Testament apostles and the Old Testament prophets spoke of the remaking of man, and Jesus of Nazareth emphasized not only its possibility but its absolute necessity. But genetic manipulation of human nature will be impotent to produce a spiritually and morally renewed man. Geneticists can guarantee no particular caliber of person or class. The potentiality for supercriminals or for sleuths is equally inherent in technological manipulation since the human will enters into the ethical use or misuse of aptitudes and skills. Genetic change therefore does not exhaust the possibilities of remedy for a flawed humanity. Special concentration upon genetic amelioration of human imperfection may in fact itself reflect an evasion of deeper concerns and profounder alternatives.

Sinsheimer lists dilemmas that beset technologists reaching for guidelines in human engineering: "Should we . . . adapt our gene pool to some hypothetical ideal society—or should we adapt our social order to a desirable gene pool? Is our social order infinitely mutable? Or would it be best always to build in some mismatch of human qualities and social structures so as to generate that discontent which is the source of innovation?" To cope with such difficult issues, Sinsheimer offers three broad principles: (1) "Go slowly and as much as possible, reversibly." (2) Preserve human individuality"—hence "avoid cloning, except for [a] very special purpose." (3) "If and when we know enough, . . . augment general qualities rather than specific talents," that is, "bequeath to our progeny sounder bodies, more alert minds, freer imaginations, sturdier emotions, perhaps even kindlier, sunnier natures."[11] But even if technology could be certain that its end product will in fact be what Sinsheimer here proposes, a physically and mentally enhanced humanity whose moral nature remains rebellious may presage hell on earth rather than a technocratic utopia. A person deficient in ethical earnestness but endowed with exceptional physical and mental powers has accelerated capacities for evil and may prove more subhuman than superhuman. To be sure, such baneful consequences are not inevitable, since possibilities of spiritual renewal are graciously proffered to mankind in every generation, but an enterprise devoted to empirical interests ought not lightly to dismiss the cumulative history of humanity and the collapse of past civilizations. To alter the human genetic balance and to heighten man's mental and imaginative powers may not be Christian imperatives; there is no doubt, however, that voluntary renewal of man's spiritual and moral nature is a divine requisite.

Yet where genetic improvement can in fact be achieved for human good, Donald MacKay suggests, our obligation is less to posterity than to the Creator. But he quickly adds that God is glorified in individual, family and social relationships where love and justice are practiced and cherished. Health holds high human value, but if it involves "artificially stock-breeding or cloning the finest specimens of manhood at the cost of destroying the biblical ideal of family relationships," says MacKay, then we "buy health at too high a cost." Does not our sense of values become hopelessly warped if family ties are made increasingly tenuous because the human species' supposed improvement is thought to depend upon stud-fathers or call-mothers? If one emphasizes, as Christianity does, the importance of the family and of interpersonal relationships, then the subtle interchange between mother and fetus or mother and child is not easily replaceable by impersonal mechanisms. In line with this, James H. Olthius, of the Institute for Christian Studies in Toronto, argues that artificial insemination is morally wrong except in the case of a blocked fallopian tube because it violates the troth relationship implicit in the biblical view of marriage. But would a childless husband and wife necessarily break troth if they were to welcome artificial insemination?

Above and beyond even the family stands, God-given, the value of human individuality. The human gene pool is exceptionally diverse. Current studies in genetic inheritance emphasize not only the vast individual variability of human beings but also the total improbability —except in the case of identical twins or possible future laboratory cloning—that any two persons have ever been or ever will be exactly alike. The genetic inheritance from each parent has been likened to "a chain of three billion nucleotide sites." The chain inherited from one's father, moreover, will differ from that of the mother at about one to 3 million sites, with the differences being scattered throughout the chains. Sinsheimer has suggested that "if we take, as an average, one thousand sites per genetic factor—that is, per gene—then up to half the genes you inherit from one parent may differ in some respect from the corresponding genes from the other parent." About 10–15 percent of the gene pairs received from the two parents are heterozygous, that is, detectably diverse. The consequences of this fact may be either negligible or extensive. In the normal fetus, remarks Sinsheimer, "three billion nucleotide sites are specifically arranged on 46 chromosomes—23 pairs. . . . Our genes will determine whether we are fair of skin or dark, fleet of foot or clumsy, keen of eye or myopic, tall and lithe or short and squat; whether we are likely to be quick of mind or retarded; whether we will be robust of health or frail; . . . prone to early heart failure, to diabetes, to cystic fibrosis, to Huntington's chorea, to manic depression, to schizophrenia. . . ." Yet the "enormous diversity of the human gene pool . . . ensures that each of us is indeed unique—an unprecedented gene combination—and that our like will not occur again."[12]

Could it be that man might venture to destroy a defective fetus which, in fact, would have potential for distinctive contributions to human greatness in certain spheres of life and experience? Since sex, race and, to a great extent, intelligence are determined before and at birth, no one has a personal basis for sexual, racial or intellectual snobbery. In respect to contrasts of genetic deformity and normalcy, V. Elving Anderson proposes five helpful guidelines to encompass both genetic diversity and human equality: (1) protect the freedom and responsibility of individuals in decisions, (2) make the means of genetic control publicly available to all, (3) explore equal opportunity for those with different genetic potential, (4) define the criteria by which equality is to be judged, and (5) respect individual worth despite genetic handicap."[12]

The need to review experimental procedures flows from many considerations—freedom and protection of scientific research, moral acceptability, financial feasibility and much else. Beyond doubt, professional scientists must have full voice in establishing the standards of their professions since the general public comprehends relatively little about technical research. The medical profession especially has gained notable reputation for devoting its energies to preserving life, although even it is not immune from the crisis of integrity now inundating Western society. The enormous social implications of modern technological research requires that the public itself increasingly have a voice in decision making. The protection of the rights and well-being of patients is of primary concern. Some suggest that a jury system of sorts be employed to evaluate proposals regarding the mentally retarded and prisoners. Review panels composed only of professional colleagues with closely interdependent interests would likely be less than adequate. Obviously, laypersons who have no scientific competence whatever are clearly out of place. But ethicists, lawyers, clergymen or theologians, and consumer advocates are sometimes highly informed and frequently represent areas of concern in which medical professionals lack expertise. A multidimensional approach to problems of ethics and values would not be amiss. To be sure, modern society reflects a considerable diversity of moral and religious perspectives. But that is no reason to abandon the determining of issues and decisions to those who view ethical and religious commitments as matters only of individual preference.

At the frontiers of biomedical advance, the rights of the community at large, no less than those of the individual, now increasingly call for a hearing. Some decisions, such as the use of brain surgery to lessen aggressiveness by a dangerously violent prisoner or the specific assignment of a kidney machine when there are numerous applications, obviously cannot be left solely to the individual. The U.S. Supreme Court decision making only the will of the mother determinative in regard to abortion has serious social consequences. Should a family have the right to decide whether a loved one gets psychotropic drugs or brain surgery if this course offers the only hope for release from a penal or mental institution? Daniel Callahan favors some responsibility by the community in deciding what is permissible, rather than obligatory, even where biomedical practice is not subject to moral criticism, such as in deciding whether to concentrate funds on the conquest of heart disease at the expense of slum clearance and unemployment problems and in deciding whether to perform open-heart surgery on those over age seventy-five.

No one group of citizens, Christians included, have any right to impose their values upon national policy. Yet on many issues the positions that prevail are not necessarily achieved by way of majority consensus. Often they reflect the well-articulated convictions of a relatively small number of people. Churches must strive to state the implications of revealed ethics not only for abortion but also for many frontiers of biomedicine—psychosurgery and cloning, to name but two. Through the public forum and mass media a consensus of committed, convincing leaders can create considerable impact upon the public at large and exert significant influence in molding public policy. Christians have as much right as any interested group to present their convictions intelligently and persuasively. In the Free World they, like others, can be effectively involved in political processes; in the United States they are free even to invite a ruling by the Supreme Court.

But the first step to an informed body of Christian opinion is a presentation of the implications of frontier learning and research by knowledgeable scholars who share a passion for scientific investigation or reflection and, at the same time, pursue their vocations as persons of evangelical faith. The scholars enlisted for this latest in the series of Contemporary Evangelical Thought symposiums seek to serve society and the religious community alike by reflecting in a Christian way upon some of the important frontiers of modern scientific learning.

NOTES

1. The final conference report, "Evangelical Perspectives on Human Engineering," will be found in appendix A.
2. Kenneth B. Clark, "The Pathos of Power: A Psychological Perspective," in *American Psychologist* 26, No. 12 (December 1971); pp. 1047–1057. Cf. also *Pathos of Power* (New York: Harper & Row, 1974).
3. Remarks at International Conference on Human Engineering and the Future of Man (hereafter designated ICHEFM).
4. Remarks at ICHEFM. Cf. Perry London, *Behavior Control* (New York: Harper & Row, 1969).
5. Remarks at ICHEFM.
6. Remarks at ICHEFM.
7. Remarks at ICHEFM.

8. Remarks at ICHEFM. Cf. Elliot S. Valenstein, *Brain Control: A Critical Examination of Brain Stimulation and Psychosurgery* (New York: Wiley, 1973).
9. Remarks at ICHEFM.
10. Remarks at ICHEFM.
11. Remarks at ICHEFM.
12. Remarks at ICHEFM.

VI

Molecular Biology in the Dock

ROBERT L. HERRMANN

My purpose in this essay is to examine the often triumphant past and the somewhat more perilous future of molecular biology. I believe that this field of study warrants the attention of thinking Christians from a wide variety of disciplines because it has provoked some of the deepest questions about life, about human nature, about how we perceive ourselves. My primary focus will be what the people who do molecular biology think about the ethical implications of their work rather than on the results of recent scientific investigation. To immediately establish my bias, however, I must add that by thus choosing to limit the discussion, I deny myself and others an act of worship, for

Robert L. Herrmann is Professor and Chairman of Biochemistry in the Schools of Medicine and Dentistry at Oral Roberts University in Tulsa, Oklahoma. He assumed this post in 1976, having served as Associate Professor of Biochemistry in Boston University School of Medicine, Boston, Massachusetts, where for seventeen years he taught medical school biochemistry. His research interest is the biochemistry of cancer and aging. After receiving a B.S. in chemistry from Purdue University and a Ph.D. in biochemistry from Michigan State University, he was a Damon Runyan Fellow from 1956–1958 and then Research Associate from 1958–1959 at Massachusetts Institute of Technology, Cambridge, Massachusetts. He is a Fellow of the American Association for the Advancement of Science and also of the Gerontological Society, and a member of the American Society of Biological Chemists and the Christian Medical Society.

to describe the exquisite workings of living organisms in molecular terms is to me a truly awesome and ecstatic experience.

MOLECULAR BIOLOGY: A CHILD PRODIGY

Molecular biology—the study of living systems at the molecular level—is a young science whose staggering growth and influence has been like an uninhibited child prodigy with an insatiable appetite for facts and a remarkable penchant for inductive reasoning. Scarcely more than three decades have passed since Oswald Avery and his collaborators at the Rockefeller Institute published the results of their study of the genetic alteration of a bacterial species, together with the astounding conclusion that "a nucleic acid of the deoxyribose type is the fundamental unit of the transforming principle. . . ." Only nine years later James Watson and Francis Crick published their model for the structure of DNA (deoxyribonucleic acid),[2] a model which at once established the prime candidacy of this macromolecule for the "genetic stuff" of cells. Experiments by others followed, verifying that DNA indeed doubled in quantity with each generation,[3] and that it was faithfully copied by the cell,[4] as an hereditary function would require. Beyond this, the field has expanded to study the molecular genetics of a wide variety of organisms and viruses and to examine a host of cell constituents at the molecular level. But most profound has been the growth in our understanding of the structure and replication of DNA, for it has brought with it the capacity to produce and multiply types of DNA molecules never seen in nature[5] and opened the door to the possibility of altering human genetic make-up.

It is interesting to compare the cataclysmic rise of molecular biology to another scientific "explosion," the advent of nuclear energy. Just thirty-two years elapsed between Niels Bohr's description of the atom in 1910 and the sustained nuclear reaction achieved by Enrico Fermi and his collaborators in the squash court of Stagg Field at the University of Chicago in December 1942. The implications of that latter discovery are well known. The blackened wasteland that was Hiroshima soon reminded us that great discoveries can be greatly misused. And we still debate the safety and usefulness of nuclear power plants and multiply sleepless nights with anxiety over the expansion of the "nuclear club" of nations that have the capacity to make the bomb. Yet the discoveries which have brought these dangers in their train have allowed us to penetrate to the very core of matter and energy. Does the risk of misuse outweigh their worth?

A similar dilemma seems to characterize molecular biology. Alongside the dangers of misuse, our knowledge of the biological world has been immeasurably enriched over the past three decades. We have succeeded in bringing physical–chemical explanation into the complex world of biology, thus providing precise mechanistic descriptions for many heretofore baffling phenomena.

ETHICAL IMPLICATIONS OF MOLECULAR BIOLOGY

These explanations have already been of tremendous importance in moving medical science closer toward finding long sought cures for cancer, autoimmune diseases and various inherited illnesses. But molecular biology has also ushered in a fresh wave of reductionist thinking. Perhaps because of its crucial location at the interface between the physical and biological sciences, it has seemed to some to provide fresh proofs that all of nature, even life itself, can be fully explained in mechanistic terms.

Evolutionist Ethics. An example of this reductionist tendency comes from the pen of the late Jacques Monod, Nobel laureate and biochemist of the Pasteur Institute. In his book, *Chance and Necessity,*[6] Monod not only brilliantly reviews the salient features of life's molecular mechanisms, but also argues that man is "alone in the unfeeling immensity of the universe" to which he came without meaning and purpose, solely by chance. Monod attacks religious beliefs with all the superiority of a high priest of science, proud of his realistic, objective outlook. He chides Teilhard de Chardin's philosophy for its "intellectual spinelessness" and "willingness to conciliate at any price."[7] After announcing the essential unpredictability of the biosphere, Monod comments: "We would all like to think ourselves necessary, inevitable, ordained from all eternity. All religions, nearly all philosophies, and even a part of science testify to the unwearying, heroic effort of mankind desperately denying its own contingency."[8]

But after having cast the first stone, Monod then makes himself a target for the same criticism when he feelingly presents his "principle of objectivity" as the condition of true knowledge, fully aware that this in itself is an ethical choice.[9] He risks this subjective decision to believe in objectivity seeking thereby to provide a new ethical system, the ethic of knowledge, which, he says, is alone consistent with our present science-derived materialistic society. Scientific knowledge (presumably especially molecular biology), he declares, has devastated our alternative value systems derived on religious grounds. "The ethic of knowledge that created the modern world is the only ethic compatible with it, the only one capable, once understood and accepted, of guiding its evolution."[10]

Monod's cure, then, for our seriously disturbed society, is to adopt something beyond our own self-interest as a goal. The ethic of knowledge is his choice. But it *is* a *choice,* and not deducible from scientific knowledge; it is a projection from his own particular subjective experience; it is his existential leap. And one cannot but sense the melodrama and pathos of it. In a volume of critical essays on Monod's work entitled *Beyond Chance and Necessity,* Arthur Peacocke recalls Bertrand Russell's words: "That man is the product of causes which had no prevision of the end they were achieving; that his origin, his growth, his hopes and fears, his loves and beliefs, are but the outcome of accidental collocations of atoms. . . . all these things, if not quite beyond dispute, are yet so clearly certain, that no philosophy which rejects them can hope to stand. Only within the scaffolding of these truths, only on the firm foundation of unyielding despair, can the soul's habitation henceforth be safely built." Peacocke adds, "This passage, written in the 1920s, represents the abyss into which both Russell and Monod peer and the noble courage with which they respond to it, as they both "whistle in the dark.""[11]

Two observations need to be made in connection with Monod's thinking. First, he ventures to build his ethical system upon the hard facts of molecular biology, but then proceeds to generalize on the basis of all science, tacitly assuming that all the scientific disciplines are equally rigorous and uniformly susceptible to precise and objective experimentation. Yet it is just those least precise *human* sciences that are the most relevant to the ethical domain. As molecular biologist Gunther Stent points out in a recent issue of The Hastings Center Report, "The physical sciences, whose propositions are those most solidly validated, have the least bearing on the realization of moral aims, whereas the propositions of the human sciences, which have the most bearing on the realization of moral aims, are conspicuously devoid of objective evaluation."[12] Stent then goes on to place Monod's conclusions in the category of *scientism*—the mistaken belief that scientific method and reasoning are applicable to all human activity, including the validation of moral acts, and that they supply the only authentic form of knowledge. This proud narrowness, this molecular myopia, should be seen as nothing more or less than a competing religion, a cult which, in Monod's case, has the ethic of knowledge as its central article of faith.

Structuralist Ethics. In place of Monod's ethic of knowledge approach, Gunther Stent proposes the existence of a kind of indeterminism in the search for an explanation for moral behavior. According to this "structuralist" approach, in the human brain "the causal connections that determine behavior do not relate to surface structures." Instead, they "are generated by covert deep structures, inaccessible to direct observation."[13] Man's moral values are seen as "programed in" as part of the innate evolutionary history of *Homo sapiens*. This "universal, ethical deep structure" which all humans share is to be distinguished from "overt ethical surface structures" which "differ significantly between diverse social groups and among members of the same social group."[14] In studying moral behavior science is not to pursue the usual Darwinian approach of providing possible explanations for the origin of ethical values in society, or explaining the "nature of evolutionary 'fitness' which morality may have conferred on *Homo sapiens*."[15] Science's role should rather be the less dramatic one of giving an account of the biological basis of moral values. This account, however, will be necessarily limited by the "fundamental inconsistencies" between deep and surface ethical structures. This is a humbling conclusion, standing in stark contrast to the optimistic clarion call of Monod and other molecular biologists who propose to explain fully all life phenomena by scientific investigation.

Both Stent and Monod do agree that present systems of morality are outmoded and unworkable. Monod claims that the Judeo-Christian moral system has been devastated by science. It would have been interesting to hear his explanation of the fact that modern science *began* in a Christian cultural setting being carried out by God-fearing

Puritans, Catholic monks, and other devout followers of the very
tradition he vilifies. Stent, on the other hand, pushes the source of the
dilemma far back into evolutionary time, explaining that "the moral
dilemmas and paradoxes with which we are wrestling today are not
simply the results of unenlightened or irrational human attitudes, but
are, instead, reflections of the fundamental inconsistency of the ethical
deep structure which underlies our morality in the first place."[16] Stent
seems to be saying that our present social mores and attitudes (the
ethical surface structures) are not at fault; rather, the erroneous,
primitive ethical mores of the deep structures are too engrained to be
overcome. But even if one assumes the structuralist argument, it is
difficult to see *which* set of ethics is *really* at fault, given the lack of
any absolute standards in Stent's epistemology.

Bioethics.   Among the relatively small group of men and women
who have made significant contributions to molecular biology in the
last three decades, Robert Sinsheimer, biochemist at California Institute of Technology, stands out, not only for his scientific contributions, but also as a leader in the fledgling field of bioethics. In a paper
delivered at the 1975 International Conference on Human Engineering
and the Future of Man, Sinsheimer examined the great breadth of
inequality among humans—economically, politically, and particularly genetically.[17] Fortunately for us, he points out, when genetic
"diversity" becomes too great, as in cases of abnormal chromosome
number, the great majority of embryos perish *in utero.* But one out
of five such embroyos do not perish. What shall we do with these?
Given the capacity of molecular biology to provide tools for the
correction of genetic defects, we seem to have an immediate solution.
But the answer is actually more complicated—as all the new technological answers are.

Sinsheimer's philosophical approach is noteworthy. From his humanistic viewpoint, the genetic defect arises through the operation of
"laws of chance," which "blindly cast their dice." Here we seem to
be presented with simply a variant of Monod's well-worn but misapplied notion of chance as a blind, chaotic and meaningless process.
The term *chance* as used in the scientific sphere is, as Donald MacKay
points out in *The Clockwork Image,*[18] a technical term denoting the
absence of the *knowledge* of prior events which could have accounted

for a certain occurrence. To speak instead of the "laws of chance" as if they were an alternative to God, is to use a metaphysical notion which has no place in strictly scientific thinking.

The God of Scripture *is* truly a God of order, but this does not demand that He *must* work in what *appears to us* to be an orderly fashion. I am tempted to parody Monod by noting that the philosophies of all atheists, nearly all humanists, and even a significant number of scientists testify to the unwearying, heroic effort of mankind, desperately denying God as the Creator and Preserver of all being. One wonders what deep antagonisms might lie behind Sinsheimer's reference to genetic defect as a "cosmic joke."[19] Perhaps in the vast sea of evil he finds no trace of a good and omnipotent God—an argument favored by many of his peers. But in this writer's opinion, the argument succeeds best when the God at fault is made most nearly in our own image, but is least applicable when we give heed to the God of Scripture. The perception of God as a doting, indulgent grandfather leaves Him helpless or capricious, if not brutal and pernicious, in view of the pain and injury that humanity experiences. But Scripture presents God as anything but helpless; rather, He is presented as omnipotent designer of this universe as an arena of faith, where His beloved creature, man, may discover Him in spite of, or sometimes even *because* of, the evil He allows. As the writer to the Hebrews tells us, "You can never please God without faith, without depending upon Him. Anyone who wants to come to God must believe that there is a God and that he rewards those who sincerely look for Him" (Heb. 11:6, The Living Bible). And that reward cannot be measured by the list of assets and debits on a balance sheet of a person's genetic health. God's drama is played out on a far larger stage, as Leon Kass once said, "The world suffers far more from the morally and spiritually defective than from the genetically defective."[20] The reward of faith may come directly, as it did in the sight of the blind man whom Jesus healed, "that the works of God should be made manifest." (John 9:3, KJV). But who can tell how many others were affected by his healing?

I am reminded of an experience related by David Allen, psychiatrist and Christian ethicist, who spent a year as a Kennedy fellow of medical ethics at the Fernald School for the mentally retarded in suburban Boston. A newborn boy was admitted, suffering from hydrocephaly, a serious congenital defect that involves the accumulation of serous fluid in the cranium and results in a greatly enlarged head and a severely reduced brain size. The child soon developed pneumonia, I believe, and as is customary in cases of severe defect, the physicians indicated that he should be allowed to die. The nurses, however, revolted, arguing that the child was a person, responding to their care, and should be cared for as such. The nurses prevailed. Sometime later Allen brought a visitor to see the child. As they came into the ward, they found a group of nurses standing around his crib singing "Happy Birthday." It was his first birthday. And Allen asked his visitor, "Do you know how I know that that child is a person? It's because these nurses have *made* him a person!" The little boy has since died, but who can measure the impact of his brief life upon those nurses—that the works of God may be made manifest?

Nonetheless one must, I think, credit Sinsheimer with more compassion for his fellow humans and deeper concern for the misuse of the new genetic techniques than anyone else of his stature in the field of molecular biology. One must admire his call for caution in the use of the new genetic technologies in the face of the enthusiasm shown by most molecular biologists to press the search for new knowledge. Sinsheimer's criticism, most recently voiced in a symposium sponsored by the American Society of Biological Chemists,[21] takes as its focus the need for wisdom in the study of recombinant DNA. Molecular biologists have developed techniques for splicing together two different DNA molecules—which may be as widely different as bacterial virus and human DNA—and introducing the resulting recombinant DNA molecules into bacterial cells where the new DNA "species" may multiply. Potential problems in these experiments were discussed in the 1973 Gordon conference on nucleic acids. This led to a call for an international moratorium on such experiments by a committee headed by Paul Berg of Stanford in the summer of 1974.[22] At a subsequent conference at Asilomar, California, in February 1975, a group of about 120 scientists and a few laypersons issued guidelines for the conduct of recombinant DNA research. The National Institutes of Health, the chief funding agency for this type of research, has since issued a similar set of guidelines and set up appropriate machinery to screen all applications coming to them for research of this kind.[23]

The major reaction to these efforts has been that they are commendable, but inadequate. The guidelines focus entirely upon the public health or "biohazard" aspect of this research, and concern such eventualities as the accidental production of organisms harboring genes for antibiotic resistance, or genes of carcinogenic viruses, or totally new pathogens "yet unborn." Sinsheimer questions the effectiveness of even these extensive containment measures, emphasizing the uniqueness of this kind of hazard. As he points out, "Living organisms are self-reproducing. They cannot be recalled, nor their manufacture ceased."[24]

Beyond this controversy lies the whole gamut of ethical, social and political issues, which most of us trained in science find vague and ill-defined. Ethical concerns find us particularly ill-equipped. My personal brief is that the Church, through its local congregations and its support of Christian colleges and individual scholars, may supply some imaginative leadership in this regard.[25] While a member of Grace Chapel in Lexington, Massachusetts, I had opportunity to help plan a lecture seminar program that included one weekend devoted entirely to the relation between science and Christianity, with epistemologist Walter Thorson as our speaker. The program provided a very useful learning experience for a number of scientists, as well as for church members. As I have said elsewhere,[26] it would be a genuine act of charity, considering the misguided opposition science has given Christianity in decades past, for the Church of Jesus Christ to extend a warm and helping hand to a branch of learning that is just now feeling its ethical depths.

A Political Dimension—Science Belongs to the People. Jon Beckwith, a professor in the Department of Microbiology and Molecular Genetics at Harvard Medical School, has become a leading spokesperson for a Boston-based group called "Science for the People." The goal of the organization is to educate the body politic to the dangers of uncontrolled scientific research, not only because of the very complicated ethical questions it poses for the recipients of the new technologies, but also because the research may well be carried out for the wrong motives. Beckwith is deeply concerned about a possible revival of the eugenics movement in America. In a paper presented at the New York Academy-sponsored Conference on Ethical and Scientific Issues Posed By Human Uses Of Molecular Genetics in May 1975,[27] he points out that when a significant segment of our society raged "against the inequalities of our political-economic system. . . . one response was the proposals by academics and others that much of the source of our social problems was in the genes or the biology of the individuals involved, rather than in the nature of the system itself."[28] He then reviews some examples of such thinking, including B. Maletzky's statement published in *The Resident and Staff Physician* that possible brain defect or injury may be source of certain social ills: " . . . nonetheless, of all those millions afflicted with poverty, social hatred and urban stagnation, only a few behave violently toward their fellow man. . . . Is it not entirely reasonable to assume that such patients are suffering attacks of a form of epilepsy?"[29]

A similar suggestion was made by Boston City Hospital neurosurgeon Vernon Mark following the Detroit race riots, as part of his justification for a Justice Department grant expanding his research on the surgical disruption of small segments of the distal brain as a treatment for temporal lobe epilepsy.[30] The suggestion earned Mark the relentless antagonism of most political liberals, doubtless led to the disapproval of the grant proposal, and prompted the hospital in early 1973 to appoint a committee to oversee any future psychosurgery on epileptics performed by Mark or his collaborators. David Allen, who was then chief resident in Psychiatry at the Boston City Hospital, was asked to chair the interdisciplinary committee, and he in turn appointed as members a Boston University law professor, a Harvard sociologist, a Tufts psychologist, a social worker, a Boston University medical student, and myself. Later, biochemist–historian Charles Thaxton of Brandeis and Gordon–Conwell Seminary professor Carlyle Saylor were added. Over the next two years our committee considered four cases—three individuals being considered for psychosurgery and one, who had been operated upon previously, serving as a comparison. Each patient was presented as a temporal lobe epileptic with a history of "rage" or "running" attacks, of very frequent episodes of violent, and largely involuntary, behavior that were generally forgotten afterwards. In each case the history of seizures was traceable to some neurological damage early in childhood, with the patient having had a subsequent medical history of family crisis and usually of innumerable drug therapies.

The overwhelming impression these cases made on me is the enormous complexity of interpretating the malfunctioning of the human brain in the family and cultural milieu. Our first patient had had long-term experience as an epileptic, apparently initiated by an attack of ether pneumonia at age three, leading to arm twitches at age ten, subsequently to periods of unconsciousness and eventually to severe attacks of rage. He seen numerous psychiatrists, neurologists and neurosurgeons with no apparent relief. Vernon Mark and his psychiatrist colleague, Paul Blumer, first presented the medical history to the committee. Following this, the patient, not then hospitalized, met with the committee in the absence of Mark and Blumer. We sought to determine (a) the degree to which his illness was in fact temporal lobe epilepsy, as Mark and Blumer claimed, and (b) how well he understood the dangers as well as the possible advantages of "stereotactic" surgery. We then met with the parents separately, since there was clearly a conflict between the thirty-eight-year-old patient and his "domineering parents." All this occurred over a two hour period. The members of the committee then reconvened a week later at David Allen's home to discuss their findings. I vividly recall the diversity of opinion. Louisa Howe, the sociologist, was convinced that the entire problem was environmentally conditioned, including the sporadic twitches of the right arm at age ten and periods of unconsciousness at age thirteen. As a trained medical scientist, I couldn't believe my ears. She didn't believe there was such a thing as pathology! But I admit that her arguments had some merit; the mother did have a strong sense of guilt, which might have been a conditioning factor in the gradual development of the rage attack syndrome. Our final decision was to recommend that the patient not be treated by psychosurgery, but rather be given some degree of independence and some help with his excessive use of alcohol. I think most of us viewed this as the lesser of two evils; we had little confidence, from our readings and discussions, in the psychosurgical techniques.

My reason for including this experience, which concerns an area presently beyond the limits of molecular biology, is to add a perspective which Jon Beckwith perhaps cannot provide in judging the motives of the psychosurgeons. You simply have to look at individual cases in order to realize that there are valid reasons for carrying out these techniques. If you could see the tragic individuals and their equally tragic families, torn apart by years of crisis and confusion, you would sense some of the motivation of the psychosurgeons to seek to relieve their suffering. And the experience of an interdisciplinary committee quickly reminds one of a debt that reasoning owes to training. Sociologists see the world *very differently* than do molecular biologists!

But Jon Beckwith is still right. All of us in science must admit that our motives are mixed, that even our good intentions may be tinged with human greed and personal ambition. Add to that the sobering lesson of science under dictatorship in Nazi Germany, where scientists quickly fell under the spell of an ideology of ethnic superiority, and we can see how easily we could be manipulated for political purposes here in the United States.

A PLEA FOR CLEMENCY

The best insurance against a perversion of the scientific quest for truth and of its application to human need is for us all to recognize that we stand in need of far greater wisdom than we presently possess. Jacques Monod's solution is to be rid of our old systems of morality and to place our faith in scientific objectivity. Gunther Stent seems to be shifting away from his faith science toward some kind of accommodation with the deep ethical structures of the human brain, rather like the Hindu mystics who, rather than seeking to change the world, ask the world—largely through meditation—to change them. Robert Sinsheimer, I think, brings to us the best of the humanist tradition, passionately longing for human beings to grow up socially and culturally so that they may discover themselves and their full potentiality. The two major factors in this growth process would seem to be time and caution, though he could hardly be cast in the mold of the reactionary. Science and the excitement of scientific discovery still have large roles in his plans. As he puts it: "It is a privilege to be a scientist. To live at the edge of knowledge, in a world forever new is to be forever young." Of the four, Jon Beckwith seems to have the most realistic view of the frailty of human institutions, though his focus seems to be on institution rather than on individual deficiencies.

From my own perspective as an evangelical Christian, I have a deep conviction that what is basically wrong with the world is not my nonobjective thinking or my ethical deep structures or sluggish social or political institutions, but *me—mankind—my species!* I believe that the historic Christian faith has the ultimate answer to the human dilemma because it presents the most apt description of who I am and why I am here. It explains the struggle, the passion for truth, the deep-seated tension between the material world and the world of meaning. As Norman Mailer says in *Of A Fire On The Moon,* "there exists at once in us a desire for the most objective scientific facts alongside a yearning to preserve the individual, subjective, and non-scientific view of man and his universe."[31] In the midst of the tension, the schizophrenia of our technologically sophisticated society, Jesus says, "And you shall know the truth, and the truth shall make you free" (John 8:32, KJV).

NOTES

1. Oswald T. Avery, C. M. MacLeod and M. McCarty, "Studies on the Chemical Nature of the Substance Inducing Transformation of Pneumococcal Types," *Journal of Experimental Medicine* 79 (1944): 137.

2. James D. Watson and Francis H. C. Crick, "Molecular Structure of Nucleic Acid," *Nature* 171 (1953): 737–738.

3. Matthew Meselson and Franklin W. Stahl, "The Replication of DNA in *Escherichia coli,*" *Proceedings of the National Academy of Science, U.S.* 43 (1958): p. 581.

4. Arthur Kornberg, "Biological Synthesis of Deoxyribonucleic Acid," *Science* 131 (1960): 1503–1508.

5. V. Hershfield, H. W. Boyer, C. Yanofsky, M. A. Lovett and D. R. Helinski. "Plasmid Col El as a Molecular Vehicle for Cloning and Amplification of DNA," *Proceedings of the National Academy of Science, U.S.* 71 (1974): 3455–3459.

6. Jacques Monod, *Chance and Necessity: An Essay on the Natural Philosophy of Modern Biology* (New York: Vintage Books, 1972).

7. *Ibid.,* p. 32.

8. *Ibid.,* p. 44.

9. *Ibid.,* p. 176.

10. *Ibid.,* p. 177.

11. Arthur Peacocke, "Chance, Necessity and God," in *Beyond Chance and Necessity,* ed. John Lewis (Atlantic Highlands, N.J.: Humanities Press, 1974), p. 13.

12. Gunther S. Stent, "The Poverty of Scientism and the Promise of Structuralist Ethics," *Hastings Center Report* 6 (1976): 32.

13. *Ibid.,* p. 36.

14. *Ibid.,* p. 39.

15. *Ibid.*, p. 38.

16. *Ibid.*, p. 36.

17. Robert L. Sinsheimer, "All Men Are Created Equal?" Paper delivered at the International Conference on Human Engineering and the Future of Man. Wheaton, Ill., July 1975.

18. Donald M. MacKay, *The Clockwork Image* (Downers Grove, Ill.: Inter-Varsity Press, 1974).

19. Sinsheimer, *op. cit.*

20. L. Kass, "New Beginnings in Life," in *The New Genetics and The Future of Man,* ed. M. Hamilton (Grand Rapids, Michigan: William B. Eerdmans Publishing Co., 1972), p. 19.

21. Robert L. Sinsheimer, "On Coupling Inquiry and Wisdom," *Federation Proceedings* 35, (1976): 2540–2542.

22. Paul Berg et al., a letter to *Science* 185 (1974): 303.

23. *Federal Register,* Vol. 41, No. 131, 7 July 1976, Part 2, pp. 27902–27943.

24. Sinsheimer, "On Coupling Inquiry and Wisdom," p. 2541.

25. Robert L. Herrmann, "Human Engineering and the Church," *Journal of the American Scientific Affiliation* 28 (1976): 59–62.

26. Robert L. Herrmann, Response to Donald MacKay's paper "Biblical Perspectives on Human Engineering", International Conference on Human Engineering and The Future of Man, Wheaton, Ill., July 1975.

27. Jon Beckwith, "Social and Political Uses of Genetics in the United States: Past and Present," *Annals of the New York Academy of Science* 265 (1976): 46–58.

28. *Ibid.*, p. 52.

29. B. Maletzky, "Roots of Violence," *Residence and Staff Physician* 19 (1973): 40.

30. Vernon Mark and Frank Ervin, *Violence and the Brain* (New York, Harper & Row, 1970).

31. Norman Mailer, *Of a Fire on the Moon* (Boston: Little, Brown & Co., 1970).

VII

Dilemmas in Biomedical Ethics

LEWIS PENHALL BIRD

The signal lesson of our scientific age has been that technology usually outpaces the ability of its creators to harness its diverse implications within completely ethical channels. As Jacques Ellul carefully observes, Christianity has long noted and criticized technological innovations with a singular concern: "Technical activity did not escape Christian moral judgment. The question 'is it righteous?' was asked of every attempt to change modes of production or of organization. That something might be useful or profitable to men did not make it right and just."[1] Consequently, the Christian clinician seeks

Lewis P. Bird is Regional Director for Christian Medical Society at its Eastern headquarters in Havertown, Pennsylvania. He holds a B.S., B.D., S.T.M., and Ph.D., the latter from New York University in the field of religion and the family. He is author of *The Ten Commandments in Modern Medicine* (1965) and of *Learning to Love* (1971). He contributed the essay entitled "Universal Principles of Medical Ethics" to the symposium *Is it Moral to Modify Man?* (Claude S. Frazier, ed., 1973). He was chairperson of the program committee of both the 1968 Christian Medical Society Conference on Abortion, Contraception and Sterilization and the 1975 International Conference on Human Engineering and the Future of Man. He is a member of Phi Delta Kappa, of the American Association of Sex Educators and Counselors, of the Advisory Board of Christian Association for Psychological Studies and of the Executive Board of Evangelical Child and Family Service (Philadelphia, Pennsylvania).

to blend ethical sensitivity with technological expertise. The burgeoning field of biomedical ethics now seeks balances between rights and responsibilities, the individual and society, costs and benefits, what can be done and what should be done.

As we have progressed from the atomic age through the computer age and into the space age, there has been a concurrent exploration of inner space. The continuing dissection of man's subconscious terrain and the discovery of the genetic implications of the deoxyribonucleic acid (DNA) molecule have unlocked further mysteries with attendant ethical dilemmas. Where the ancient Psalmist stood in awe of the heavens (Ps. 19:1–6), many moderns now stand in awe of the laboratory.

Although the average patient is usually aware of the benefits a relatively recent repertoire of scientific gadgetry may provide, the special patient may be tempted to pray for mercy as the remaining days of life are punctured with needles, tubes, scalpels, roentgen rays and experimental pharmaceuticals. The development of medical care from an art to a science now may be in danger of becoming merely a technological support system. A balance of these three components of modern medical practice—art, science and support system—would probably gratify most clinicians and patients today.

For the Christian researcher, the Creation Mandate ("have dominion over . . . every living thing," Gen. 1:28, RSV) has particular applicability to the life sciences. While the Church has inhibited scientific inquiry at times,[2] in its finer moments it has also enhanced medical progress by matching morality with medicine,[3] desacralizing nature,[4] inaugurating the charity hospital movement,[5] and extending health care delivery to Third World peoples.[6] Consequently, ecclesiastical involvement in bioethics[7] calls for both courage and caution.

While Holy Scripture provides the framework within which the Christian clinician seeks to refine ethical judgment,[8] mortal finitude limits one's rational and moral consistency. However, at bedside the specialist must think incisively and act decisively in the patient's best interest. Here, professional competence, ethical sensitivity and human compassion are required. While the Christian physician may not exhibit all of these skills on every occasion, nonetheless, with professional excellence as one's vocational goal, the Christian in the health sciences finds a ready resource in biblical revelation for both motivational renewal and moral reflection. Such a heritage is no small treasure in a world where cynicism too frequently erases humanistic ideals.

Coping with constant change taxes even the best minds, as refinements continue in organ transplantation, surgical techniques, prosthetics, reproductive technologies and behavior controls. The problems confronting the clinician, regardless of how well read one may be in the journals and irrespective of one's standing as an amateur philosopher, are no abstraction; a living—or dying—*person* needs attention. Sheri Finkbine,[9] Karen Quinlan,[10] and Renee Richards[11] have each contributed in their own unplanned way to the lexicography of contemporary bioethics. The debates over abortion (Finkbine), artificial life-support systems and euthanasia (Quinlan), and transexual surgery (Richards) all found special focus in these patients. The families, along with the physicians related to each of these persons, have had to rethink medical morals as well as cultural mores. In two of these three cases, new frontiers in medico-legal jurisprudence were drawn.[12]

As a diversity of value systems increasingly characterizes modern life, the differing belief systems of individual patients and colleagues will have to be understood if total patient care is to have meaning. Respect for the rapport with individual persons amid ethical and ethnic pluralism may only be possible where similarities may be celebrated and differences at least clearly comprehended. Since Evangelical Protestants know they are answerable to revealed truth, their values will be formulated from a biblical baseline under the continuing guidance of God's Spirit. This may result in the sponsorship of unpopular causes or lonely vigils for forgotten principles. In a relativistic age such a stance may be readily misunderstood, but for those who seek ultimate meaning in life's diverse adventures, such a world view may have compelling relevance. In the wider context of bioethical debates, this essay will highlight the work of some clinicians for whom theism and the scientific method have not been mutually exclusive avenues.[13]

When the apostle Paul affirmed a citation from Epimenides before Athenian intellectuals ("In Him we live and move and have our being," Acts 17:28, RSV), he fully acknowledged the role of Divine Providence in human affairs. Our mortal breath, our motor control and our meaningful existence are all viewed as gifts from God's hand. As the presence of evil in human suffering cripples physical function and clouds rationality, therapists and clinicians ("made a little less than God," Ps. 8:5, RSV) may appropriately intervene with curative measures where possible. Such is the healing task in the service professions, in full accord with the compassionate concern of the Church.

At least four prime philosophical questions haunt medical wards with diverse new implications: What is the nature and meaning of human personhood? Human suffering? Human death? Human responsibility? Each will be addressed in turn; however, because of its foundational importance, the first question will be given fullest development.

ISSUES IN DEFINING HUMAN PERSONHOOD

The ancient Psalmist queried, "What is man that thou art mindful of him?" (Ps. 8:4, RSV). Nicholas A. Berdyaev considered the problem of man to be the basic theme of modern philosophy.[14] With increasing urgency this philosophical quest confronts those who consider transplanting organs, implanting artificial prostheses, modifying the genotype, aborting the fetus, controlling the mind or shutting off the respirator. This problem continues to be the central question in contemporary bioethics.

At least three significant subproblems are involved: What do we mean by *human personhood?* When does *human* life begin? When may human life *justifiably* be taken? Physicians, philosophers, theologians, lawyers, sociologists, psychologists, anthropologists, ethicists, biologists and the general public all have vested interests in the assumptions made and in the replies given to these ultimate questions. But it is the clinician at the front line of disease and sudden trauma whose responsibility it is to act, not speculate. If one is to be more than society's technician, the physician must reflect on the ethical principles which undergird and safeguard one's practice. A review of the "human personhood" debate in bioethics begins this section.

Whether man be viewed as "cosmic orphan" or the "lethal factor" in modern life,[15] his dignity is increasingly being both assumed and debated. With humanistic values informing more and more bioethic forums, the frequently used but seldom defined term *human* is receiv-

ing increased attention. At a 1971 symposium on genetic counseling
and the use of genetic knowledge, biochemist Robert L. Sinsheimer
advanced the following agenda in a desire "to commence an inquiry"
into defining our *humanum:*[16]

1. our self-awareness
2. our perception of past, present, and future
3. our capacities for hope, faith, charity and love
4. our enlarged ability to communicate and thereby to create a
   collective consciousness
5. our ability to achieve a rational understanding of Nature
6. our drive to reduce the role of Fate in human affairs
7. our vision of man as unfinished.

Joseph Fletcher joined the discussion with his catalogue of twenty
criteria:[17]

Positive Human Criteria	*Negative Human Criteria*
1. Minimal intelligence	Man is not:
2. Self-awareness	1. Non- or anti-artificial
3. Self-control	2. Essentially parental
4. A sense of time	3. Essentially sexual
5. A sense of futurity	4. A bundle of rights
6. A sense of the past	5. A worshiper
7. The capability to relate to others	
8. Concern for others	
9. Communication	
10. Control of existence	
11. Curiosity	
12. Change and changeability	
13. Balance of rationality and feeling	
14. Idiosyncrasy	
15. Neocortical function ("cardinal indicator")	

In an effort to lend specificity to the inquiry, Fletcher risked significant censure with the following amplification of his first point, "minimal intelligence": "Any individual of the species *homo sapiens* who
falls below the I.Q. 40-mark in a standard Stanford-Binet test, am-

plified if you like by other tests, is questionably a person; below the
20-mark, not a person. *Homo* is indeed *sapiens,* in order to be *homo.*[18]
Coming from a theologically trained mind, Fletcher's clarification of
the last criterion was also surprising: "Mystique is not essential to
being truly a person. Like sexuality, it may arguably be of the fulness
of humanness but it is not of the essence."[19] For Fletcher, this assertion followed from his premise, namely, ". . . that a viable biomedical
ethics is humanistic. . . ."[20]

After two years of reflection, Fletcher modified the list to "Four
Indicators of Humanhood":[21]

1. Self-awareness.
2. The relational potential.
3. Euphoria and affectionate responses to caresses.
4. Neocortical function (the human *sine qua non*).

Since semantic confusion results when definitions incorporate the
term to be explained within the exposition, the use of *human* in the
fourth point clouds Fletcher's meaning. Remove *human* from this list
and one may wonder whether Fletcher is describing our schnauzer
Heidi or our daughter Susie. Seeking to probe core concepts may be
critically necessary, but one must be forewarned that what may clarify
at one level may serve only to confuse at another.

The Institute of Situational Ethics prepared an ethical aptitude test
". . . as part of a program to determine the ethical quotients of persons
applying for admission to professional schools and of those seeking
positions of responsibility in business, in government, and in other
occupations involving policy decisions." For the question, "What are
the principal criteria for establishing the relative value of human
lives?", the essential criterion cited by almost all respondents in a
representative sample of 435 adult Americans was "potential economic productivity."[22] Utilitarian value judgments persist in American culture, with dangerous implications for defining our *humanum*
and for regulating our future.

The effort to lend specificity to definitions of human personhood
continues to elicit a wide range of responses. Some seek to distinguish
between *human* and *person.*[23] Others attempt to delineate human
from animal capacity. For instance, reflecting on animal and human
experimentation, anthropologist Margaret Mead concluded: "Guinea

pigs are not able to invoke their experience or fears or cognitive powers. . . . These are distinctively human and noble aspects of humanity."[24] Sociologist Amitai Etzioni emphasizes the relational aspect of humanness: "To lead a *human* life . . . is to be aware, to communicate, be loving, or function on his or her own."[25] Some scholars emphasize potentiality; thus, for example, philosopher Baruch Brody affirms that "what is essential for being human is the possession of the potential for human activities that comes with having the structures required for a functioning brain."[26] The ethicist James M. Gustafson similarly asserts that "to be human is to have a vocation, a calling; . . . it is to become what we now are not. . . ."[27]

Not all bioethicists, however, view the effort to define human personhood as a legitimate pursuit. For instance, Paul Ramsey, with typical tenacity, disapproves of this whole debate: "Any product of human conception is, by definition, human. Tracing the development of human personhood is appropriate in the areas of morality, cognition, and psychosexuality. Such an effort is inappropriate in the field of medicine; it can only lead to the slippery slope to Nuremberg."[28] Given the history of holocaust in this century, a number of ethicists view with alarm the dehumanizing tendencies implicit in the sociopolitical practices of many modern societies. Debates of this kind rekindle anxieties about the public policies which led to the Nazi experience.[29] Biologist Gunther S. Stent sounds a valid warning of the limitations with which such a quest for definition may be inevitably confronted:

> . . . I think that it is important to give due recognition to this fundamental epistemological limitation to the human sciences, if only as a safeguard against the psychological or sociological prescriptions put forward by those who allege that they have already managed to gain a scientifically validated understanding of man.[30]

Ramsey and others[31] argue that the qualities of human personhood reside in each individual *sui generis.* This is not to say that human personhood lodges wherever human protoplasm is found, but it underscores the view that where human genes combine, the newly formed zygote is obviously human; genetic programming is still species aligned.

Where philosophers speak of the dignity of human life, theologians usually refer to its sanctity. Some, such as Hans Jonas, mourn the fact that religious categories have been rigorously banned from most philosophies of science: "Nature had been 'neutralized' with respect to value, then man himself. Now we shiver in the nakedness of a nihilism in which near-omnipotence is paired with near-emptiness, greatest capacity with knowing least what for."[32] Jonas goes on to suggest that the category of the sacred is needed now more than ever: "It is a question whether without restoring the category of the sacred, the category most thoroughly destroyed by the scientific enlightenment, we can have an ethics able to cope with the extreme powers which we possess today and constantly increase and are almost compelled to use."[33]

The category most compellingly employed to define the sanctity of human life in both Jewish and Christian theology is that of the *imago Dei,* the doctrine that man is the image of God. This concept of innate human dignity has historically fostered respect for all forms of human life and has encouraged programs to alleviate human suffering. As Evangelical morality has found an ultimately authoritative source in the biblical revelation, so its confidence in attaching definite value to human life, in distinction from all other forms of animal life, has been grounded in an absolutism which contrasts increasingly vividly with the ethical relativism of our age.

Turning to Scripture for a definite answer regarding precisely when human life begins has not produced unanimity of opinion among Evangelicals. At a 1968 symposium on abortion, one participant recalled Lutheran theologian J. Theodore Mueller's opinion that the question of when the soul joined the body was an open one; that is, a problem "on which the Word of God is silent."[34] Having acknowledged this difficulty, however, John Warwick Montgomery went on to conclude that "for the biblical writers, personhood in the most genuine sense begins no later than conception; subsequent human acts illustrate this personhood, they do not create it. Man *does* because he *is* (not the reverse) and he *is* because God brought about his psychophysical existence in the miracle of conception."[35]

Other participants were not so certain. Kenneth Kantzer argued that "Scripture does teach us that a human fetus is of immeasurable value because of its potential, in spite of the fact that it is not yet fully human. . . ."[36] In his concluding summation, Kantzer considered the problem of balancing competing values: "From conception, the fetus is of immeasurable value because of its potential humanity; and, therefore, to destroy it is an evil which can only be willed by man in obedience to God as a lesser evil so that not to destroy it would be to destroy other immeasurable values which are yet known to be greater (i.e., not just the well-being as in the sense of greater pleasure but the greater humanity of man—as life, sanity, and *perceptible personhood*)."[37]

According to Daniel Callahan three basic answers have been given to the question of when human life begins.[38] The genetic argument reasons that human life begins at the moment of conception, since the DNA coding of all the characteristics of specific individuality is present then. The developmental argument postulates that at some point during the zygote-blastocyst-embryo-fetus development the conceptus becomes human. The social consequences argument theorizes that defining the conceptus as "human" must be done only in the face of the social implications such a judgment would have. Few Evangelical Protestants have written in defense of the third answer,[39] since the Evangelical community shuns utilitarian arguments of this kind.

Evangelical defenders of the first point of view include pediatric surgeon C. Everett Koop,[40] theologian Harold O. J. Brown, [41] and pastoral counselor Clifford E. Bajema.[42] Koop asserts: "Once there is the union of sperm and egg, and the twenty-three chromosomes of each are brought together into one cell that has forty-six chromosomes, we have an entirely different story. That one cell with its forty-six chromosomes has all of the DNA, the whole genetic code, that will, if not interrupted, make a human being just like you, with the potential for God-consciousness."[43] An Old Testament scholar who has contributed to the Evangelical debate on abortion should also be included among defenders of the genetic point of view. Bruce K. Waltke has now shifted from an earlier, moderate position[44] to a more conservative judgment: "The fetus is human and therefore to be accorded the same protection to life granted every other human being."[45]

The developmental point of view is found in both Evangelical and orthodox Protestant circles. Psychiatrist Merville O. Vincent concludes: "I am convinced of the sanctity of human life, but I find it difficult to maintain with certainty that human life comes into existence at the moment of conception. . . . I feel that it is a valid position to state that the fetus develops a body and soul in utero. I am not

convinced from either Scripture or science that the early embryo has
a value equal to the value of a fully developed body and soul."[46] Also
arguing for the developmental view is pastoral counsellor Eldon Weisheit; he reasons that " . . . understanding the birth of a child as a part
of God's continuing creation does not require a moment of ensouling.
. . . The beginning of a new life is not just a moment in history but
is a spin-off of the continuing life cycle.[47] Gynecologist R. F. R.
Gardner likewise opts for the developmental view: " . . . while the
fetus is to be cherished increasingly as it develops, we should regard
its first breath at birth as the moment when God gives it not only life,
but the offer of life."[48] Theologian Paul King Jewett underscores the
ambiguous state of the fetus when he asserts that "there is nothing in
scripture bearing directly on the question of the participation of the
fetus in the divine image."[49]

John Warwick Montgomery, on the other hand, unequivocally
states in a recent issue of *Christianity Today:* "The Bible stands abso-
lutely against the killing of fetal life. Among Bible-believing theologians, Protestant and Catholic, this issue is no longer in dispute.
. . . For a genuine evangelical, there is no option but to regard the
Supreme Court's decision in *Roe v. Wade* as monstrous—and no
alternative, in our government of checks and balances, but to counter
that decision by a constitutional right-to-life amendment. . . ."[50] Such
a unilateral judgment, however well-intentioned, overlooks a significant body of data. A statement which reflects the deep concern many
evangelical clinicians express over abortion, yet acknowledges diversity of opinion, was drafted at the 1975 International Congress of
Christian Physicians:

> Legalised termination of pregnancy is now established in many countries
> throughout the world and it is becoming an accepted way of conducting
> human affairs. The Christian will continue to regard it as an evil and hope
> society will before long remove [it] from the statute books of nations.
>
> The will to terminate life arises out of disorder in human relationships
> which society should be concerned to remedy. Some Christian doctors oppose
> the termination of a pregnancy for any reason; others are prepared to termi-
> nate a pregnancy when its continuance is likely to result in serious damage
> to the health of the mother or the child. Unanimity of Christian judgment in
> these matters is not likely to be achieved but all Christians are agreed on the
> principle of reverence for human life at any stage of development.[51]

John R. W. Stott, a respected British voice in Evangelical circles, also has wrestled with these difficult issues. He concludes:

> Even sin has not entirely destroyed God's image in man. If then the morally deformed are still said to be made in God's image (James 3:9), the physically deformed certainly are. We have no liberty to say that a damaged, deformed baby is not a human being. The case of so-called monster babies is, I think, different. . . . I take as my example the anacephalic [sic], born . . . without any cerebral cortex (and therefore, it seems, entirely without any capacity to think or choose or love or in fact grow into a human being). One can argue, of course, that every creature conceived and born of human parents is human. It is significant, however, that the Roman Catholic Church is prepared to entertain a doubt and will baptize "monster" babies only conditionally, saying, "If you are a man, I baptize you. . . ."[52]

Stott's effort to balance a deep sense of sanctity for human life with the realization that ambiguity attaches to some forms of human existence aligns with this writer's judgment. Using the anencephalic (an infant born without a brain) as an example readily pushes any definition of human personhood to its logical limits. These infants usually die upon delivery once their sustenance from the mother is severed. Offering conditional baptism to hydranencephalics (lacking cerebral hemispheres) and other severely retarded newborns bears witness to an historic lack of certainty about the status of these infants. Yet administering conditional baptism is a strikingly different moral act than practicing infanticide on severely retarded nurslings. In the face of ambiguity, the practice of most Evangelical clinicians is one of caution. Extraordinary measures would likely be suspended, but minimal sustenance would be supplied; better economically certain expenditures than ethically uncertain experimentations in caring for these puzzling forms of humanity.

Another dimension to this problem also colors Evangelical social ethics. Moses and the prophets were routinely concerned about justice for the alien, the orphan and the widow (Deut. 27:19; Isa. 1:17; Jer. 22:3). Unfortunately, every culture has its own way of defining what particular forms of humanity it will consider alien to its own central interests. While fetal experimentation becomes an issue, Hans Tiefel stresses the biblical concern for protecting the discards from various social programs:

A dominant motif in the biblical traditions is God's special compassion and care for those who are outcasts, for those who are given no place in the human community. The widow, the orphan, the poor, the foreigner were favored in the eyes of God if not of men. And Jesus's identification with the least of human beings (Matthew 25:40) expresses the same concern. Now, there are no better candidates for the "despised and rejected," for the unwanted and outcast, than abortion fetuses. And if God is on their side and keeps us from treating living abortion fetuses as merely useful research material, believers ought also to insist upon their protection.[53]

Christians of various denominations will be increasingly insistent upon protecting clinicians who are members of academic departments or hospital staffs where abortions on demand and fetal experimentation are mandated in the face of freedom of conscience clauses. In reviewing recent British experience, Paul Ramsey concludes that ". . . contrary to the wording of the Abortion Act, Great Britain has by administrative decision instated a policy of abortion on demand, and . . . more than one sort of medical consultant is now required to acquiesce."[54]

Logical argumentation may proceed more easily if assumptions about human personhood posit full rights and sanctity from the moment of conception, but such a view has yet to be found persuasive by all the Evangelicals whose professional responsibilities bring them face to face with this question. But whatever their view of the origin of human life, clinicians of this persuasion would permit an abortion when the life of the mother is threatened, with some favoring selective abortion and only a few advocating an open abortion policy.

Defining what is meant by *human personhood* is an urgent task in bioethics today. To conduct this debate on sociopsychological grounds may be necessary; however, such measurements have an ethically vexing way of becoming socioeconomic and sociopolitical policy. What began as an exercise in medical metaphysics may end tragically in utilitarian quantifications far removed from initial concerns. Ultimately, society's valuation of human forms of life measures as well something about that culture's own humane instincts.

ISSUES IN DEFINING HUMAN SUFFERING

In a society saturated with hedonism, talk of human suffering is an anachronism at best and an embarrassment at worst. Our contemporary culture teaches us to have little tolerance for discomfort, disease, pain or suffering. Not only have the terminally ill often been abandoned by attending health care personnel,[55] even the temporarily ill know the sense of isolation sickness brings when nuclear family life cuts them off from extended family support. The permanently disabled routinely witness untold dehumanizing episodes in their struggle with the able bodies for a place in the sun.

Following his 1963 lecture tour of the United States, Helmut Thielicke was somewhat surprised at the American avoidance of the problem of suffering: "Not a single person ever raised it in any discussion I had in this country. . . ."[56] His evaluation: ". . . Americans do not have this color on their otherwise so richly furnished palette."[57] The subsequent political assassinations of John F. Kennedy, Martin Luther King, Jr. and Robert F. Kennedy notwithstanding, the topic of suffering still triggers an awkward silence in most American conversations.

Such was the case in the ancient world, notes medical historian Fielding Garrison: ". . . the spirit of antiquity toward sickness and misfortune was not one of compassion, and the credit of ministering to human suffering on an extended scale belongs to Christianity."[58] While suffering was frequently correlated with sinful behavior (sometimes correctly so), Jesus clarified for the disciples how one man's blindness occurred so "that the works of God might be made manifest in him" (John 9:3, R. S. V.).

Suffering may be defined as "an anguish which we experience, not only as a pressure to change, but as a threat to our composure, our integrity, and the fulfillment of our intentions."[59] As one of life's universal experiences, authentic suffering may find meaningful resolution through at least three different interpretations: as moral consequence, as a maturing process and as meritorious atonement. In the first instance, the cause–effect equation provides a rationale. In other circumstances, the mystery of suffering may find resolution in the personal maturation such trauma makes possible. H. E. Hopkins reminds us that "just as it is possible, by setting the sails correctly, to travel fast and securely into the wind, or alternatively to allow the wind to take control and drive one in the opposite direction, so, in relation to the onslaught of suffering, more depends on the attitude we adopt towards it than on its own particular vigour and vehemence."[60] Finally, as Christian theology affirms in Christ's atonement, suffering may find a meritorious dimension which lends a transcendent meaning to personal agony. In this instance, "there is no greater love than this, that a man should lay down his life for his friends" (John 15:13, NEB).

While pain and suffering may be overlapping experiences, they do differ. Dorland's *Medical Dictionary* defines pain as "a more or less localized sensation of discomfort, distress, or agony, resulting from the stimulation of specialized nerve endings. It serves as a protective mechanism insofar as it induces the sufferer to remove or withdraw from the source."[61] Pain, as nature's early warning system, is a very valuable physical sensation. It operates at both physiological and psychological levels; individual perceptions of pain may be altered significantly because of differing threshold levels or diverse environmental circumstances.[62]

Pain and suffering have been ethically interpreted, in some circumstances, as experiences essentially without meaning. While physical trauma may be part of the moral consequences of human misbehavior, prolonged, intense pain may lack moral or medical justification. As humans understand more clearly their basic interdependence, meaningful suffering would likely be found in a context where these criteria prevailed: physically, the individual would be relatively free from prolonged, excruciating pain and the patient would be free from a prolonged coma, and psychologically, elements of courage, grace, realism, insight, faith, hope and love would characterize the attitude of the patient in a social context where elements of support, compassion and interpretation from significant friends supplemented the patient's own personal point of view. Meaningful suffering could demythologize the illusion of personal autonomy and self-sufficiency, dematerialize corrupted value systems and demonstrate the bonds of love which surround us.

The twin goals of preserving life and relieving pain often collide. Traditionally a variety of analgesics have been used to ameliorate intractable pain. The advice of one Christian clinician is certainly echoed by many of his colleagues: ". . . let suffering have its full relief at the conscious risk to life, for to allow suffering of that intensity to proceed for long is to kill the mind and to distort the life to something foreign to the purpose of God."[63]

Two specific options confront the seriously ill patient with increasing frequency and with diverse ethical implications: clinical experimentation and organ transplantation. The issue of human experimentation has received impressive treatment in recent years.[64] The ethics of informed consent detail a multitude of problems.[65] The Nuremberg Code (1946), the Declaration of Geneva (1948) and the Declaration of Helsinki (1964) all exhibited particular concern for clinical experimentation with human subjects. In summary, they sought to establish these safeguards: (1) only scientifically qualified persons should conduct the clinical research, under the supervision of other qualified scientists; (2) only after extensive laboratory and animal experimentation should human subjects be used; (3) only as foreseeable benefits, either to the subject or to others, outweigh inherent risks should the research project proceed; (4) only when a reasonably informed consent has been obtained should the experimentation begin; and (5) only when rigorous measures have been taken to safeguard the personality of the subject from unintended mind alterations should the experiment be undertaken.[66]

Risk–benefit ratios, cost–benefit ratios, reward systems, experimentation with captive groups (prisoners, military personnel, etc.) or subjects who cannot give an informed consent (children, the mentally incompetent, comatose patients, etc.), patient coercion and scientific motivations—all merit continuing ethical scrutiny. If the trust between patient and physician is to remain secure, then principles like the Golden Rule, with its "intelligent anticipation of the well-being of another,"[67] must guide clinical experimentation.

Mitigating human suffering with organ transplantations, provided the donor's own interests have not been violated, accords with Christian ethics. One Christian surgeon involved with tissue transplants, John E. Woods, suggests that an experimental procedure is morally acceptable when

. . . all other modes of accepted therapy have been explored and exhausted; death or total incapacitation is inevitable within a short and predictable period of time; the surgeon has optimally prepared himself through laboratory experience; there is a definite, if small, chance of the procedure succeeding; and the patient is fully aware of the experimental nature and the risks of the procedure. If these criteria are fulfilled and if the procedure does not entail undue suffering or loss of human dignity, the physician may in good conscience proceed. The aim in organ transplantation is not simply prolongation of life with possible attendant suffering, but total rehabilitation of the patient.[68]

In Christian perspective, organ transplantation offers promising new options for sustaining human life; its potential abuse appears when elemental human rights are violated and when utopian delusions of physical immortality are nourished.

ISSUES IN DEFINING HUMAN DEATH

The shift toward a definition of human death in terms of cerebral cellular activity rather than cessation of the heart beat disturbs few Christians. The Bible has poetically described human emotion and function as emanating from various physical organs (the heart, bowels, kidneys and liver). Biblical anthropology emphasizes the totality of human functions rather than organic pathology. With the advent of transplantation operations, coupled with the technological means to sustain various physical functions, more sophisticated definitions and clinical measurements of human death were needed.

Many Evangelical Protestants join with those who propose "death with dignity," while recognizing as well the indignity of death itself.[69] Compassion mandates that responsible care be extended to the hopelessly ill patient[70] so that any "Living Will,"[71] while perhaps psychologically reassuring, would only document what sound clinical judgment already commends. Given modern technology's impressive means to extend the process of dying, "orders not to resuscitate"[72] may have ethical sanction in carefully guarded circumstances. Following physical death, Christian ethics would support and encourage the donation of anatomical parts, where they could alleviate another's suffering or advance scientific inquiry, or both.

Two Evangelical clinicians who have translated Christian compassion into pragmatic programs in the medically forbidding arena of the terminally ill have been Cicely Saunders[73] and Balfour M. Mount.[74]

With an optimistic realism which Christian hope can provide, coupled with a capacity for consistency of concern, these pioneers in the sphere of thanatology have established hospice facilities, where isolation, neglect, dishonesty and needless surgical interventions have been replaced with trust, realism, support, fulfillment and reconciliation in an essentially pain-free state.[75] In a quiet disclaimer of any meritorious achievement, Mount recalls Hinton's insight: "We emerge deserving of little credit; we who are capable of ignoring the conditions which make muted people suffer. The dissatisfied dead cannot noise abroad the negligence they have experienced."[76] Until recently, only a few medical centers have offered hospice care for the dying; the recent strides in managing terminal illness merit wider application. Furthermore, the recent emphasis on honesty with the terminally ill finds strong support in Evangelical medical ethics.

The resuscitation of interest in euthanasia must concern thoughtful clinicians and ethicists alike. Just as the medical indications for abortion are diminishing, so the medical management of the terminally ill is removing a number of the traditional arguments for active euthanasia. What in some instances may be a fine line of ethical judgment separates in clinical practice active euthanasia (the administration of a drug or other agent to induce death) from passive euthanasia (the withholding of a treatment program likely to prolong the dying process).

British clinician Duncan Vere has argued that advocates of active euthanasia presuppose total hopelessness in the situation and thereby launch "death acceleration" programs which may incorporate suicidal instincts usually inimical to most Christian and public values.[77] Interestingly, when Dr. and Mrs. Henry P. Van Dusen, members of the Euthanasia Society and active participants in the American theological community, both swallowed overdoses of sleeping pills, the front page headline read: "Theologian Dies in Suicide Pact."[78] Helmut Thielicke's ethical perception is particularly pertinent here: ". . . euthanasia, . . . which ends the suffering by prematurely induced death, is contrary to the meaning of the life of the sufferer. For man, unlike the animal, is a being who can suffer ethically. Therefore there can be a *'coup de grace'* for a dog, but not for man."[79]

In a classic legal essay, Yale Kamisar considers one aspect of the "wedge principle" (i.e., where a narrow criterion later broadens into a sweeping policy) in the context of the sociopolitical climate of the twentieth century, no mean correlation. Kamisar concludes that "another reason why the 'parade of horrors' argument cannot be too lightly dismissed in this particular instance . . . is that the parade *has* taken place in our time and the order of procession has been headed by the killing of the 'incurables' and the 'useless.' "[80] The lessons of history should not be lost and the lessons the "incurables" and the "useless" can teach all of us need to be sounded abroad, not silenced. Erickson and Bowers argue persuasively that "the advocacy of euthanasia disregards the Biblical perspective on suffering" and that "passive euthanasia would suffice" in many cases where the extensive use of extraordinary measures supports only a minimal level of human existence.[81] Happily, with Evangelical clinicians in the forefront of providing truly palliative measures for the terminally ill, arguments for active euthanasia find little appeal in the Evangelical community. And the hope of resurrection, grounded in the miraculous event of that first Easter, provides the believer with a powerful antidote to the fear and despair death holds for many.

ISSUES IN DEFINING HUMAN RESPONSIBILITY

Article 25 of the Universal Declaration of Human Rights speaks with special relevance to the medical profession:

> Everyone has the right to a standard of living adequate for the health and well-being of himself and of his family, including food, clothing, housing and medical care and necessary social services, and the right to security in the event of an unemployment, sickness, disability, widowhood, old age or other lack of livelihood in circumstances beyond his control.[82]

Such an ambitious creed has obvious socioeconomic implications. Its justification, either philosophically or theologically, may not be as self-evident.[83]

"Rights" rhetoric, of necessity, branches out into related issues: rights versus responsibilities, rights versus obligations, and rights versus wants, to name a few. Philosopher Ronald Nash defines a right this way: "To have a right is to have a legally or morally justifiable claim to possess or obtain something or to act in a certain way."[84] In response to the obvious query, By what authority does one claim a given right? arguments from natural law theory, contract theory, utilitarian theory or totalitarian theory are usually advanced. Melden's observation that ". . . the notion of a right that is one's moral title opens up a complex conceptual structure . . ."[85] underscores the treacherous terrain over which such an inquiry must journey.

For Nash, natural human rights are implicitly rather than explictly discovered in Scripture; they are grounded in the human dignity possessed by humans created in the image of God.[86] While theists or humanists may legitimately assert their own rights on various occasions (as the apostle Paul did before Festus, Acts 25), there are circumstances where such rights are relinquished for a greater good.

Of particular interest to this discussion is the relationship between patients' rights and health care services. One physician has argued that "the concept of medical care as the patient's right is immoral because it denies the most fundamental of all rights, that of a man to his own life and the freedom of action to support it. Medical care is neither a right nor a privilege: it is a service that is provided by doctors and others to people who wish to purchase it."[87] Gene Outka rather effectively counters this kind of reasoning: "Modern physicians depend on the achievements of medical technology and the entire scientific base underlying it, all of which is made possible by a host of persons whose salaries are often notably less. Moreover, the amount of taxpayer support for medical research and education is too enormous to make any such unqualified case for provider-autonomy plausible."[88] The debate over the right to health care services needs to focus as much on the motivations which will assure appropriate and compassionate patient care as on the mechanisms by which such aid will be funded. Duncan Vere, familiar with both the British and the American medical milieu, hopes "to hold complementary truths in a just balance. . . . It may well be that the urgent needs today are for British doctors to improve standards of individual care, for Americans to improve collective care."[89]

Another issue challenging human responsibility concerns the way we will seek to balance dwindling energy resources with expanding population margins. In referring to inadequate food supplies, physiologist John Brobeck raises the question, "Should we limit our own food intake so that our body weight is reduced to, and remains at, a level perhaps 5% to 10% below standard values for our height and age?"[90] He calls for responsible sacrifice: "There is no way to circumvent the principles of physiological energy exchange. What we can do is to agree—perhaps as a general Christian covenant—to respond to these impending crises by using less gasoline and fuel oil, and by habitually eating less food."[91]

In a society where interdependency between individual and society, between rights and responsibilities, between resources and their allocation, between physician and patient, and between patients and their families is more clearly understood, decisions about responsibility may be more easily implemented.

CONCLUSION

This survey of issues, though only touching numerous problems which have larger implications than suggested here, nonetheless may demonstrate ways in which responsible Evangelical clinicians are seeking to respond creatively to current issues while maintaining fidelity to God's revelation in Jesus Christ. Questions about embryo transplants, deviant versus variant sexual behavior,[92] sociobiology, and other major problems will continue to concern Christian clinicians, as they will all thoughtful researchers.

The Christian psychiatrist Paul Tournier provides a fitting final note for this chapter: "Reduced to the elements of science and technique, medicine is in danger of losing its human quality, of becoming dangerously impersonal. . . . Neither science nor technique can give physicians an adequate or whole view of the human person."[93] If one is to treat the whole person, perhaps one needs to be a whole person. In a broken world, Christian clinicians have found grace and strength from a Great Physician who calls for both ethical sensitivity and personal compassion amid diverse patient problems.

NOTES

1. Jacques Ellul, *The Technological Society,* trans. John Wilkinson (New York: Alfred A. Knopf, 1973), p. 37.
2. Cf. Arturo Castiglioni, *A History of Medicine,* trans. E. B. Krumbhaar (New York: Alfred A. Knopf, 1958), pp. 409 ff.

3. Cf. James B. Nelson, *Human Medicine: Ethical Perspectives on New Medical Issues* (Minneapolis: Augsburg Publishing House, 1973), pp. 14 ff.

4. Ellul, *op. cit.,* pp. 35 ff.

5. Cf. Fielding H. Garrison, *An Introduction to the History of Medicine,* 4th ed. (Philadelphia: W. B. Saunders Co., 1929), pp. 141 ff.

6. Cf. Edward M. Dodd, *The Gift of the Healer* (New York: Friendship Press, 1964).

7. A term originated and defined by Van Rensselaer Potter, *Bioethics: Bridge to the Future* (Englewood Cliffs, N.J.: Prentice-Hall, Inc., 1971).

8. Cf. James M. Gustafson, *Theology and Christian Ethics* (Philadelphia: Pilgrim Press, 1974); Gene H. Outka and Paul Ramsey, *Norm and Context in Christian Ethics* (New York: Charles Scribner's Sons, 1968); Roger R. Nicole, "Authority" in *Dictionary of Christian Ethics,* ed. Carl F. H. Henry (Grand Rapids, Michigan: Baker Book House, 1973), hereafter *DCE;* and Sidney S. Macaulay, "The Use of Scripture in the Ethics of Paul Ramsey" (Master's thesis, Columbia Theological Seminary, 1976).

9. Cf. discussion of the Finkbine case in Daniel Callahan, *Abortion: Law, Choice and Morality* (New York: MacMillan Co., 1970), p. 93.

10. Cf. cover story, "A Right to Die?" *Newsweek* 86, No. 18 (November 3, 1975): 58–69.

11. Cf. Ray Kennedy, "She'd Rather Switch—and Fight," *Sports Illustrated* 45, No. 10 (September 6, 1976): 16–19.

12. Cf. Thomas W. Hilgers and Dennis J. Horan, eds., *Abortion and Social Justice* (New York: Sheed and Ward, 1972) for an analysis in the aftermath of the January, 1973 U.S. Supreme Court decision and see also the Matter of Karen Quinlan, Supreme Court of New Jersey, A–116, September term 1975, decided 3/31/76, Slip Opinion pp. 1–59.

13. International Congresses of Christian Physicians have been held in Amsterdam (1963), Oxford (1966), Oslo (1969), Toronto (1972) and Singapore (1975); their *Proceedings* are available from the Christian Medical Society (USA). Christian Medical Society co-sponsored with *Christianity Today* a symposium on abortion, contraception and sterilization in 1968; these papers are available in Walter O. Spitzer and Carlyle L. Saylor, eds., *Birth Control and the Christian* (Wheaton, Ill.: Tyndale House, 1969); CMS also convened a symposium to explore the meanings of demon possession, the occult and mental illness; major addresses available in John Warwick Montgomery, ed., *Demon Possession* (Minneapolis: Bethany Fellowship, Inc., 1976); and a consortium of Evangelical professional societies sponsored a symposium in 1975 on "Human Engineering and the Future of Man"; these papers are to be available in Craig W. Ellison, ed., *Modifying Man: Implications and Ethics* (Washington, D.C.: University Press of America, 1977).

14. Cf. Nicholas A. Berdyaev, *The Destiny of Man* (London: Geoffrey Bles, 1948).

15. Both terms were coined by anthropologist Loren Eiseley; cf. "The Cosmic Orphan," *Saturday Review/World* 1, no. 12 (February 23, 1974), pp. 16–19.

16. Robert L. Sinsheimer, "Prospects for Future Scientific Developments: Ambush or Opportunity?" in *Ethical Issues in Human Genetics,* ed. Bruce Hilton et al. (New York: Plenum Press, 1973), p. 350.

17. Joseph Fletcher, "Indicators of Humanhood: A Tentative Profile of Man," *The Hastings Center Report* 2, No. 5 (November 1972): 1–4.

18. *Ibid.*, p. 1.

19. *Ibid.*, p. 4.

20. *Ibid.*

21. Joseph Fletcher, "Four Indicators of Humanhood—The Enquiry Matures," *The Hastings Center Report* 4, No. 6 (December 1974): 4–7.

22. Leonard C. Lewin, "Ethical Aptitude Test," *Harper's* 253, No. 1517 (October 1976): 20.

23. Cf. Lisa S. Cahill, "Correspondence" column, *The Hastings Center Report* 5, No. 2 (April 1975): p. 4.

24. Margaret Mead, "Research with Human Beings: An Anthropological Model," *Daedalus* 98, No. 2 (Spring 1969): 374.

25. Amitai Etzioni, "The Next Karen Quinlan Case?" *Parade* (November 7, 1976): 24. (Italics in original.)

26. Baruch Brody, *Abortion and the Sanctity of Human Life: A Philosophical View* (Cambridge, Mass.: MIT Press, 1975), p. 114.

27. James M. Gustafson, "What Is the Normatively Human?" *The American Ecclesiastical Review* 165, No. 3 (November 1971): p. 207.

28. Paul Ramsey in his lecture, "The Ethics of Fetal Research," delivered at Albany Medical Center, January 26, 1976. The developmental work of Jean Piaget, Erik Erikson and Lawrence Kohlberg was envisioned in Ramsey's discussion.

29. "Biomedical Ethics and the Shadow of Nazism," Special Supplement, *The Hastings Center Report* 6, No. 4 (August 1976): 1–20.

30. Gunther S. Stent, "Limits to the Scientific Understanding of Man," *Science* 187 (March 21, 1975): 1052–57.

31. Cf. J. D. Zizioulas, "Human Capacity and Human Incapacity: A Theological Exploration of Personhood," *Scottish Journal of Theology* 28, No. 3 (1975): 401–447.

32. Hans Jonas, *Philosophical Essays: From Ancient Creeds to Technological Man* (Englewood Cliffs, N.J.: Prentice-Hall, Inc., 1974), p. 19.

33. *Ibid.*, pp. 19 f.

34. J. Theodore Mueller, *Christian Dogmatics* (St. Louis: Concordia Publishing House, 1934), p. 58.

35. John Warwick Montgomery, "The Christian View of the Fetus," in Spitzer and Saylor, *op. cit.*, p. 83.

36. Kenneth Kantzer, "The Origin of the Soul as Related to the Abortion Question," in Spitzer and Saylor, *op. cit.*, p. 556.

37. *Ibid.*, p. 558. (Italics are mine.)

38. Callahan, *Op. Cit.*, chap. 11.

39. However, one should note the article by Roger W. Rochat which urges consideration for "the greater values of individual health, family welfare, and social responsibility" in "Abortion, the Bible and the Christian Physician," *Christian Medical Society Journal* 7, No. 3 (Summer 1976): 19–26.

40. C. Everett Koop, *The Right To Live; The Right To Die* (Wheaton, Illinois: Tyndale House Publishers, 1976).

41. Harold O. J. Brown, "The American Way of Death," *Moody Monthly* 77, No. 4 (December 1976): 32–35; and "What the Supreme Court Didn't Know," *Human Life Review* 1, No. 2 (Spring 1975): 5–21.

42. Clifford E. Bajema, *Abortion and the Meaning of Personhood* (Grand Rapids, Michigan: Baker Book House, 1974).

43. Koop, *op. cit.*, pp. 26 f.

44. Bruce K. Waltke, "Old Testament Texts Bearing on the Issues," in Spitzer and Saylor, *op. cit.*, pp. 5–24.

45. Bruce K. Waltke, "Reflections from the Old Testament on Abortion," *Journal of the Evangelical Theological Society* 19, No. 1 (Winter 1976): 3–13.

46. Merville O. Vincent, "Birth Control" in *Our Society in Turmoil*, ed. Gary R. Collins (Carol Stream, Illinois: Creation House, 1970), p. 168.

47. Eldon Weisheit, *Should I Have an Abortion?* (St. Louis: Concordia Publishing House, 1976), pp. 81 f.

48. R. F. R. Gardner, *Abortion: The Personal Dilemma* (Grand Rapids, Michigan: Wm. B. Eerdmans Publishing Co., 1972), p. 126.

49. Paul K. Jewett, "The Relationship of the Soul to the Fetus" in Spitzer and Saylor, *op. cit.*, p. 58.

50. John Warwick Montgomery, "Will an Evangelical President Usher In the Millennium?" *Christianity Today* 21, No. 2 (October 22, 1976): p. 66.

51. Lawrence Chan et al., "Statement on Abortion," *Proceedings* of the Fifth International Congress of Christian Physicians (Singapore: Christian Medical Fellowship, 1976), p. 155.

52. John R. W. Stott, "Reverence for Human Life," *Christianity Today* 16, No. 18 (June 9, 1972): 8–12.

53. Hans O. Tiefel, "The Cost of Fetal Research: Ethical Considerations," *The New England Journal of Medicine* 294, No. 2 (Jan. 8, 1976): pp. 85–90.

54. Paul Ramsey, "Abortion After the Law," *Christian Medical Society Journal* 7, No. 3 (Summer, 1976): 12.

55. Cf. Balfour M. Mount, "The Problem of Caring for the Dying in a General Hospital," *Canadian Medical Association Journal* 115 (July 17, 1976): 119–121.

56. Helmut Thielicke, *Between Heaven and Earth*, trans. John W. Doberstein (New York: Harper & Row, 1965), p. 185.

57. *Ibid.*

58. Garrison, *op. cit.*, p. 176.

59. Daniel Day Williams, "Suffering and Being in Empirical Theology," in *The Future of Empirical Theology*, ed. Bernard E. Meland (Chicago: The University of Chicago Press, 1969), p. 181.

60. H. E. Hopkins, *The Mystery of Suffering* (Chicago. Inter-Varsity Press, 1959), p. 87.

61. *Dorland's Illustrated Medical Dictionary*, 25th ed. (Philadelphia: Saunders, 1974).

62. Cf. Henry K. Beecher, "Pain," *Surgical Clinics of North America* 43 (June 1963): 609–617.

63. Duncan Vere, cited in Douglas MacG. Jackson, *The Sanctity of Life* (London: The Tyndale Press, 1962), p. 20.

64. Cf. particularly P. A. Freund, ed., "Ethical Aspects of Experimentation with

Human Subjects," *Daedalus,* 98, No. 2 (Spring 1969); and the Forum of the National Academy of Sciences, *Experiments and Research with Humans: Values in Conflict* (Washington: National Academy of Sciences, 1975).

65. Cf. Paul Ramsey, *The Patient As Person* (New Haven: Yale University Press, 1970), chap. 1.

66. Cf. Paul S. Rhoads, "Medical Ethics and Morals in a New Age," *The Journal of the American Medical Association* 205, No. 7 (August 12, 1968): 517–522.

67. Cf. Harold B. Kuhn, "Golden Rule," in Henry, *DCE,* p. 267.

68. John E. Woods, "Organ Transplantation," in Henry, *DCE,* p. 475.

69. Cf. Paul Ramsey, "The Indignity of 'Death with Dignity,' " *The Hastings Center Studies* 2, No. 2 (May 1974): 47–62.

70. Cf. A Report of the Clinical Care Committee of the Massachusetts General Hospital, "Optimum Care for Hopelessly Ill Patients," *The New England Journal of Medicine* 295, No. 7 (August 12, 1976): 362–364.

71. Cf. Michael T. Sullivan, "The Dying Person—His Plight and His Right," *New England Law Review* 8 (Spring, 1973): 197–216.

72. Cf. Mitchell T. Rabkin et al., "Orders Not To Resuscitate," *The New England Journal of Medicine* 295, No. 7 (August 12, 1976): 364–366.

73. Cf. Cicely Saunders, "The Last Stages of Life," *American Journal of Nursing* 65 (March 1965): 70–75.

74. Cf. Mount, *op. cit.*

75. *Ibid.*

76. J. Hinton, *Dying,* 2nd ed. (London: Penguin, 1972), p. 159.

77. Duncan W. Vere, *Voluntary Euthanasia: Is There An Alternative?* (London: Christian Medical Fellowship, 1971).

78. *The Philadelphia Evening Bulletin,* February 26, 1975, p. 1.

79. Helmut Thielicke, *The Ethics of Sex,* trans. John W. Doberstein (New York: Harper & Row, 1964), p. 266.

80. Yale Kamisar, "Some Non-Religious Views Against Proposed 'Mercy-Killing' Legislation," *Minnesota Law Review* 42, No. 6 (May, 1958): 969–1042. Quotation is on p. 1031. (Italics in original.)

81. Millard J. Erickson and Ines E. Bowers, "Euthanasia and Christian Ethics," *Journal of the Evangelical Theological Society* 19, No. 1 (Winter 1976): 22 f.

82. Appendix IV, "Universal Declaration of Human Rights," in *Human Rights,* ed. A. I. Melden (Belmont, Calif.: Wadsworth Publishing Co., 1970), pp. 147 f.

83. Cf. Joseph L. Allen, "A Theological Approach to Moral Rights," *The Journal of Religious Ethics* 2, No. 2 (Spring 1974): p. 138.

84. Ronald H. Nash, "Rights," in Henry, *DCE,* p. 590.

85. Melden, *op. cit.,* p. 2.

86. Nash, *loc. cit.*

87. Robert M. Sade, "Medical Care as a Right: A Refutation," *The New England Journal of Medicine* 285, No. 23 (December 2, 1971): p. 1289.

88. Gene Outka, "Social Justice and Equal Access to Health Care," *The Journal of Religious Ethics* 2, No. 2 (Spring, 1974): p. 23.

89. Duncan W. Vere, "Health For One—For Many," *Christian Medical Society Journal* 21, No. 4 (September/October 1969): 4 f.

90. John R. Brobeck, "The Natural History of Christian Man," Supplement to *In the Service of Medicine* 22, No. 3 (July 1976): p. 3.

91. *Ibid.*, p. 4.

92. Cf. Lewis Penhall Bird, "Deviance vs. Variance in Sexual Behavior," *Christian Medical Society Journal* 6, No. 3 (Summer 1975): 9–17.

93. Paul Tournier, *To Resist or To Surrender?*, trans. John S. Gilmour (London: SCM Press, Ltd., 1964), p. 10.

VIII

Biological Engineering and the Future of Man

V. ELVING ANDERSON

When G. Rattray Taylor wrote *The Biological Time Bomb*[1] almost ten years ago, his choice of title had two implications. First, recent developments in biology and medicine may turn out to be "as earth-shaking as the atom bomb" in their significance for the understanding and control of human nature. Second, although the precise timing and nature of dramatic breakthroughs was not predictable, enough real possibilities could be imagined that an "explosion" appeared imminent.

The reaction of the general public to this prospect can take several forms. There is the fear that someone may do something to me without my knowledge or consent. There is the possibility of unexpected

V. Elving Anderson is Professor of Genetics and Assistant Director of the Dight Institute for Human Genetics at the University of Minnesota in Minneapolis. His research interests include the study of genetic factors in mental retardation, psychotic disorders, and other human behavioral problems. He is currently on the board of the Institute for Advanced Christian Studies, and has been on the boards of Sigma Chi, Minnesota Academy of Science, American Scientific Affiliation, Behavior Genetics Association, American Society of Human Genetics, and Bethel College and Seminary in St. Paul, Minnesota. He has been a visiting Research Fellow at University College, London, where he helped plan research strategies for combining the study of genetics, behavior, and biochemistry in human subjects. He is co-author of *Psychotic Disorders: Family Studies* (1973).

and unintended consequences or accident. Furthermore, there is the possibility that the use of some technologies may lead to an erosion of currently held beliefs or values.

New knowledge often is controversial in this way. Within a surprisingly short time, however, the human mind adapts to the changed circumstances, the new technology becomes routine, and fear is reduced. This tendency to adapt may not, however, be entirely beneficial, since one can imagine some developments that one should continue to resist. Jacques Ellul has pointed out that propaganda is an essential feature of any technological society, since it is only through propaganda that the general public will learn to accept new techniques.[2]

It is now clear that some of the time estimates in *The Biological Time Bomb* were off the mark. Taylor had quoted Sir Peter Medawar's prediction that "transplantation not only of hearts but of liver and lungs may be established practice within five years."[3] In fact, although kidney transplants have become quite routine, heart transplantation has essentially stopped and those of liver and lungs have not increased. Currently there is much more concern about the possibility that "wild viruses" might be brought into being by unpredictable accidents associated with gene transfer experiments.

In this context it sometimes is claimed that our science and technology will outstrip our cultural tools for dealing with the issues these new developments raise. In response we must ask what techniques in biology and medicine are indeed new. Are the underlying ethical questions also novel? What are the implications for our understanding of human nature, of the meaning of life and of death?

An initial list of "new" technologies might well include the following:

1. The feasibility of organ transplants, including the ability to tissue-match donor and recipient and to suppress the immunological rejection of the transplant.

2. A knowledge of neurotransmitters (the chemicals that communicate between nerve cells) sufficiently detailed to explain the action of mood-altering drugs and to synthesize a variety of drugs for the treatment of neurological and psychiatric disorders.

3. Prenatal diagnosis of genetic conditions (chromosomal and bio-

chemical) sufficiently early that selective abortion becomes possible.

4. Such an extensive knowledge of DNA (the basic genetic material) that it is possible to synthesize specific genes and insert them in target cells, although many details must be resolved before an application to the human can be considered seriously.

I have chosen to group biomedical advances under three headings: detection, treatment, and general improvement. The list cannot be exhaustive, but some of the major issues can be considered, along with the implications for personal choice, for public policy, and for further research.

DETECTION AND DIAGNOSIS

A number of important biomedical advances involve methods for detecting disease conditions: (1) more accurately, (2) less obtrusively, and (3) earlier. Such developments are for the most part welcome, yet there are some troublesome consequences. The newer technologies are expensive, and this limits their availability to the general population. Ability to detect always runs ahead of ability to treat, and this leaves a shifting category of diagnosable but inadequately treated conditions. Perhaps most important is the identification of human variability that may or may not cause a problem, but nevertheless stigmatizes the individual.

In the development of more accurate diagnostic measures, the key word is *heterogeneity*. What initially seemed to behave as a single disease (such as epilepsy or diabetes) turns out to involve a number of distinguishable subtypes, often with different modes of treatment and differing prognosis for the future of the affected person. In the case of mental retardation, it is possible to name about 150 rare genetic causes, each resulting from mutations within a gene. In 1959 it was discovered that the presence of an extra chromosome is associated with one form of retardation. More recently, the development of "banding" techniques permits identification of the addition or loss of even small portions of chromosomes that can lead to retardation.

Chromosome studies became sharply controversial when it was discovered that some males have an XYY set instead of the usual XY.

In 1965, 9 such males were reported out of 197 in a special security institution in Edinburgh. Eight of these were mildly retarded and six were at least six feet tall. Seven months later a tall man of low mentality murdered eight women in a Chicago apartment. Somehow the impression grew (and was reported widely) that this man had the "XYY syndrome," in spite of the fact that chromosome studies showed this to be false.[4]

The presumed association between aggressive behavior and a deviant chromosome count appeared to challenge strictly environmental explanations for such behaviors. Questions about the accountability and responsibility of XYY males for their behavior were raised. Research workers who identified XYY boys through routine screening of newborns were confronted with the problem of what to tell the parents. Did they have the right to withhold the information? How could they inform the parents without creating an emotional climate in the home that could be harmful to the child? The negative reaction by groups opposed to XYZ research was sufficiently vigorous that several research studies were brought to a halt.

This situation might be seen as a classical illustration of the old adage that a little knowledge is a dangerous thing. It seems almost inevitable that similar controversies will emerge along the frontiers of biomedical research. The underlying ethical issues do not seem novel, however.

In addition to becoming more accurate, diagnostic and detection procedures have become less obtrusive and invasive. Tests that once required a biopsy now can be performed on the cultured white cells from a blood sample. Heart catheterization permits a detailed analysis of blood flow patterns and the diagnosis of cardiac anomalies. Computerized axial tomography (CAT) involves a sophisticated X-ray procedure that often can replace air-contrast and other techniques for neurological studies. These safer and more informative procedures do not entail any obvious new ethical problems except the high cost which may restrict their use to relatively few individuals in highly industrialized nations. In his book *Small is Beautiful* E. F. Schumacher[5] stressed the need for "intermediate technology" in Third World countries. Surely, a continuing goal of research can be to develop simplified procedures that will be accessible to a larger number of people in many parts of the world.

A third type of change involves the earlier detection of conditions on three levels—postnatal, prenatal (diagnosis in the fetus), and pre-conceptional (genetic screening for carriers who could produce an affected child).

The case of phenylketonuria (PKU) illustrates the first of these levels of detection. PKU is one of the better known causes of severe mental retardation, one in which the effects can be alleviated significantly by an altered diet. The former means of diagnosis involved a urine test that is only reliable on infants at least six weeks old, but many children are not examined routinely at that age. By 1965 a screening test began to be used which requires only a few drops of blood and can be performed by three to five days of age. However, this test also picks up milder versions of the disease. When the symptoms are mild, physicians can be placed in a double-bind situation. Their clinical judgment of the individual case might suggest that treatment would be undesirable or even harmful, yet withholding treatment could be considered evidence of malpractice. Such dilemmas can be resolved only by further experience and research, but advances in diagnostic accuracy can be expected to create a period of uncertainty, involving difficult decisions with ethical implications.

The development of techniques for prenatal diagnosis has turned out to be more controversial. Amniocentesis (the withdrawal of a small amount of amniotic fluid surrounding the embryo) had been used late in pregnancy to detect Rh problems. In 1961 the procedure was suggested as a means of early detection of genetic problems. Now it has been extended to cover three types of conditions—chromosome anomalies, enzyme defects, and neural tube defects. The first two depend on fetal cells grown in tissue culture, and the third on a specific type of protein that leaks from openings in the brain or spinal cord of the developing fetus. The usefulness of direct visualization of the fetus (fetoscopy) also is being explored.

In general, this approach is accurate and safe when the amniocentesis and the analysis are carried out by specialists in the respective procedures. Spontaneous miscarriages occur no more often than in other pregnancies followed from the same initial state. Subsequent psychological testing of those children who were carried to term after amniocentesis indicates no detectable effect.

It is now considered good medical practice to inform the family at risk for a specific disorder about the possibility of prenatal diagnosis, but what are the possible courses of remedial action that can be taken? Efforts have been made to find means of prenatal treatment, but these generally must be indirect (via the mother), and there may be a delicate trade-off between the possible benefit to the fetus and the possible harm to the mother. Most often, the results of amniocentesis are used as a basis for selective abortion.

Christians (both lay and professional) are divided about the acceptability of abortion in this situation. Parents must take responsibility for children, but does this extend to a decision that, a given fetus should have its existence terminated? Is this a situation in which one should pray for the strength (for one's self and the child-to-be) to cope with a serious disability? Or may one pray for forgiveness and the strength to make a difficult decision to terminate the pregnancy?

The nature of such choices will be altered continuously by advances in biomedical knowledge. Conditions will be added to the diagnosable list. Means of treatment, prenatally or postnatally, will be found that ameliorate the severity of the disease. Furthermore, families will differ in their ability or willingness to cope with conditions in an intermediate range of severity.

I am more concerned about the more general implications of prenatal diagnosis. It is one thing to request amniocentesis for any one of a series of relatively rare conditions. It is quite different to assume that families have a natural "right" to expect that every child should be healthy. There is no medical way to provide such an assurance. A fetus that has no obvious chromosomal anomaly still runs the risk of other disorders for which no test has been made. Furthermore, it seems utterly frivolous to request a prenatal test in order to abort a fetus of the "wrong" sex. One of the serious effects of rapidly advancing technology is the level of expectation that appears to result in the public mind.

Detection can be pushed back one more step. Families who have one child with a specific genetic defect can be given a "recurrence risk" estimate for the same defect in the next child. More recently it has become possible in some conditions (notably sickle cell anemia and Tay-Sachs disease) to test for carrier status and to state such risks for couples before they have any children at all.

When the risks for serious defect are 25 percent or more, does a family have the right to proceed with another pregnancy? There are no legal sanctions in such a case, and genetic counselors in general do not make strong recommendations against such a response. On the other hand, Paul Ramsey[6] has argued that couples never had a "right" to produce children simply for their own sakes. Thus he calls proceeding in such a case "gravely immoral."

The significance of such a choice was emphasized by Pope Pius XII: "Better warned of the problems posed by genetics and of the gravity of certain hereditary diseases, men of today have, more than in the past, the duty to take account of this increased knowledge so that they might forestall countless physical and moral difficulties for themselves and others. They should be attentive to whatever could cause lasting harm to their descendants and involve them in an interminable succession of miseries. . . . Although the formal elements of every human community are of the psychological and moral order, the lineal descent is its material basis, which must be respected and in no way harmed."[7]

It may be difficult to accept such information, however, especially if an individual is only a carrier and has had no direct experience with someone who is affected with a double dose of the gene. In sickle cell testing, furthermore, carriers have been stigmatized unfairly and have been refused employment, education, and insurance unnecessarily. Among American blacks about one person in twelve is a sickle cell carrier, and this has obvious implications for finding a mate and for deciding about children. To say that such knowledge affects one's "self image" seems an understatement.[8]

At present there are relatively few conditions for which screening methods are sufficiently accurate and inexpensive to justify routine population studies. Some persons call before marriage to request a "genetic test" on the assumption that they can be given some guarantee of genetically healthy children, but such broad assurances are not possible.

TREATMENT AND CONTROL

As diagnosis becomes more accurate, treatment can be more precise. When our knowledge about a condition is limited, the search for effective drugs seems almost random. But when a basic molecular understanding is reached, theories emerge to guide the synthesis of drugs that will maximize beneficial results and minimize harmful effects. The miniaturization and complexity of electronic instrumentation is as helpful for treatment as for diagnosis.

On the other hand, it may be tempting to overuse a medication in an effort to obtain a "quick fix," as in the widespread use of drugs for "hyperactive" children. In other conditions, the treatment itself may cause harm, or relax natural selection so that any genes involved may increase in frequency. Four recent advances in therapy may serve to illustrate these points: organ transplants, psychosurgery, psychoactive drugs, and genetic therapy.

Organ transplants became feasible when there were developments along several lines—mechanical procedures for maintaining blood and oxygen flow to organs, tissue typing to match donors and recipients, and immunological suppression to reduce organ rejection. Further advancement in these areas has led to significant increases in basic knowledge, such as in our understanding of cancer.

The early successes with heart transplants led to enthusiastic predictions for the future, but now, as we noted, after less than ten years, very few such operations are being reported. Meanwhile kidney transplants have become routine in larger medical centers. Why this difference? It is partly because the kidneys are paired organs, so that one will suffice, and because hemodialysis permits survival even without any kidney. Also the immunological problems of rejection may be less critical for this organ. A more general implication is that biological mechanisms are sufficiently complex that predictions on the research frontiers are always tenuous and there are more unknowns than on manned flights to the moon. The human costs of experimentation in this area have been detailed carefully by Fox and Swazey.[9]

Two problems with ethical implications arose in transplant operations: (1) the definition of death in the donor, and (2) the selection of donors to receive the few organs available. The first is more a medical and legal question and appears to have been reasonably well settled for most situations. The principle of having different physicians responsible for determination of death and for the transplant procedures helps to reduce the inevitable conflict of interest. The second problem also has been handled on the medical level, with decisions based mainly on tissue match and severity of disease. There were some early efforts to consider the potential value of the possible recipients, but relative judgments as to the "worth" of a life proved impossible to make.

Knowledge about the human brain has progressed rapidly in the last several decades. Specific pathways have been defined anatomically and biochemically, and the function of the various brain areas is reasonably well understood. A tumor or traumatic lesion can on occasion lead to episodes of aggression and violence, and removal of that brain area sometimes will alleviate the behavior. Psychosurgery has been extended to other cases of behavioral disorder with a less well-defined anatomical basis. The overuse of the procedure has led to rather drastic restrictions.[10]

This fluctuation in practice and policy seems regrettably inevitable. Procedures become adopted widely before careful research evaluation is completed. They are applied to situations in which the evidence for an underlying disorder is weak or completely missing. (In fact a careful definition of what we mean by *disorder* may be what is needed.) Understandably there is a reaction, but a complete prohibition of the therapy may be no more justifiable than its original careless application. Meanwhile we must hope and work for a more judicious policy that permits a procedure but provides for monitoring and evaluation.

The situation is somewhat similar for *biochemical* intervention in the brain. The behavioral effects of harmful drugs have clearly demonstrated the importance of biochemical events in brain function. Expanding knowledge about neurotransmitters and receptor sites at nerve endings has provided a rational basis for developing more effective means to treat psychiatric disorders. Both lines of evidence make more plausible a genetic explanation for some individual variations in behavior. Meanwhile the widespread and poorly monitored use of drugs to control "hyperactivity" of school children in some localities has elicited criticism.[11] Here, again, one must conclude that technology must be applied carefully, that its use may be necessary but is not sufficient.

Early methods of treating genetic disorders involved dietary restrictions (such as for PKU) or replacement of a missing gene product (such as thyroid hormone in genetic forms of hypothyroidism). The modes of therapy are now much more diversified and include vitamin supplements (to serve as cofactors for enzymes) and bone marrow transplants for immunodeficiency diseases.[12] Currently work is underway to develop effective means for enzyme replacement.[13] This involves methods to purify and stabilize the enzymes, and to administer and deliver them to specific tissues in the body. The technical problems are considerably more difficult than in hormone therapy, but the results will be important to many patients and families, and the prospects look good.

Enthusiasm for new means of therapy must be tempered with two cautionary themes. First, some treatments have harmful side effects. Of particular concern recently is the evidence that medications taken during pregnancy (such as anticonvulsants and female hormones) increase the risk of congenital defects (mainly of the heart) in their offspring.[14] Further research will be needed to find ways to control the problem in the mother while reducing the side effects for the fetus. Second, the treatment of genetic disorders reduces the effect of natural selection, allows new mutations to accumulate, and leads to an increase in frequency of disease. Some popular discussions of this phenomenon have grossly exaggerated the rate of change. For example, it is by no means true that insulin treatment of diabetes means that half the population will require insulin within a few generations. Nevertheless, in the "cost accounting" of the gene pool, current gains must be balanced by future payment.

MEANS FOR GENERAL IMPROVEMENT

Some biomedical advances can be used to provide a more general improvement in human health status. Methods for detecting environmental contaminants (such as lead) can be applied to environmental samples or to blood samples from children. Efforts to reduce radiation will benefit the entire community and posterity as well. Recent attention has been directed toward monitoring possible chemical mutagens, which may be more common and more deleterious than sources of radiation.

In an effort to further improve the human gene pool, H. J. Muller proposed a frozen sperm bank.[15] The technology for deepfreezing human sperm has been worked out recently and such sperm banks are used as a source for artificial insemination. (Methods for ovum transplant also are technically feasible.) One limitation is that there is no generally utilized procedure for screening the family medical history of donors or for identifying any problems that may develop in children fathered by a given donor. Muller's proposal provided for such screening and further suggested that donors be selected on the basis of general intelligence and cooperativeness. Information about donors would be made available to the couple requesting insemination so that they could make an informed choice. As compared with suggestions for cloning and introduction of genetic material from other species, Muller's ideas appear modest and workable. It is difficult to imagine any widespread public acceptance however.

Does cloning really represent anything more than interesting science fiction? The scientific basis for it arises from experiments with nuclear transfer, mainly in frogs. The nucleus is removed from a frog egg, and a nucleus from some other frog tissue is inserted in its place. The biological problem is to find out if the nucleus from an adult can be reprogramed to guide the developmental steps from the egg to a tadpole and on to maturity. The procedure has become routine if a nucleus from an embryo is used, although only a small fraction of the renucleated eggs will proceed to the adult stage.

If the technical problems of differentiation can be resolved, and if the methods can be adapted to the much smaller mammalian ova, then some use for domestic animals can be expected. There would be some advantage to producing animals with a known genetic constitution instead of accepting the continual reshuffling of the chromosomes in normal reproduction. On the other hand, the reduction in variability could be a serious drawback if a genotype turned out to have a specific disease susceptibility.

The application of cloning to humans has evoked lively discussions about the desirability of a thousand Mozarts. I cannot take the option seriously, however, because it seems unlikely that anything short of a massive authoritarian plan would bring acceptance. The procedure does not solve any problems, and it imposes our selection criteria upon the next generation.

At the present time the most controversial area of biomedical research is clearly the topic of gene transfer. The major concern at the · moment is with technical research questions, but these may be resolved within a short time. The more long-term questions about the possible uses of the methodology should be considered as well.

For some time gene therapy has been considered as one means of treating genetic diseases. Instead of altering the diet or continuously replacing an enzyme, why not add the gene that makes the enzyme that takes care of the dietary component? (This is not "genetic surgery," at least in the usual sense of *surgery,* since the defective gene is not removed.) What is needed is a supply of the normal gene and a method for delivering it to the cells so that the added gene can be incorporated into a chromosome and the active enzyme can be produced. The procedure would be carried out on a child as soon as a defect was discovered, and the need for other types of continuing therapy would be reduced or eliminated. It would have to be done again each generation (since it is unlikely that many cells in the gonads would be altered), and the effective treatment would contribute to the slow increase in the frequency of the gene involved.

Serious problems have been encountered, however, in trying to develop the means of delivery.[16] The most likely carriers are viruses or plasmids, but some of the most effective plasmids have the additional property of conferring antibiotic resistance to bacteria. If new DNA is inserted into these plasmids, genetic recombination would occur and give rise to variants that would be harmful to the human population and could not be easily controlled. Some scientists involved in such research proposed an embargo on such genetic experiments until safety guidelines could be developed that would provide for the physical containment of any recombinant organisms. At the same time there have been efforts to find carriers for the experiments that would not be infectious to humans. The present guidelines, however, apply only to recipients of federal grants and not to industries.

Even more troubling is the temptation to try "shotgun" experiments. The DNA from an organism can be cut up into gene-length pieces by enzymes that are readily available. These pieces can be inserted essentially at random into cells of another organism to see what will happen. To these experiments, Robert Sinsheimer has responded: "The guidelines reflect a static view of nature as wholly under our control and of our own evolutionary niche as secure. Is it that secure? I'm concerned about irreversible processes. We lack the knowledge, both of the scientific and the social impacts of this work, to be confident that this new knowledge will not lead to disastrous consequences."[17]

If the technical problems can be solved, I do not see any moral objections to the use of gene transfer to treat specific genetic disorders. The introduction of novel DNA (from another species or from *de novo* synthesis) into the human gene pool, however, would be a very different matter. To imagine a possibily favorable situation, let us consider adding genes for the synthesis of vitamin C (present in many mammals, but not in man). In order to influence the human gene pool, the new genes must be incorporated into eggs and sperm cells. Furthermore, the genes must become part of a regulatory system for turning genes on and off at appropriate times in development (a topic that is poorly understood for mammalian cells). Finally, any newly introduced gene would almost certainly cause a number of deaths before changes in other genes provide a suitable genetic environment. At the very least, such gene transfer must be explored in domestic animals before its use in man is considered seriously.

Occasionally one finds claims like this one by Alvin Toffler: "We are hurtling toward the time when we will be able to breed both super- and sub-races. . . . We shall also be able to breed babies with supernormal vision or hearing, supernormal ability to detect changes in odor, or supernormal muscular or musical skills."[18] These are complex traits which are not understood genetically. There would be serious technical problems, whether he means levels of "ability" at the upper end of the range in the present human population or novel extremes never encountered before. Furthermore, such a concept of directed breeding is most questionable.

It should be clear that methods proposed for the general *improvement* of the human status are more controversial than those for *treatment* of specific disorders, for at least three reasons: (1) It is easier to reach consensus about what constitutes a disorder or defect than about goals for improvement. (2) The causes of defects are simpler and more readily remedied, while features selected for improvement are complex and depend upon a number of factors. (3) Treatment of defects requires only the consent of the individual or guardian, while general improvement needs broader social agreement or authoritarian coercion.

INDIVIDUAL CHOICE

Some may have hoped that science and technology would make life simpler, but a more realistic view is that the future will increase our options. Furthermore, the mix of choices available to us will continue to change, so that the task of weighing alternatives never can be finished.

How much choice can an individual tolerate? Fortunately we meet the future stepwise, and no person is confronted by all possible choices at once. What would happen, for example, if it became possible to select the sex of a child by some safe method for treating sperm cells? Would this add another source of conflict to the relationships between husband and wife? Studies of preference suggest that many families would choose a boy for the first pregnancy, but that the overall sex ratio would not be altered significantly. My own guess is that the sex-choice technique would not be used for the majority of pregnancies, either because the method would be somewhat cumbersome or because the couple would have no strong preference. The choice would be reserved for special situations, and could be most welcome.

There may be an increasing number of situations in which there is a tension between several deeply held values. This relates to our view of the process of valuing. It is easier to think of moral decisions as always involving one principle at a time. We are uncomfortable when two values come into tension and no single choice seems right. On the other hand, Frank Stagg, having reviewed the biblical data carefully, concludes that "we can find our authentic existence only in polar situations with their inescapable tension."[19] This is not to be confused with compromise or with "situation ethics" but reminds us that even in Eden humankind faced alternatives.

Future research surely will provide more precise information about our physical nature and predispositions for disease. This knowledge will raise problems for our sense of self-esteem. We will have to learn to tolerate such evidence for individual differences—in ourselves and in others.

What inner resources will individuals have for coping with future discoveries. It is sometimes claimed that questions of the future will be so unique that "old values" will be inadequate or even positively harmful. In my opinion, that kind of position misinterprets the evidence. To be sure, the technical aspects of new research can be puzzling and the implications may be frightening, but I have not found any basic questions that will not profit from consideration of a biblical perspective. With all honesty we can assure individuals that they will find the resources and help they may need to make difficult decisions.

PUBLIC POLICY

An individual perspective about biomedical research is not sufficient, however. A number of issues must be treated as matters of public policy. The importance of public involvement in policies concerning research seems well established, although not always welcomed with enthusiasm. Some of the earlier programs for sickle cell screening met with much misunderstanding and criticism, but consultation and active planning with community leaders have provided more effective programs and better acceptance. The involvement of the Cambridge city council in regulations concerning recombinant DNA research at Harvard University was interpreted by some as unwarranted. Nevertheless, it appears that the council members rapidly learned much about the technical details and arrived at a reasonable conclusion.

Furthermore, there may be situations in which biomedical research directs attention and energy away from efforts to deal with related social problems. Jon Beckwith has been very critical of the "medicalizing or biologizing of social problems,"[20] particularly with reference to the XYY controversy. I would agree that it is possible to explain away social problems as if they derived from defects in individuals, but I do not think that this argument justifies the termination of all XYY-related research. The more fitting answer, in my opinion, is not a choice between social action and biomedical research, but an appropriate emphasis on both.

A parallel situation can be seen in the growing evidence for individual differences in response to various environmental factors, an area of research termed "ecogenetics" by Arno Motulsky.[21] If only a small proportion of individuals are affected by an industrial contaminant, a company might decide to exclude such persons from employment rather than take the necessary precautions to reduce the level of the contaminant. The combined ethical and legal issues in cases such as this may not be easy to resolve.

THE NATURE OF RESEARCH

There is not likely to be any time when we have done enough research and can give full attention to practical applications. Each research finding brings new questions to the surface. But we must guard against the assumption that more technology alone will solve problems.

Are there questions which should never be raised? This is difficult to answer, in part because boundaries for research set in the past have been disregarded with no apparent harm. Perhaps more important is whether or not research is carried out with an awareness of human limitations. Our knowledge is always finite; therefore, proceed carefully and reversibly. Our motives are suspect; therefore, proceed with humility.

Gerald Helton[22] has pointed out, however, that experiences encountered in the development of a research career select for a belief that research goals can be accomplished. This might lead to the assumption that anything that can be done will be done; and if it will be done, why not by me? Furthermore, there is a tendency to focus on more answerable questions, an attitude that may account for the "biologizing" of social problems. "The psychodynamic vectors that propel a scientist in to the bright world of solvable problems turn out, on examination, to have components that originate in the flight from the dark world of anguished compromises and makeshift improvisations that commonly characterize the human situation."[23]

Others have commented lucidly on the importance of the scientist's attitude. I have appreciated Daniel Callahan's insistence that "the scientific researcher has an obligation to be as active in his moral imagination as in his scientific imagination."[24] And Victor Weisskopf has remarked: "Science cannot develop unless it is pursued for the sake of pure knowledge and insight. But it will not survive unless it is used intensely and wisely for the betterment of humanity and not as an instrument of domination by one group over another. There are two powerful elements in human existence: compassion and curiosity. Curiosity without compassion is inhuman; compassion without curiosity is ineffective."[25]

One possible response on the part of a concerned scientist is to devote some time toward activities that are socially sensitive even though they may not contribute to scientific prestige. In the excitement of recombinant DNA research, apparently little time has been given to ways for detecting and limiting any new harmful products that might emerge. Effort spent in educating lay people is another desirable form of public service. A scientist who is opposed to abortion might concentrate on possibilities for prenatal therapy in genetic diseases. Similarly, if a woman has a pregnancy at risk for genetic disease but is opposed to abortion, she might volunteer for research about prenatal treatment.

GUIDELINES FOR THE FUTURE

My own view of the future is one of cautious optimism. Some of our fears are an understandable reaction to the novel and complex. Some of our expectations represent an unrealistic overestimate of what technology can provide. The passage of time will clarify most of these points.

The potential for real danger, nevertheless, remains. Enthusiasm for new technologies or a crisis view of problems could precipitate authoritarian programs that compromise individual freedom. Recent regulations about "informed consent" sometimes appear to be so stringent that reasonable research is restricted unnecessarily, but they do provide an important safeguard. The inclusion of lay participants in science policy discussions similarly protects public decisions.

Even more fundamental are the issues that depend upon views of human nature. Individuals and families need a basis for personal choice. Efforts for improving the human gene pool require thoughtful elaboration of what is meant by "improvement." I approach this area as a committed Christian, but realize that many of my views are shared by those of other persuasions.

There is no need, however, to accept the claim that completely new ethical systems are required. It may be true that the rate of change in the future will be more rapid and that some truly new choices may emerge. But guidelines such as the following will continue to be both helpful and adequate:

1. In general, we can accept and use new technologies with gratitude, but technologies by themselves never will be enough. At the frontiers of knowledge there will be a band of uncertainty which calls for caution in research and modest expectation by the public. We

must avoid the temptation to assume that complex social problems can be solved by biomedical research alone.

2. In the future, as in the past, research workers should be constrained by two boundary conditions. On the one hand is the requirement to *avoid harm,* but on the other is the obligation to *do good.* More thought should be given to the ethics of valuing in such polar situations.

3. God's command to "have dominion" should be understood as stewardship, carried out in love, and answerable to Him.[26] Vigorous research and energetic application of results are appropriate, but there is no need for arrogance. Deliberate modification of human biological nature might even be accepted, but only if it will enhance our capacity to behave responsibly toward God and our fellows and thus honor His purpose in bringing us into being.

NOTES

1. Gordon Rattray Taylor, *The Biological Time Bomb* (New York: World Publishing, 1968).
2. Jacques Ellul, *Propanganda. The Formation of Men's Attitudes* (New York: Vintage Books, 1965).
3. Taylor, *The Biological Time Bomb,* p. ix.
4. Saleem A. Shah, "The 47, XYY Chromosomal Abnormality: A Critical Appraisal with Respect to Antisocial and Violent Behavior," in *Issues in Brain/Behavior Control,* ed. W. Lynn Smith and Arthur Kling (New York: SP Books, 1976), pp. 49–66.
5. E. F. Schumacher, *Small is Beautiful* (New York: Harper & Row, 1973).
6. Paul Ramsey, *Fabricated Man: The Ethics of Genetic Control* (New Haven: Yale University Press, 1970), pp. 35–57.
7. Pope Pius XII, "Discourse to the International Congress on Blood Transfusion, September 5, 1958," *Dight Institute Bulletin* 11 (1958): 13.
8. Philip Reilly, "Genetic Screening Legislation," *Advances in Human Genetics* 5 (1975): 319–376.
9. Renée C. Fox and Judith P. Swazey, *The Courage to Fail. A Social View of Organ Transplants and Dialysis* (Chicago: University of Chicago Press, 1974).
10. D. Gareth Jones, "Violence, Psychosurgery and Human Responsibility," *Journal of the American Scientific Affiliation* 28 (1976): 49–54.
11. Robert J. Grimm, "Brain Control in a Democratic Society," in *Issues in Brain/Behavior Control,* ed. W. Lynn Smith and Arthur Kling (New York: SP Books, 1976), pp. 120–121.

12. Robert J. Desnick and Morris B. Fiddler, "Advances in the Treatment of Genetic Diseases: An Overview," in *Birth Defects, Risks and Consequences,* ed. S. Kelley, E. B. Hook, D. T. Janerich, and I. H. Porter (New York: Academic Press, 1976), pp. 329–356.

13. Robert J. Desnick, William Krivit, and Morris B. Fiddler, "Enzyme Therapy in Genetic Diseases: Progress, Principles, and Prospects," in *The Prevention of Genetic Disease and Mental Retardation,* ed. Aubrey Milunsky (Philadelphia: W. B. Saunders, 1975), pp. 317–342.

14. Olli P. Heinonen, Dennis Slone, Richard R. Monson, Ernest B. Hook, and Samuel Shapiro, "Cardiovascular Birth Defects and Antenatal Exposure to Female Sex Hormones," *New England Journal of Medicine* 296 (1977): 67–70.

15. H. J. Muller, "What Genetic Course Will Man Steer?" in *Man's Future Birthright. Essays on Science and Humanity by H. J. Muller* ed. Elof A. Carlson (Albany: State University of New York Press, 1973): pp. 117–152.

16. George Wald, "The Case Against Genetic Engineering," *The Sciences* (September/October 1976): 7–12.

17. Robert Sinsheimer, quoted in Robert C. Cowen, "Should Biologists Redefine Life?," *Christian Science Monitor,* February 3, 1977, p. 15.

18. Alvin Toffler, *Future Shock* (New York: Random House, 1970), p. 179.

19. Frank Stagg, *Polarities of Man's Existence in Biblical Perspective* (Philadelphia: Westminster Press, 1973).

20. Jon Beckwith, "Social and Political Uses of Genetics in the United States: Past and Present," *Annals of the New York Academy of Sciences* 265 (1976): 46–56.

21. Arno Motulsky, "Ecogenetics: Genetic Variation in Susceptibility to Environmental Agents" (paper presented at the V International Congress of Human Genetics, Mexico City, October 10–15, 1976), *Excerpta Medica International Congress Series* 397 (1976): 13.

22. Gerald Holton, "Scientific Optimism and Societal Concerns: A Note on the Psychology of Scientists," *Annals of the New York Academy of Sciences* 265 (1976): pp. 82–101.

23. Gerald Holton, *op. cit.,* p. 82.

24. Daniel Callahan, "Ethical Responsibility in Science in the Face of Uncertain Consequences," *Annals of the New York Academy of Sciences* 265 (1976): 6.

25. Victor Weisskopf, "The Significance of Science," *Science* 176 (1972): 138–146.

26. D. Gareth Jones, "Making New Man: A Theology of Modified Man," *Journal of the American Scientific Affiliation* 26 (1976): 144–154.

IX

Brain Research and Human Responsibility

DONALD M. MACKAY

Scientists are like exploratory map makers. Their map making, like that of geographers, may require them to feel their way where few others have gone before, to pry into territory in which many others claim an interest, and to exercise discretion as to whether, when and to whom to disclose what they discover. Their aim, of course, like that of modern geographers, goes far beyond mere description. The purpose of their explorations is to understand what must be reckoned with in the world around them, to discover the motive forces of what they study, to identify resources that may be tapped by future map

Donald M. MacKay is Granada Research Professor in the Department of Communication at the University of Keele, Staffordshire, England. A distinguished specialist in analogue computing and brain physiology, he holds a B.Sc. from St. Andrews University and a Ph.D. from London University. He is a Fellow of the Institute of Psychology, and a member of the Experimental Psychological Society, the Physiological Society, and the International Brain Research Organization. His numerous published articles include "The Sovereignty of God in the Natural World," *Scottish Journal of Theology,* vol. 21, (1968); "Information Technology and the Manipulability of Man," *Zeitschrift für Evangelische Ethik,* 12, no. 3 (1968), English translation in *Study Encounter,* vol. 5/1, (1969); and various papers on information theory, automatous theory and cerebral organization. He delivered the Eddington Memorial lecture at Cambridge University on *Freedom of Action in a Mechanistic Universe* (1967). He is author of *The Clockwork Image* (1974).

users. Their maps, in a word, are *functional.* Their duty is to guide
intelligent agents and not mere sightseers. Brain scientists are not
exempt from any of these obligations. Their chosen domain has an
organized structure more complex than any other known to man.
New tools of investigation create constantly expanding frontiers of
pioneering effort. Every one of their fellow humans claims a natural
interest in the territory they explore. The proper use of their knowledge is thus for brain scientists a matter of constant and inescapable
concern.

THE AUTHORITY FOR BRAIN RESEARCH

Fundamental for anyone in this position is the question of *authority.*
By what authority are the maps being made? To whom are the map
makers accountable? Whose is the territory they explore? For the
Christian, the answer is clear. The world is God's. It is to Him that
we are ultimately accountable. It is by His authority that we are
commissioned to explore and have dominion over the works of His
hands, in a spirit, not of arrogant exploitation, but of humble and
compassionate stewardship. In contrast to the pagan image of the
gods as jealous of their secrets and resentful of man as an inquisitive
interloper, the biblical emphasis is on man's duty to apply his mind
to the understanding of the natural world, as an expression of reverence for its Creator and in gratitude for the benefits that deeper
understanding can bring.

Inasmuch as the human brain is one of the works of God's hands
and a part of the natural world, the Genesis mandate to "subdue"
nature presumably makes brain research not just a legitimate but an
obligatory sector of our responsibility to our Creator. But there are
two singular features that set the human brain apart from other
objects of investigation. First, map makers of the brain are in a certain
sense mapping (or trying to map) part of themselves; and the logic of
such an enterprise must present certain difficulties and pitfalls that
map makers of other domains can escape. Second, our common experience in choosing and acting, let alone the Christian doctrine of the
human soul, might seem to raise a question as to whether the human
brain is in fact a purely "natural" object, conforming to the same
physical laws as the rest of the natural world.

It must be said straight-away that this last question is still an open one. Despite all recent advances in brain science, our ignorance of the causes of brain events still vastly exceeds our knowledge. Nobody can rule out on scientific grounds the possibility that some events in the human brain may violate the physical principles that apply in other parts of the natural world. What I hope to show, however, is that it would be both unnecessary and dangerously misleading for Christians to try to defend any such theory in the interests of the biblical doctrine of man. It would be unnecessary, I believe, because nothing in biblical teaching requires the brain to be exempt from normal physical principles; and dangerously misleading, because such an emphasis would deflect attention away from the distinctive points that the Bible does make about our human nature and destiny.

In this context, then, my title has an obvious double meaning. First —and vital for a healthy relationship between brain research and Christianity in particular—there is the question of our human responsibility to explore, map and gain understanding of the vastly mysterious territory in which we are embodied as conscious agents. Have we any right to probe the mystery that surrounds the springs of human action? The biblical answer to this, I have suggested, is in principle straightforward. If there is need to be met, and good to be done, by gaining knowledge of God's world not forbidden us by Him, then we would need a good excuse to neglect its pursuit. We have not merely a right, but an obligation to our Creator and our fellow humans, to learn all we legitimately can about the way the brain works, the ways it can go wrong and the ways it may be mended. Increasing knowledge will of course bring enlarged responsibility for its proper use, but to gain that knowledge, in that spirit, is a matter of obedience.

This, however, in turn raises the much more complex question implied in my title, namely, that of the implications of what we learn about the brain for our concept of human responsibility itself. Science has a long-standing reputation for demonstrating that things are not always what they seem to common sense. Brain science is likely to be no exception. Is there not a risk, then, that it may end by showing up as "illusions" those very aspects of our commonsense view of man that make meaningful our idea of responsibility? Might not brain science, for all its biblical warrant, end by debunking the biblical view of our human nature? It is this second question that will occupy us for most of the present essay.

MAJOR DEVELOPMENTS

The great surge forward in brain science in the present century has resulted from a coincidence of advances on many different fronts. Developments in microscopy, including the art of selective staining of nerve cells, have told us more about the way cells interconnect than we know how to use. The rise of electronics has produced a whole battery of sensitive tools that allow us to stimulate, record and analyze the chatter of electrical activity that goes on in the ten-thousand-million-strong neural population and even in the minute individual members of it. Workers in biochemistry and related fields have begun to trace intricate patterns of chemical interaction that add a new dimension to our already complex map of the brain and greatly enlarge the cabinet of drugs whereby its behavior can be modified for good or ill.

But perhaps the most far-reaching influence on brain science has come from quite another direction. The need for automatic machinery to take the place of human operators in dangerous, boring or otherwise undesirable occupations has forced engineers and psychologists to cooperate in an unprecedented effort to understand and specify the mechanisms of intelligent action. Although this hybrid "cognitive science" (whose components go by such names as "automata theory," "autonomics," "communication and control theory," "cybernetics" and "artificial intelligence") is only a few decades old, it has already revolutionized the way in which brain scientists think of their problems. Let me emphasize that this does *not* mean they draw detailed analogies between brains and present-day computing machines. Our present electronic computers work on quite different physical principles from the nervous system, and the differences between them and the brain are probably more significant than the resemblances. What it does mean is that the *habits of thought* of the automation engineer have powerfully shaped the kind of question brain scientists ask, and the kind of answer they may accept as satisfactory. It now comes as second nature to them to think of the brain as a protoplasmic way of engineering the kinds of information-processing functions that we have found necessary to produce intelligent, goal-directed behavior in our automata. The brain may well be *more* than that; but it is at least amenable to a great deal of detailed explanation in these mechanistic terms. Hypotheses framed in such terms have led to an astonishingly fruitful crop of experimental results, and they show every sign of continuing to do so. Conversely, the merchants of "artificial intelligence" are becoming ever more sophisticated in the kinds of tasks for which they can produce formal written instructions. In working out their ideas, they find that a computer serves as an invaluable "test bed," because it can relentlessly expose any flaws in a hypothetical model and allows them to discover (or obliges them to face) unexpected as well as expected consequences of their speculations.

ROOM FOR THE SOUL?

In biblical thought, man is distinguished from all other animals as "made in the image of God." What this means in theological depth has been the subject of unending debate.[1] For our present purposes, however, we can extract three essential ingredients:

1. Man has rational faculties capable of apprehending not only concrete facts of his immediate environment, but also abstract ideas, including truths revealed by God.
2. Man's death on earth does not annul his relationship (whether of love or rebellion) with his Creator.
3. Man is *answerable* to God for his actions: he can be *called to account* by his Creator.

Our question in this and the following two sections is whether, and if so, how, these ingredients mesh with the kind of understanding of man being developed in brain science, particularly in its mechanistic aspects.

In tackling this question we must beware of a presupposition that has no basis in biblical doctrine, but is widely accepted, even by some Christians, as "common sense." According to the mechanistic model, which was popularized by Descartes, the brain and body is to be thought of as a steerable machine, like a car or an aircraft. The "soul" is then thought of as the invisible pilot, exerting quasi-physical influences on suitably sensitive parts of the machine. I am not concerned here to argue that this model is wrong. Our ignorance of brain mechanics is so great that nobody can dogmatize about the details of its control system; and no less an authority than Sir John Eccles, Nobel

Prize winner in neurophysiology, has opted for something very like the Cartesian picture.[2]

What I do want to emphasize, however, is that this model is not required by the biblical data. The teaching of chapter 1 of Genesis is that man "became" a living soul, not that a "soul" was coupled to his body as an extra *part*. The mechanistic notion of the soul as an invisible and independent entity, capable of exerting *forces* on parts of the brain, goes far beyond anything taught in Scripture. It implies, in addition, that unless there are suitable "gaps" or indeterminacies in the chain mesh of physical cause-and-effect patterns in the brain, there can be no effective connection between the workings of the soul (so conceived) and the activity of the body. It suggests that if brain science were ever to swing in a completely deterministic direction, the soul would find itself squeezed out, having no effective part in determining human behavior.

Christians brought up to accept a "bipartite" (if not a "tripartite") idea of man may at this point feel restive. Surely, body, mind and spirit are biblically distinct concepts? How can we do justice to them if we do not postulate forcelike connections between the body and the soul?

Oddly enough, I think that the example of computer technology itself illustrates the answer. When mathematicians say their computer is "solving an equation," they mean that the behavior of the machine is *determined* (note the term) by that particular equation. This does not imply that there are "gaps" in the physical cause-and-effect chain mesh linking its components through which some invisible entity called an "equation" exerts quasi-physical influences on the transistors. Indeed, the electronic engineer in charge of the machine will insist that every physical event in it is *determined* (note the same word) by other physical events in its depths. Far from contradicting this, the mathematicians will insist that they *rely* on its being true as the basis for their own claim that the behavior of the machine as a whole was determined by their equation! They will insist equally strongly that computer hardware and mathematical equations are distinct concepts, in quite different categories.

Any appearance of conflict here is of course illusory. A computing machine is simply one example of a situation that *needs explanations at more than one level* in order to do it justice. Each explanation may specify in its own concepts what determines the behavior at that level *without necessarily conflicting* with the claims of another. No matter how complete the electronic engineer's explanation, the mathematicians' is *necessary* if we are not to miss the whole point of what a computer is and does. The equation determines what the network transistors do, not by prodding them with quasi-physical "forces," but by *being embodied in it.*

The point of this illustration is not of course to argue that computers have minds, still less that men are "nothing but" computers. (I have discussed the fallacies of such arguments elsewhere.)[3] Its purpose is only to suggest an alternative way of doing justice both to biblical data and to common experience, by regarding body, mind and spirit as entities recognizable at three different *levels of significance* of our mysterious and complex human nature, rather than as three different kinds of "stuff" that somehow exert forces on one another. According to this alternative view, which I like to call *comprehensive realism,* mental activity determines brain activity by being *embodied in it.* Spiritual life similarly shapes mental life by being *embodied in it.* This does not mean that these are only three names for the same thing, nor that mental activity is "nothing but" brain activity. That is the fallacy of metaphysical reductionism, or "nothing-buttery." It would be as absurd as to suggest that the equation embodied in the computer is "only another name" for the transistor network, or that mathematical relations are "nothing but" relations between computer parts. If there were any conflict here, it is our immediate experience as conscious agents that would have to take priority over any story about our brains and bodies, however persuasive. But the point is that there need be no conflict. Each story bears witness to facts to be accounted for, although at different levels of significance. As we shall see, this way of thinking about man—as a unity with at least three levels of significance—is, if anything, more consonant with biblical emphasis than the Cartesian (tripartite or bipartite) model.

The moral I wish to draw is, not that we should all espouse comprehensive realism (although I personally do), but only that there exists at least one viable alternative to *Cartesian interactionism,* the doctrine that the mind or soul *interacts* with the brain or body by exerting *influences* on certain physical parts. The alternative we have considered, moreover, has nothing to fear from advances in mechanistic brain science; it can indeed positively welcome them. If that is so, Christians have a responsibility to avoid giving the contrary impression, as if the biblical doctrine of the soul logically required some breakdown of physical cause-and-effect relationships in the brain. Here, as on so many other scientific questions, our Christian duty is to keep both our minds and our eyes open and obedient to whatever further data God may give us.

LOWER ANIMALS AND AUTOMATONS

If our capacity for conscious experience depends so directly on the structure of our brains, what are we to say of the capacities of lower animals, or, for that matter, of automata? The nerve cells making up the brain of a monkey, a dog or a cat are very similar to our own. The principles on which our behavior is organized can, to some extent, be imitated by automata. Is there not then a "thin end of the wedge" argument for attributing some kind of mind or soul both to such animals and to automatons?

Once again, our concern here is not to decide the issue one way or the other, but rather to evaluate the *logic* of such arguments from continuity, or "thin-end-of-the-wedgery." I see no biblical reason to deny that animals have conscious experience and (limited) mental ability; indeed the term *nefesh,* translated in Genesis, chapter I, as *living soul* is elsewhere applied to lower animals. Recent work[4] has shown that even the rudiments of symbolic communication are within the capacities of chimpanzees trained to use the deaf-and-dumb alphabet. Similarly, as I have argued elsewhere,[5] the Bible offers no objection in principle to the possibility that artificially constructed "brains" might embody some kind of conscious mentality—however speculative and impracticable such science-fiction notions may be. But the "argument from continuity" by itself is quite invalid. To take an obvious counterexample, a weak mixture of gas and air may contain the same kinds of molecules and lie on the same continuum as a richer mixture that burns; but this does nothing to prove that some kind of flame must be possible from the weaker mixture. Below a certain minimum concentration, the mixture is simply nonflammable. By the same token, the fact that a human brain organized in a specific way can embody conscious mental and spiritual life does nothing to prove that similar mental and spiritual capacities must be present in the brains of animals, still less in the artificial brains of automata built of different elements.

Having made this negative point, however, it is important to put it in perspective. Why do so many atheistic propagandists try to make anti-Christian capital out of advances in the scope of "artificial intelligence"? Why have some Christian apologists felt it to be in their interests to minimize the powers of lower animals or of automata? I suspect the reason may be, on both sides, a hangover of the same "nothing-buttery" thinking. If the biblical claim were that man is distinguished from lower animals and automata by having a brain sensitive to nonphysical influences, and that these nonphysical influences are what made his behavior essentially human, then of course the question of the capacities of animals or automata built of ordinary physical matter would become crucial. Once this claim is recognized as without biblical foundation, however, the polemical pressure disappears, and the whole issue becomes one of marginal interest to the biblical apologist, whose primary duty on this issue is to keep an open mind.

IMMORTALITY

So far, our discussion has been tied strictly to experience here and now. But the example of the computer, with its two levels of significance, may seem to raise a difficulty when we face biblical teaching regarding the hereafter. After all, if a computer were destroyed physically, that would be the end also of its mathematical significance. Does not this suggest that when our brains are destroyed at death, our mental and spiritual life ends, too?

Although such arguments from analogy must be handled with care, I believe that this one has an element of truth in it. There is a real biblical sense in which death is the end of our agency in this space-time framework. But the very same example suggests a possibility which, in fact, seems more in harmony with the biblical emphasis on resurrection of the body than the Cartesian solution. If a computer solving an equation is destroyed, the mathematicians can, if they wish, set up the very same equation again in some new embodiment. This need not be a computer identical to the old, and certainly need not re-use the original components in order to be recognizably an embodiment of the same equation.

In 1 Corinthians, chapter 15, which gives our most explicit teaching on the Christian hope of eternal life, we find a remarkably similar emphasis. We are given no promise of *physical* continuity, let alone identity, between our present body and the resurrection body. As when a grain of wheat is sown, the blade that rises from the ground is a quite different structure, so at death we are "sown as an animal body, . . . raised as a spiritual body" (1 Cor. 15:44, NEB). The continuity implied is, rather, at the level of our personal relationship with God; the personality that is ours will find expression in a new embodiment, perhaps unimaginably different from our present one, but still having the same essential characterological structure that identifies and distinguishes us as individuals here and now.

Attempts have been made to discredit this biblical doctrine by suggesting that such a resurrected individual ought to be regarded as a mere *copy* of the original. This argument seems strangely perverse. Nothing is more universally accepted than our daily experience of waking up to find ourselves *the same individuals* who went to sleep the night before, despite all kinds of metabolic changes in our bodily tissues. Mysterious though the idea of resurrection may be, there would seem to be no basic *logical* difference between the problem of personal identity upon waking up in another world and that of waking up in this world. The objective reference in either case must of course be ontologically to the *fiat* of our Creator, to whom we owe our continual identity moment by moment, day by day. If He knows and recognizes us in the resurrection as those whom He knew in the days of our flesh, then by the same token, that is who we are in fact, for it is our Creator who alone determines and gives being to what is the case.

Even the most mechanistic brain science, then, offers no objection in principle to the possibility that our Creator might bring into being a sequel to our earthly career and in that sequel bring to eternal fruition (for good or ill) the solemn consequences of our dealings with Him here and now.

RESPONSIBILITY

Here (if not before) someone may be inclined to protest. Even if mechanistic brain science has no objections to the doctrine of the soul or of the resurrection, surely it must question whether we as individuals can be held *responsible* for "the deeds done in the body"? If my brain were as mechanical as a computing machine, would it not be physical forces, rather than my decisions, that determined my actions?

I have discussed this question at length elsewhere[6] and must here be brief. I believe that it rests on a fallacy—the same fallacy of "nothing-buttery" that we noted earlier. The question presupposes an *either–or form: either* my actions are determined by my decisions *or* they are determined by physical forces. But where we are dealing with explanations at different levels, this assumption is baseless. At one level, it is true that a computer's behavior is determined by the equation it is solving, and at another level, that it is determined by physical forces. To suggest that if one of these explanations is true, the other must be false or redundant, would be to talk sheer nonsense.

It is equally nonsensical, and for the same logical reason, to argue that my brain processes *must* be inexplicable in mechanistic terms if my actions are determined by my decisions. This ignores the possibility that the brain processes are precisely the *necessary correlate,* at the mechanistic level, of the mysterious process I know in conscious experience as "making up my mind." In view of our present ignorance, nobody can say whether, in fact, my brain workings always proceed entirely according to physical laws; but even if they did operate in that way, I could not on those grounds rationally deny, or be denied, responsibility for my actions.

But, you may say, if physical laws ruled all my brain workings, would not the outcome of my making up my mind be inevitable? Here we must make a crucial distinction. *For an observer* who was physically incapable of interfering with me, the outcome of my decision process could well be inevitable, in the sense that (by definition) he could do nothing to affect it and might even be able *(ex hypothesi)* to predict it with certainty. But—and this is the crucial point—even though inevitable-for-him, the outcome would not in general be *inevitable-for-me. Inevitability* is essentially a *relative* term. An event inevitable-for-A need not be inevitable-for-B. In particular, we shall see that there will be some future events in B's brain that would not be inevitable-for-B, even if his brain were as mechanical as a computer.

The proof of this is quite short, though the result digs deep. According to brain science, there must be some mechanism in B's brain which represents by its physical state *what B believes.* Let us call this mechanism *M.* By definition, no change can take place in what B believes without a correlated change in M. It follows that no completely detailed specification of the present or immediately future state of M could be equally correct whether or not B believed it. (If it were correct *before* B believed it, then it must be incorrect in some detail *after* B comes to believe it; conversely, if the specification were adjusted so that it would *become* correct if and when M were changed by B's believing it, then it would not be correct *unless* B believed it.) In this strict sense, then, the immediate future of M is not *inevitable-for-B.* By this I mean that no complete specification of it exists, unknown to B, with an *unconditional claim to B's assent.* The truth is, rather, that in some details at least, the immediate future of M is *up to B,* in the sense that what B thinks and believes will determine the correctness or otherwise of any purported specification of it, and there is no unique specification of it that B would be logically bound to accept as inevitable, to the exclusion of all others, if only he knew it. The details in question are *logically indeterminate* for B.

It follows that B cannot logically argue that any decision causally dependent on those details of M was inevitable-for-him. The truth, rather, is that such decisions were strictly *up to him* in the foregoing sense, no matter how physically determinate the workings of his brain.

Note that so far we have been discussing a normally functioning individual in whom the process of deciding and acting depends directly or indirectly on what he knows and believes. If through brain damage, drugs, *force majeure* or the like, the normal link between M and the action centers of the brain is cut or overridden, then the outcome may cease to be logically indeterminate for the agent, and may become inevitable for him. To the extent to which this happens, there would then be logical grounds for denying or diminishing the responsibility we attribute to him for that outcome. One of the challenges offered by brain science to Christians especially is to clarify the rationale of arguments for reducing the accountability of criminals for their actions, arguments which are often quite inadequately based on claims that "physical causes" or "psychological causes" made them "inevitable." In the light of the foregoing, there is a clear need to distinguish two questions. The first concerns the strength of the alleged evidence for casual connections between particular factors and behavior. The notorious "XYY-chromosome" abnormality, for example, seems to have been much overrated as an indicator of criminal tendencies.[7] Explanations of behavior in social terms are often even more shaky. It would be a great mistake, however, to imagine that such explanations ought to be minimized *in order to* maintain a belief in human responsibility. The force of the argument above is that even if causal explanations of behavior in such terms were complete, this would not necessarily diminish the responsibility of the human agent.

The relevant question highlighted by the argument is not whether (or how far) an action was *predictable* (by a detached observer) in practice or in principle, but whether and to what extent it was *inevitable for the agent.* All too often, an answer to the first question is taken (by both sides) as if it were an answer to the second. The foregoing argument makes clear that it is not. Christians accustomed to living responsibly under divine sovereignty should not find this too surprising.

THE DAMAGED BRAIN

Despite the delicate intricacy of the nervous system, a remarkable amount of damage can be done to certain large areas of the brain without causing death. A bullet wound in the occipital lobes at the back of the head, for example, may merely leave the patient with a permanent localized "blind spot." Excision of tissue to remove a tumor from so-called association areas may have still less easily detected effects. Even after such a drastic operation as the separation of the two hemispheres by cutting the millions of connecting fibers in the corpus callosum,[8] a patient may seem surprisingly normal to superficial observation.

If the brain embodies the human personality in the sense we have been exploring, a Christian is bound to ask how such brain damage may affect the spiritual status of the individual and the spiritual significance of any resulting changes in his personality. Whereas damage to the occipital lobes of the brain may make no more difference to the personality than the loss of an eye, a corresponding loss of brain tissue or connecting fibers from the frontal lobes (above the eyes) can turn a formerly civilized and restrained individual into an uninhibited and inconsiderate boor.[9] Damage to one of the parietal lobes (roughly above the ear) can lead to a patient's completely neglecting the opposite side of his body, and even denying that it is his. Most dramatically of all, after the split-brain operation mentioned above, it is possible for opposite halves of the brain to develop *incompatible* goals.[10] One unfortunate patient found that when he was buttoning up his trousers with his right hand, his left hand would push past the right and unbutton them again!

Startling though such observations are, it would be a mistake to overemphasize the novelty of the issues they raise. Mankind has known since the discovery of alcohol that damage to the functioning of the brain (in this case via its blood supply) can radically transform personality. Because drunkenness is normally a reversible condition, we tend to solve the problem by associating the identity of the individual with his sober state, saying that he is "not himself" when drunk. Deterioration of the brain in senility presents a different, though equally long-standing, problem. Here we find ourselves having to say that the patient is "not the man he was."

Doubtless, as we grow more accustomed to the newer forms of personality disturbance caused by brain surgery, we shall develop verbal ways of coping with the mystery of the resulting transformation. A mystery, however, it remains: a mystery of which death itself is the ultimate exemplar. In a case of sudden death we are spared the need to speculate about the status of half-mangled personalities. What cases of brain damage force us to consider is the possibility of the death of a personality without the death of the body that once expressed it, leaving a half personality that may be so different as to lack essential spiritual continuity with the one who is no more.

In this context what the Christian must recognize is that the entry into eternal life offered by Christ is something far more and other than a mere extrapolation of the personality as it exists at the point of death. The stuff of eternal life, as the Gospel of John in particular makes clear, is the relationship formed in our present life with the eternal Son. It is by virtue of this relationship that we can be known by the Father and can be welcomed to eternal bliss in the resurrection. The events in our lives that have sealed our relationship with Christ are in no way annulled by death. Thus if, through brain damage, the death of our personality takes place by stages, there is no more reason to fear the eternal consequences than if those stages were telescoped into one. What matters is always and only the covenant of grace entered into while the personality was entire and undamaged.

I am painfully aware that this does not answer all the theological questions raised by the aftereffects of surgery on or accident to the brain; but I believe that, for spiritual purposes, the general principle of focusing on the relationships formed with God while the individual was capable of them, and thinking of brain damage as a first install-ment of death, is fully consonant with biblical teaching. If no person can snatch from Christ's hand those to whom He has given eternal life, we may be sure that no brain damage can do so either, however horrendous the behavioral consequences of that damage for the re-maining span of bodily existence.

THE CHALLENGE TO THE CHRISTIAN.

Let me end by mentioning a few summary implications of what I have said.

1. It is vital that Christian apologists for the dignity of man should not rest their case upon arbitrary "postulates of impotence" such as, "You'll never find a scientific explanation for such-and-such." We may or may not in the end succeed in explaining or predicting the bulk of human behavior on a scientific basis; but to pretend that there are any *biblical* grounds for predicting failure would be totally unwar-ranted. Christianity has no stakes in our ignorance of the physical causes of brain events. Its concern is that we should see and reckon adequately with what they *mean*.

2. We must beware of confusing claims about *brains* with claims about *people*. For example, it is not brains but people—conscious cognitive agents—that think. Their brains doubtless go through corre-sponding motions, embodying people's thoughts much as a computer embodies an equation; but it makes no sense to describe the brain (or the computer, for that matter), *qua* physical mechanism, as "think-

ing." Similarly, it is people, not their brains, who make choices, freely or otherwise. As we have seen, there need be no contradiction in saying that a person's brain is physically determinate, and saying that the person (as a cognitive agent) has several possible courses of action —any more than in saying that a computer is physically determinate, yet the equation that determines its behavior has several possible solutions.

3. One of the greatest temptations of Christian apologists is to *go beyond their biblical brief* in their eagerness to erect would-be lines of defence. With regard to those aspects of human nature that concern the scientist, the biblical data is much more reticent than is commonly supposed. As Professor R. Hooykaas has remarked in another connection,[11] we are all too ready, like Uzzah, to put out our hands unbidden to steady the ark (2 Sam. 6:6). We cannot remind ourselves too often that our brains, like the rest of our world, are God's workmanship in all their intricate detail. It is He who is affronted if we presume to tell Him in advance how they must—or must not—function in order to leave room for our spiritual nature and eternal destiny.

4. In contending with destructive reductionism, or "nothing-buttery," one of the best services that Christian apologists can render is to remind people of simple ontological priorities. For biblical thesists, the only ultimate reality is God, what is real is what God holds in being. It is God who brings into being and holds in being the world in which we find ourselves, including our own brains. It is He who gives us moment by moment the flux of our experience as conscious agents. Since it is only in and through that experience that we gain scientific (or any other) knowledge of the world of physical objects, including our own brains, there can be no question of our scientific knowledge throwing in doubt the reality of ourselves as conscious agents. If there were any conflict, the doubt would have to be the other way around! Even in science it is to the conscious experience of other observers that we appeal in order to resolve questions of objectivity and reality. Thus the practice of science itself is built on a recognition that people have ontological priority over things: our fellow scientists, as conscious beings, are more indubitably "real" than anything we may collectively believe about the world around us. Nothing could be more fraudulent than the pretence that science requires or justifies a materialist ontology in which ultimate reality is granted only to what

can be weighed and measured, and in which human consciousness is reduced to a mere epiphenomenon. Even apart from biblical considerations, this is to stand reality on its head.

5. But the greatest challenge offered by brain research, I suggest, is not to our theoretical understanding of ourselves so much as to our practical compassion for our fellow humans. Once the nonsense of "nothing-buttery" has been exposed, each advance in our knowledge of brain processes is to be welcomed in principle as enhancing our sensitivity to one another's vulnerabilities, as increasing our respect for one another's strengths, and as extending our capacities to do one another good. The fateful effects of malnutrition on infant brain development;[12] the vital importance of social and environmental factors in the maturation of personality;[13] the risks of unethical manipulation, whether by psychological or physico-chemical means;[14] the possibilities (as yet, alas, primitive and limited) of scientifically based psychotherapy[15]—our rapidly growing knowledge under these and similar heads daily adds fresh dimensions to our responsibility both to discern its right use and to guard against its abuse. Here science as such is not enough. Although knowledge of the scientific "map" is essential and would-be guides who are ignorant of its details can be a menace, the choice of a route is not exclusively the business of the map maker. Christians can claim no monopoly of wisdom in such a task, but they surely have a special duty to contribute positively and constructively to the effort to do it justice, as in the sight of God its giver.

NOTES

1. A detailed survey of the biblical evidence is given in: G. C. Berkouwer, *Man: The Image of God* (Grand Rapids, Michigan: William B. Eerdmans Publishing Co.; London: InterVarsity Press), 1962.

2. See, for example, his *Facing Reality* (New York: Longman, 1970).

3. Donald M. MacKay, "A Mind's Eye View of the Brain," in *Cybernetics of the Nervous System,* ed. Norbert Wiener and J. P. Schade; Progress in Brain Research, vol. 17 (New York: Elsevier, 1965), pp. 321 f. Also see, Donald M. MacKay, "The Use of Behavioural Language to Refer to Mechanical Processes," *British Journal of the Philosophy of Science* 13 (1962): 89–103; also in *Human and Artificial Intelligence,* ed. F. J. Crosson (New York: Appleton-Century-Crofts, 1971).

4. B. T. Gardner and R. A. Gardner, "Two-way Communication with an Infant Chimpanzee," *Behaviour of Non-human Primates,* ed. A. M. Schrier and F. Stollnitz (New York: Academic Press, 1971).

5. Donald M. MacKay, "From Mechanism to Mind," *Transactions of the Victoria Institute* 85 (1953): 17–32; cf. also *In Brain and Mind* ed. J. R. Smythies (London: Routledge and Kegan Paul, 1965) pp. 163–200.

6. Donald M. MacKay, "Brain and Will," *The Listener,* May 9 and 16, 1957; also in (revised) *Faith and Thought,* 90 (1958), pp. 193–215, and in *The Art of Philosophy* ed. F. A. Westphal (Englewood Cliffs, N.J.: Prentice-Hall, 1972), pp. 162–167; "On the Logical Indeterminacy of a Free Choice," *Mind* 69 (1960): 31–40; "Information and Prediction in Human Sciences," in *Information and Prediction in Science* eds. S. Dock and P. Bernays, Symposium of the International Academy for Philosophy of Science, 1962 (New York: Academic Press, 1965), pp. 255–269; *Freedom of Action in a Mechanistic Universe* (Eddington Lecture) (London: Cambridge University Press, 1967), reprinted in *Good Readings in Psychology* ed. M. S. Gazzaniga and E. P. Lovejoy (Englewood Cliffs, N.J.: Prentice-Hall, 1971), pp. 121–138; "The Logical Indeterminateness of Human Choices," *British Journal of Philosophy of Science* 24 (1973): 405–408; and *The Clockwork Image: A Christian Perspective on Science* (London: InterVarsity Press, 1974), especially chap. 8 and appendix.

7. D. S. Borgaonkar and S. A. Shah, "The XYY Chromosome Male—or Syndrome?" in *Progress in Medical Genetics,* vol. 10 (New York: Grune & Stratton, 1974); also, E. B. Hook, "Behavioural Implications of the Human XYY Genotype," *Science* 179 (1973): 139–150.

8. This has occasionally been done in an attempt to mitigate epileptic seizures.

9. H. L. Teuber, "The Riddle of Frontal-lobe Function in Man," *The Frontal Granular Cortex and Behavior,* ed. J. M. Warren and K. Akert (New York: McGraw-Hill, 1964), pp. 410–444; also Teuber, "Unity and Diversity of Frontal Lobe Functions," *Acta Neurobiologiae Experimentalis* 32, (1972): 615–656.

10. M. S. Gazzaniga, *The Bisected Brain* (New York: Appleton-Century-Crofts, 1970); see also Chapter 1 of *The Neurosciences,* Third Study Program, ed. F. O. Schmitt et al (Cambridge, Mass.: MIT Press, 1974).

11. R. Hooykaas, *Religion and the Rise of Modern Science* (Edinburgh: Academic Press; London: Chatto and Windus, 1972).

12. R. J. Wurtman and J. D. Fernstrom, "Nutrition and the Brain," *The Neurosciences, op. cit.*

13. See also the essay by M. A. Jeeves in this volume.

14. Gordon Wolstenholme, ed., *Man and his Future* (London: Churchill, 1963).

15. A. E. Bergin and S. L. Garfield, eds., *The Handbook of Psychotherapy and Behavior Change* (New York: Wiley, 1971).

X

Psychological Knowledge and Christian Commitment

MALCOLM A. JEEVES

The almost explosive growth of behavioral and social science in general and of psychology in particular has been a salient feature of scientific development in this century. Already by 1950 Professor E. G. Boring of Harvard, a distinguished experimental psychologist and historian of psychology, estimated that if the number of professional psychologists continued to increase at the same rate that they had during the first half of the twentieth century, then by the year 2000 every other person in America would be a psychologist! The extensive public funding of psychological research indicates the importance governments now attach to the need for continued growth in firmly based psychological knowledge.

Malcolm A. Jeeves is Professor and Head of the Department of Psychology at the University of St. Andrews, Fife, Scotland. From 1959–1969 he was Head of the Department of Psychology at the University of Adelaide, Australia. His research interests include the experimental psychology of complex thinking and neuropsychology, with particular reference to the study of cerebral asymmetries and functions of the corpus callosum. He is a Fellow of the British Psychological Society and of the Australia Psychological Society. Among his scientific books are *The Effects of Structural Relations on Transfer* (1968) and *Experimental Psychology: An Introduction for Biologists* (1974). He has also written extensively on psychology and religion. He is author of *The Scientific Enterprise and Christian Faith* (1969) and of *Psychology and Christianity—the View Both Ways* (1976).

Even so, psychologists themselves are aware of the difficulty of defining precisely where psychology as a discipline begins and where it ends. There is no clear dividing line between physiology, neurology and psychology. Nor is it easy to say where social psychology merges into sociology or where humanistic psychology becomes more an ideology or philosophical system than a behavioral science. Because such a wide range of subject matter is included under the general heading of psychology, it is difficult to focus on specific contact points along the frontiers of psychological knowledge and Christian belief and practice. We can, however, examine divergent models used in contemporary psychology and try to identify their common underlying assumptions. We may then ask what implications such assumptions have for a Christian assessment of man, his behavior and experience. The need to undertake such a preliminary review of the nature and scope of modern psychology, including its models and theories, arises because not a few of the problems said to exist at the frontiers of psychology and Christianity appear on close examination to be pseudo problems resulting from misunderstandings either of the claims of psychologists or of Christian beliefs, or both.

After briefly tracing their historical roots, we shall describe some of the conceptual models most prominent in contemporary psychology and note their underlying assumptions. We shall then ask how psychological statements relate to Christian beliefs that purport to be concerned with the same data, events, experiences or behavior. Finally, we shall discuss the implications of Christian doctrine for the scientific enterprise pursued by psychologists.

CONTEMPORARY PSYCHOLOGY: ITS ROOTS AND BRANCHES

During the last century, a psychology based more upon fact than upon opinion began to emerge. Some of the early psychologists, frequently trained in medicine and physiology, were interested in questions such as how the physical intensity of an applied stimulus was related to subjective experience. Others, strongly influenced by the work of Charles Darwin, were intrigued by behavioral similarities between men and animals. In addition to carefully observing animals in their natural surroundings, they began to study animal learning and problem-solving abilities in laboratory situations. They noticed, for example, that learning ability seemed to be systematically related to the complexity of an animal's nervous system. At the same time, still others, sparked by renewed interest in the care of the mentally ill, made sustained attempts to classify such illnesses systematically and to search for underlying common causes.

By the turn of the century William James, physiologist, physician and philosopher, had produced his now classic work on psychology. Shortly before this, in 1879, William Wundt had established in Leipzig the first psychological laboratory. This event was soon followed by the establishment of laboratories elsewhere in Europe and in North America. The prevailing emphasis on the introspective method precipitated a strong reaction, led by John B. Watson in America. Influenced by the work of the Russian physiologist Pavlov on classical conditioning, he attempted to produce a scientific psychology emphasizing the study of behavior. Although Watson's approach was not new, he particularly emphasized objective psychology and insisted on the study of behavior to the exclusion, as far as possible, of introspection and of reference to mental events. This emphasis has carried through into modern psychology. Today, however, to label psychologists behaviorists indicates little more than that in their research they emphasize the study and analysis of behavior and that they avoid as far as possible any reference to hypothetical, unobservable mental processes. To be a behaviorist is not necessarily to be anti-Christian. There are Christian behaviorists and non-Christian antibehaviorists.

While Watson was propagating his special brand of behaviorism, Sigmund Freud was capturing the imagination, and soon the allegiance, of psychologists and psychiatrists on both sides of the Atlantic. Psychoanalysis held the public, and often the academic, eye. But other psychologists with more modest aims and more limited objectives were quietly working away in new and steadily growing departments of psychology especially in North American universities. During the Second World War psychologists turned their attention to concrete applications of their theories, such as how to select the most suitable men and women for different branches of the armed services, how to design weapons and machinery to match men's capabilities, and how to cope with such wounds of war as brain injury and shell shock.

Out of the explosive increase in psychology that followed in the post-war years, there emerged a wide variety of specialist branches. Some specializations today differ so much from others that members of one branch at times find it difficult to communicate with those of another. A psychologist studying the biochemical bases of behavior has very little in common with a colleague studying how people behave in small groups. Yet each recognizes and values the contribution the other makes to the understanding of the complex problems of behavior.

To ignore the diversity of subject matter in contemporary psychology and to fail to recognize the range of concepts employed in theory-building, is to multiply the prospect of producing pseudo conflicts with Christian beliefs. There is special need, therefore, for semantic hygiene in this area of science. Nonspecialists need to appreciate the diversity of contemporary psychology. Any attempt to discredit Christianity that begins with the assertion that "psychology says" is more likely to signal a superficial acquaintance with psychology on the part of the speaker than the start of a considered critique of the Christian faith.

SCIENTIFIC METHOD IN PSYCHOLOGY

Most people today agree that a measure of objectivity differentiates scientific knowledge from what we variously call common sense, popular opinion or everyday knowledge. We must not, of course, ignore or deny the the scientist's personal involvement in acquiring scientific knowledge, a point developed convincingly by Michael Polanyi.[1] Because none of us can hold in mind too vast a catalogue of facts, we make generalizations in order to summarize our collected facts or experience. Psychology faces special problems in this regard. We are so influenced by our particular upbringing, experience and environment that objective judgments become very difficult. Our private "psychological theories" about other people illustrate this well. We tend to select experiences that fit our hunches and to ignore those that do not. In this way we can retain generalizations hallowed by time but not necessarily scientifically supportable. How often, for example, have we heard that "fat people are good humored," that "people with high foreheads are highly intelligent," that "a protruding chin goes with guts and determination"?

Because psychologists are so aware of the effects of bias and prejudice, they have developed systematic methods for studying behavior which aim at reducing to a minimum the influence of such subjective factors. They are also aware that hopes and fears about the outcome of an experiment can influence findings, and thus feel somewhat more confident when other psychologists working separately are able to repeat their findings. When data gathering involves interviewing, as in psychoanalysis, the effects of personal bias and selective perception increase enormously, and the chances of objectivity recede markedly.

MODELS AND THEORIES

In common with scientists in other disciplines, psychologists use concepts which, by their nature, are not directly observable but which nevertheless help to make sense of observable events. Such concepts —sometimes termed *theoretical constructs*—are not fundamentally different from those used in physiology or in physics. The physiologist talks about the sodium pump much as the physicist does about atoms, protons, neutrons and so on.

Theoretical constructs are given operational definition by reference to models—frequently mental models, though occasionally mechanical or electronic ones. Since the subject matter of contemporary psychology covers the behavior of organisms from molluscs to mice to men, it is not surprising that no unifying theory has yet emerged. Most psychologists believe that it is still too early to even look for a comprehensive model. Certainly the Einstein of psychology has yet to appear. Most psychologists are content to construct models which can cope with only the data within their specialist area. We shall later consider how some psychological models are related to models of man traditionally offered in religious and in other nonscientific literature. Those described below are chosen merely to illustrate the wide spectrum of models employed by psychologists today.

Freudian Psychoanalytic Theory. For many persons, psychology remains synonymous with psychoanalysis. The vocabulary of Freudian psychoanalysis has found its way into common usage. People now speak freely about repression, inhibition and the unconscious, though rarely using such terms in the way that Freud would have approved.

Freud believed that the human personality is organized around three major systems, the interaction among which could account for such normal and abnormal behavior. The id concerns the discharge of a person's basic drives. The ego, that part of the personality normally described as the conscious mind, regulates a person's interaction with the environment. The superego encapsulates the moral standards by which a person attempts to live. This is not the place to attempt a detailed exposition of Freudian theory. But Jerome S. Bruner notes its essential flavor: "Freud's is a theory or a proto-theory peopled with actors. The characters are from life; the blind, energetic, pleasure seeking id; priggish and punitive super ego; the ego, battling for its being by diverting the energy of others through its own use. The drama has an economy and a terseness. The ego develops canny mechanisms for dealing with the threat of id impulses; denial, projection, and the rest. Balances are struck between the actors, and in the balance is character and neurosis. Freud was using the dramatic technique of decomposition, the play whose actors are parts of a single life."[2]

One of the curious things about psychoanalytic theory is that it continues to be accepted by the average person and by intelligent people in the arts despite its rejection by many academic psychologists. Why this should be so is itself an interesting question. Some suggest it is because the notions of psychoanalytic theory are sufficiently similar to what we might call "common sense" that it meets an immediate felt need. Others, less charitably inclined, point out that it is the lazy person's way of explaining *post hoc* almost any behavior one can think of.

Among professional psychologists debate continues unabated over the scientific foundations, if any, of psychoanalytic theory. One recent survey of studies designed to test psychoanalytic theory is presented in P. Klein's *Fact and Fantasy in Freudian Theory*. After examining hundreds of studies Klein concludes that "any blanket rejection of Freudian theory as a whole simply flies in the face of the evidence."[3] The care with which Klein carries out his critical appraisal makes his conclusion a compelling one, even to the skeptical professional psychologist. How much more convincing then to the nonpsychologist, particularly if predisposed accept Freudian theory. A word of caution, however, is required even here. In a recent book, H. J. Eysenck looks again at the papers which Klein regarded as the best evidence in favor of Freudian theory and claims on reexamination, that they all fail to provide any conclusive proof.[4] As Eysenck puts it, "I would conclude . . . that this conscientious, scholarly and well-documented summary of the most convincing evidence for Freudian theories leaves the reader little option but to conclude that, if this is the best that can be offered by way of support, then the only conclusion can be that there is no evidence at all for psycho-analytic theory."[5] Eysenck's criticism may be somewhat extreme. Nevertheless, numerous others, such as Orval H. Mowrer[6] in the United States, tend to to share Eysenck's view, though this does not mean that they necessarily deny Freud's contribution to the development of psychology.

The debates surrounding Freud and his views will doubtless continue for many years. One thing at least is clear: it is unwise and inadvisable for theologians, apologists or anyone else to build upon a foundation so liable to change or rejection as psychoanalytic theory. Although Freudian psychoanalysis may turn out to be lacking in any secure scientific foundation, this does not mean that a more securely based psychodynamic theory of personality will not emerge and prove important in understanding personality. If, however, any claim approaching the status of a scientific theory is made, it will have to be free from the unscientific characteristics of early Freudian theory which made it so vulnerable to attack.

Information Processing Model of Man. By contrast with the Freudian psychoanalytical model, the information-processing model of personality is little known outside professional circles. It has close connections with aspects of communication theory and computer science, to which it owes much of its development. The model focuses on the human organism's sensitivity to energy changes occurring in the environment. Such changes, detected at receptor surfaces, are transformed and transmitted via the peripheral nervous system to the brain. There they are processed according to certain established routines and an appropriate response is made. Using this model, input/output relations may at times be expressed in precise mathematical terms.

Ethological Model of Man. Another contemporary model owes much to the work of biologists such as Konrad Lorenz and Nikolaas Tinbergen. Describing themselves as ethologists, those who believe in this model regard their task as the scientific study of behavior. The distinctive feature of the ethological approach is an interest in understanding what a particular segment of behavior achieves for the animal. What function does this or that behavior fulfill in the life of the animal, and what function may it have fulfilled in the survival of the species? Such an approach, based on careful and painstaking observation, has already made it possible to specify with detailed precision how, for example, stimuli emitted by one member of a species may evoke or inhibit the behavior of other members of the same or of different species. Typically, such models refer to sign stimuli, action potentials, innate releasing mechanisms and so on. Applying an ethological approach to the behavior of human and nonhuman primates has provided the starting point for popular ethological best sellers such as Desmond Morris's *The Naked Ape.*

The Behavorism of B. F. Skinner.   The final model to which we devote attention sits firmly in the behaviorist tradition of J. B. Watson, though its creator would almost certainly object to it being given the label of "model" at all. It has received wide publicity in recent years through the writings of Harvard psychologist B. F. Skinner. His influence is felt not only through reports of his laboratory studies of conditioning and learning but also through their application and through his philosophical and speculative writings.

Skinner's basic notion and the method he uses is, to quote a recent book on behavioral control, "no different in principle from one that Grandma might have selected, but is used more systematically."[7] Starting from the fact that behavior of all kinds has consequences, Skinner has systematically studied the ways in which, by manipulating those consequences, behavior can be shaped, established or erased. Writers in this field, following the terminology introduced by Skinner, regard the most influential "shapers" of behavior as basically of two kinds. These are "reinforcers," known to us more familiarly as rewards for actions, and "punishers," consequences which are in one way or another unpleasant. As a result of work by Skinner and his colleagues over the last thirty years we now understand much better how reinforcers and punishers shape and control the behavior both of animals and humans.

It is important to distinguish carefully between Skinner's scientific contribution and his speculative writings. Into the latter he freely imports his own values, beliefs, hopes and fears. But this importation should not detract from the importance of his scientific contribution. Neither, of course, does his scientific contribution give any grounds for accepting his speculations about how the techniques he has devised might be applied in order to produce an ideal society. This society he equates with the Utopia long sought by social and political reformers. One of Skinner's basic contentions is that we must not formulate psychological theories which involve nonobservable mentalistic entities. This being so, it is difficult to point to Skinner's psychological model since, as we have said, in a sense he shuns model-building.

The models we have described are only a few examples of the wide variety available in today's psychological marketplace, and are constructed because psychologists, like other scientists, are not satisfied simply to discover empirical relationships between events. They also construct theories, which embody generalizations from which, in turn, further deductions can be made and applied for testing. As in other sciences, such theories serve two principal functions. They help to make sense of data gathered from observation and experiment, to summarize it and to integrate it with existing data. They also help to suggest further lines of research.

It is important to emphasize that psychologists do not claim to hold a monopoly on understanding people. They certainly do not claim exclusive rights to notions of why people act (as we say) "in character," of why they act predictably in certain situations. Wise persons deeply involved in practical affairs become very shrewd judges of the behavior of their fellow humans. Where psychology differs from these persons is that it tries to move from intuitive, largely private, hunches to the formulation of testable hypotheses, formulated as rigorously as possible. It seeks to move from the description or explanation of behavior in everyday terms toward the statement of explanations using terms defined as precisely as possible. Such terms are said to be "operationally defined" and refer explicitly to events observable by anyone with the appropriate training, assisted where necessary by specially developed instruments. Moreover, psychologists seek to make their observations under carefully controlled conditions, rather than under everyday conditions, where so many random occurrences make the isolation of causal sequences extremely difficult.

Although acknowledging the diversity of psychological models, we may still ask whether there are any shared assumptions which underlie and guide the research and model-building of most psychologists. If there are such, then we can ask further whether any conflicts exist between these and Christian beliefs.

ASSUMPTIONS COMMONLY HELD BY PSYCHOLOGISTS

In so far as humans and animals share common properties as regards their anatomy, physiology and biochemistry, it is not surprising that they are also found to share behavioral properties. Most psychologists, therefore, accept the premise that a proper understanding of animal behavior may substantially increase our understanding of human behavior. Many basic aspects of human behavior such as perceiving, learning, remembering and problem solving, as well as many emotional and instinctive reactions, can thus be profitably studied by looking at nonhuman primates, and in some instances at animals considerably lower on the phylo-genetic scale. The existence of such similarities between the behavior of animals and humans does not of itself produce any particular or immediate problems for Christian doctrine. Such similarities are analogous to those already familiar in physiological functioning, which certainly pose no threat to Christian beliefs about man. Indeed, we may be thankful that such similarities at the physiological level provide important avenues for deepening our understanding of human physiology. Why, when one then discovers certain similarities of behavior between human and nonhuman primates, one should therefore become unduly concerned from a Christian point of view, remains a puzzle.

To argue thus is not in any sense to accept the excessive and misleading accounts of man given in publications such as *The Naked Ape*. Extrapolations in such writings go far beyond the evidence and are more likely to cloud real issues and to impede the development of a true science of ethology. Similar highly speculative books such as Konrad Lorenz's *On Aggression*[8] have been subjected to searching criticisms by other ethologists. When Lorenz's book appeared, a group of specialists in the same area of scientific enquiry thought the issues he raised sufficiently important, and his treatment of them so controversial, that they published a volume under the title *Man and Aggression*[9] specifically designed to refute Lorenz's more extreme claims. Thus S. A. Barnett wrote: ". . . I have read the book through more than once. On each reading more self-contradictions, confusions and questionable statements have emerged. . . . It makes statements on two crucial features of our existence: the growth of social behavior in children, and the prevention of violence and war. These are not topics in which loose thinking can be accepted with a tolerant shrug; such work should be based on a respect for facts, for logic and for the researches of others. Instead, the method of *On Aggression* is essentially anti-rational. This method should be repudiated by all scholars —indeed, by all responsible people."[10]

A second assumption shared by many psychologists is a form of determinism linked with a mechanistic approach to theory building. Such an approach may take the form of one or another of the models given above or of similar ones. Put in simplest form, this means two things. First, the psychologist assumes that what he or she does one day under a particular set of conditions in the laboratory will be reproducible another day provided that the same set of conditions is observed. Some would assume that what happens on the two occasions will be precisely the same (usually referred to as strong determinism), while others assume simply that on the two occasions the outcome will be similar within close statistical limits (often referred to as weak determinism). Second, as a starting point he or she will assume that even the most complicated forms of behavior should ultimately, and in principle, be capable of description in mechanistic terms. Another way of expressing this is to say that we find it useful to adopt a "what if" kind of approach in our model building and theorizing. Such an approach can only lead to error, if from asking a "what if" type of question, one goes on to say that, therefore, man is "nothing but" a complex machine. In short, each of the "what if" approaches can unthinkingly lead to a variety of forms of "nothing-buttery." The information processing approach may lead to the assertion that man is "nothing but" a complex machine, the ethological approach to the notion that man is "nothing but" a particularly highly developed animal, or the Skinnerian approach to the verdict that man is "nothing but" the product of environmental forces. To be sure, from a Christian point of view, nothing is at stake in recognizing that, as part of the tactics of scientific research, much is to be gained by developing and testing models of man as a complex machine, in recognizing that important clues to brain and behavior relations in man can be found from studies in animals, that to some extent man shares features of his behavior with animals, and that, within limits, a man's behavior is heavily dependent upon the circumstances within which he has developed. What must be resisted is the implication that such procedural and research benefits necessarily lead to the conclusion that man is therefore "nothing but" each of the things that we have listed. That there are research benefits to be derived from adopting such a deterministic and mechanistic approach to the study of behavior is amply born out in practice. At the same time, few psychologists doubt the reality of their *own* freedom of action or that of their colleagues. That such a mechanistic approach does not lead to a denial of human responsibility has been demonstrated by Donald MacKay.[11]

A further assumption shared by most psychologists is that it is futile to regard approaches to the study of behavior made at one level as being in competition with complementary approaches made at other levels. When it comes to deciding what level of explanation is the most appropriate for any particular problem, one may well find different psychologists holding different views. Such views, however, are not based on scientific data but on personal philosophies, values and hopes. Some—today a minority—believe that the goal of all explanation is ultimately to reduce everything to the most fundamental level possible, such as the subatomic one. Others take the view that the level of explanation invoked must be appropriate to, and do justice to, the complexity of the behavior being studied.

The notion of a hierarchy of explanations in which psychology would appear below anthropology but above physiology, is a familiar one. To attempt to expand the terms of reference of physiology so as to embrace psychology is as much to expand physiology as to reduce psychology, a point not always apparent in the writings of some reductionists. Whether science is to be unified by proceeding upwards or downwards through this hypothetical hierarchy remains an open question. Most psychologists, however, make the tacit assumption that their primary concern is with the behavior of the whole organism. This is not to deny the importance or relevance of levels of explanation which are given by those who concentrate on the behavior of the individual in a social context, or upon the study of mechanisms and processes going on within organisms which gives rise to explanations at what may be called an intraorganismic level. *All* levels are necessary if we are to do full justice to the complexity of man's behavior.

A question remains, however. If the different explanations of the same set of events (horizontal plane) offered by psychologists as well as those offered at other levels (on a vertical plane) by sociologists or physiologists are not to be regarded as competitors, then how are they to be related? Are there no limits to the number of explanations we must accept? Are there any criteria for helping us to decide whether two explanations are complementary or competitive? Since Christian apologists have treated this question in considerable detail in recent years, we may simply refer the reader to such papers as that by Donald MacKay.[12] The somewhat negative, but nonetheless important, point which emerges from his and similar discussions is that before explanations at different levels are debated as rivals, they need to be shown to be not in fact complementary. This is important, because what applies to the relation of these different scientific explanations applies also to the task of relating religious and psychological accounts of behavior. In both cases, however, it is essential to realize that proof of complementarity does not establish that either account is true.

What we are arguing is that it is mistaken, both on logical and on empirical grounds, to assert that psychology leads inevitably to reductionism. That would logically be tantamount to saying that a "Fasten your seatbelt" sign is "nothing but" wires and bulbs and that, therefore, you may ignore it, or that the words addressed to you by a friend are "nothing but" sounds analyzable without remainder on a sound spectrograph. It is evident empirically that there are questions—for example, about interpersonal relations—that cannot even be properly formulated, let alone answered, if reference is made only to physiological mechanisms. The choice of one approach, which in itself may be extremely productive and lead to important discoveries, can at the same time exclude even the formulation at a different level of equally important questions about the same events.

Failure to grasp this simple but basic point is at the root of a good deal of meaningless and fruitless debate today, both within psychology and between psychology and religion. The necessity of studying behavior simultaneously from a variety of standpoints in order to do justice to its complexity does not mean that any and every explanation is acceptable, however far out and fanciful. Each must be justified as necessary to a full understanding of what is being studied, and each must bring forward evidence relevant to the level being advocated. We shall return to this matter of complementary descriptions when we discuss the specific issue of how and why psychological explanations have at times been presented as competitors with religious explanations of behavior.

IMPLICATIONS OF PSYCHOLOGY FOR CHRISTIAN EXPERIENCE, BELIEFS AND PRACTICES

We have already mentioned that the majority of psychologists regard their discipline as the science of behavior. In principle, there is no reason why the same approach should not be used in the investigation of aspects of religious behavior. Although the psychology of religion has never formed a major part of contemporary psychology, a steady stream of publications has appeared on the topic, including the better known works of William James, Freud, Robert Thouless, Gordon Allport, Michael Argyle, and Mowrer. In addition, other, more speculative, contributions have from time to time aroused considerable interest, particularly if they have been presented as alternatives to traditional religious explanations of behavior. The few illustrative examples of psychological explanations of religious behavior which follow are given so that we may go on to ask how they are related to the more familiar religious explanations.

Because those who take seriously the words of Christ cannot regard conversion as an optional extra for some Christians only, we may take it as our example. Conversion is certainly of the essence of being a Christian, for Christ himself said, "Except ye be converted . . . ye shall not enter into the kingdom of Heaven" (Matt. 18:3, AV).

The tremendous variety of explanations of religious conversion offered by psychologists may be reduced to three broad categories: those involving social learning theories, those involving psychophysiological theories, and those involving psychodynamic theories. The first group stresses the formative influence of the social and cultural environment on a person's religious beliefs and practices. Such influences include family, church and denomination. Certain religious groups establish norms about the kind of experience that a young person shall report and the kind of behavior which is acceptable within that group. For this reason, if for no other, it is not surprising that among certain Christian groups sudden conversions are reported more frequently than among others. Theories of the second type discuss conversion as a form of brainwashing. It is claimed that in some religious meetings, particularly during high-powered evangelistic campaigns, it is possible to detect certain recurring ingredients. These include a respected speaker whose considerable prestige has been built up through the media and who preaches with great fervor, conviction and seeming authority. Such meetings are frequently crowded and emotional hymns are sung before and after the main address. In addition, there may be bright lights, massed choirs dressed in white and rhythmic, stirring music. Such factors taken together— so it is argued—increase the likelihood of sudden conversions. Situations of this kind were described and analyzed in detail by William Sargant in *Battle for the Mind* and *The Mind Possessed.*[13]

There seems little doubt that some practices listed above do influence the thoughts and actions of those attending such meetings. The extent of this influence remains to be clarified by further studies. Such studies constitute a proper labor for those engaged in the scientific study of religious behavior. Christians will be as interested as non-Christians in their outcome. Sargant believes he finds important similarities between what is happening in the brains of people subjected to brainwashing and those suddenly converted in highly emotional evangelistic meetings. His detailed descriptions and analyses of such situations are contained in his two books *Battle for the Mind* and *The Mind Possessed.*[13] The Christian psychologist is as concerned to understand the nature and function of any psychophysiological mechanisms as is the non-Christian one. Both, moreover, must realize that to understand such mechanisms does not bear one way or the other on the truth or falsehood of the beliefs held at the end of the conversion process. That simple logical point is, perhaps, more readily appreciated if one takes a slightly less emotionally tinged example. One day we may understand the psychophysiology of the processes involved when scientists are making discoveries and producing theories, or the processes that occur when mathematicians are working out proofs. In neither case, however, should we attempt to evaluate the truth of the scientist's theory or the validity of the mathematician's proof by analyzing the brains that created it. If we want to judge the truth of what the innovator says, we should examine it in the light of the appropriate evidence.

A somewhat different approach to the psychological understanding of religious experience, and one which illustrates our third broad category, is that of Sigmund Freud. Freud believed that religion and all that it involves is an illusion.[14] What his theory and others like it tell us, is principally something about the person who believes in a god, and little about the god in whom he or she believes. The particular function of religion in the life of an individual will not tell us anything about the existence or nonexistence of the god in whom he or she believes, nor about the truth or falsehood of the statements made about that god. Those questions must be settled on other grounds.

Having just indicated how psychologists reflect on conversion, let us compare it with the biblical account and then see how we may relate the two. The first thing one notices, if one takes the Bible at all seriously, is that it does not stipulate only one type of genuine Christian conversion experience. What Scripture offers is a record of people with widely differing backgrounds, brought to faith in Christ through different circumstances, and yet at the end all sharing a common faith. Within the space of a few chapters of the Acts of the Apostles, for example, we find the accounts of the conversion of an Ethiopian leader, of Saul of Tarsus, of a military commander in the armed services, of a woman named Lydia and of a jailer. From a psychological point of view, a variety of psychological mechanisms was doubtless at work in these five individuals. In each case, however, the outcome was the same—belief in God and faith in Christ. To focus on psychological aspects of conversion does not mean that one either ignores or denies that above all else the truth grips the mind of the hearer and is a prime ingredient in coming to faith in Christ. Moreover, the Bible makes clear that, despite the diversity of background and circumstances involved, each conversion occurred because God had acted initially—in a word, that hearers respond to the Gospel when God first begins to work in them.

How then are the biblical accounts of conversion to be related to the accounts offered by psychologists and physiologists? Each has its own distinctive features. The religious account is what may be described as an "actor" account of what is going on; it is the account given by the person being converted. By contrast, the psychological and physiological accounts may be regarded as "spectator" accounts; they are given from the particular viewpoint of the observing scientist. One, as we have seen, may be interested in environmental factors which accompany the conversion experience, another in the physiological brain processes occurring at conversion. Each selects for study only one set of events which, for purposes of analysis and understanding, may be usefully analyzed from several different viewpoints.

By viewpoints, we mean here the psychological, physiological, the biochemical and so on, as well as the distinctly personal. The personal experience certainly cannot be dismissed as a mere epiphenomenon. The experience of conversion is just as real as the scientist's experience in reading his measuring instruments. Moreover, the various accounts should not be regarded as competitors. An account of the physiological processes underlying behavior does not compete with the psychological account of the same event. Neither is the psychological account a competitor of the account which the person converted gives in his own personal or religious language. Within its own language system, each of the different accounts may be regarded, at least in principle, as exhaustive, but none may claim to be exclusive. Thus, the personal account, which refers to a personal encounter with God, does not have to be "fitted into" either the psychological or the physiological or the biochemical account, any more than the psychological account has to be "fitted into" the physiological account. In general, we find that the personal account of the event is much more concerned with the personal significance of the event than with the particular psychological, physiological or other mechanism which may have been at work at the time.

Personal accounts will include, as indeed do those in the Bible, mention of God as personal and of the Holy Spirit. That is not to suggest that the Holy Spirit can be used as an explanatory concept to supplement the psychological account of religious behavior. That would be to ignore the important truth that the Holy Spirit is God Himself, and is not to be "fitted into" any psychological or other kind of explanation that we choose to give. The God of the Christian is one who upholds and sustains all things at all times (Heb. 1:3). It is extremely important to remember this when we think about the relationship between the psychological accounts of conversion and the significance of the event to the convert. The point is that the whole pattern of events leading up to a person's conversion is to be regarded as God-given. What, therefore, the converted person is asserting is that to do full justice to the whole of the experience, he or she finds it necessary to interpret that experience in religious terms. The non-Christian can always, of course, say that such an explanation is superfluous or that such an interpretation is meaningless. As far as I can see, no amount of arguing can ever produce an incontestable proof that the non-Christian is right, and that the Christian is wrong, or vice versa. It is not that the Christian has, so to speak, a special set of religious sense receptors, which he can tune into the religious wavelength to pick up information which is not available to the non-Christian. Rather it is that, the Christian's experience makes sense to him at the deepest level as personal dialogue between himself and God. That is not to say that the Christian does not have substantial reasons for his beliefs. He most certainly does. While the grounds for belief emphasized by different Christians vary considerably, no account can claim to be true to biblical Christianity which denies the historicity of the life, teaching, death and resurrection of Christ.

PSYCHOLOGY AND THE NATURE OF MAN

What implications, if any, do developments in psychological science have for our Christian understanding of the nature of man? Some have argued that if it could be shown that the scientific, psychological model of man fits with the biblical model, then this would give added support to Christian belief as a whole, especially in an age of widespread disbelief. The motivation behind this way of thinking is understandable and the intention well-meaning. On closer scrutiny, however, it is evident that, for a number of reasons, such an approach is mistaken. In the first place, it is based upon a misunderstanding of the nature of psychological models as they are constructed and used by psychologists today. As we saw earlier, these models are projected in order to make sense of the accumulated empirical data. By their nature, therefore, models change as more data comes to light; they are modified or, at times, totally rejected and replaced by new ones. In some cases, for example, that of the information processing model, with its descriptions partially expressed in terms of mathematical equations, it is very difficult to see just how one could fit it to a Christian model of man. In other cases (perhaps the Freudian model is a good example), it is easier to see how a model which uses very loosely defined terms within an extremely flexible conceptual framework could, with a little ingenuity, be bent to fit what is thought to be the Christian model of man.

A recent attempt to link a psychological model with Christian beliefs has been made by some Christians who have appropriated the ethologists' description of man as "innately aggressive." These Christians find it natural to regard this description as justification for their belief in man's fallen state, or, as some choose to call it, his innate depravity. But, as I have tried to indicate, the views put forward by some ethologists are today seriously challenged by their scientific contemporaries and have already been shown to be almost certainly wrong in some respects. If one makes the passing theories of certain scientists the grounds of belief in the fallen state of man, what becomes of that belief when the theories are changed or dispensed with altogether?

To try to fit scientific models to the Christian view of man is, I believe, to misunderstand what each is about. It certainly reveals a misunderstanding of the Christian picture of man, which is not confined to any particular age, but embodies enduring truths about man which apply in scientific and prescientific eras alike. The Christian picture of man makes sense of the common experiences of life in every age. Scientific models, by contrast, are deliberately limited in their scope and application.

Psychological models of man remain silent on questions of good and evil, sin, redemption and eternal life—themes which are central to the Christian view of man, concerned as it is with man's relation to God as he lives in a God-created, but sin-ridden, world. On such matters, psychologists differ in their personal views. There are Christian psychologists and there are non-Christian psychologists. And Christian and non-Christian psychologists alike are found to be working across the spectrum of current psychological research.

So far we have taken examples of advances in psychological knowledge which have implications for Christian doctrine. At times the application of psychological knowledge to practical problems raises ethical and moral issues of concern to Christians. When this happens it is all too easy, and from the highest motives, to espouse positions without pausing to scrutinize issues with the care they deserve. Take as an example an issue currently debated in both Christian and non-Christian circles, that concerning the practice and theory of behavior therapy. Some Christians, believing it derives from a behaviorist approach in psychology, have taken a very negative attitude toward behavior therapy, having decided it is anti-Christian because it is linked to the work of B. F. Skinner. Those who oppose the methods of behavior modification used by behavior therapists sometimes do so on the grounds that the techniques employed are inhuman and use "merely" mechanical procedures to manipulate people as things. One basic assumption underlying behavior therapy is that we may usefully regard a variety of conditions, including neurotic anxiety, compulsive behavior, homosexual activity and uncontrolled drinking, as examples of inappropriate behavior, which can be modified, shaped, and eliminated, by the application of operant conditioning and related techniques. Undesirable responses can be extinguished and desirable responses evoked and strengthened.

Ethical problems certainly do arise in instances where there seem to be grounds for attempting to modify people's behavior without their consent. For example, should one submit the continuance of self-destructive behavior in a severely retarded child, if there are good grounds for believing that the application of behavior therapy techniques can eliminate such behavior? The answer is that, in so far as it allows the child to become more truly human and in control of himself, behavior modification should surely be attempted.

The issue of the property of behavioral techniques is being actively debated by practicing psychologists at the present time. We raise it here in order to point out that there do not seem to be any specifically Christian grounds for opposing the ethical use of such new therapeutic techniques. Indeed, it needs to be said that any technique, as a technique, is ethically neutral, and any method, whether depth therapy based upon psychoanalytic theory, or behavior therapy, can be applied in an inhuman way. Depth therapy can be used to assault the mind just as effectively, and, some would contend, with more lasting consequences, as any alleged physical assault used in aversive stimulation by behavior therapists. It is not very meaningful therefore to ask, Is this or that psychological technique Christian or non-Christian? Ethically it is neutral; but it may be used by good persons or bad to benefit or to degrade their fellow humans. If Christians wish to take sides on these issues, let them do so on the basis of a critical evaluation of the relevant evidence and the likely validity of the psychological theories that are put forward, not on the basis of supposed matches of one particular psychological model with some particular supposed Christian model of man.

A CHRISTIAN PERSPECTIVE ON CONTEMPORARY PSYCHOLOGY

We have concentrated on the implications that psychology may have for Christian beliefs, experience and practices. But there is another side to this question: What implications has the Christian view of man for the psychologists' notions of man and his behavior? The biblical view of man is a God-centered one. Its emphasis is upon man made by God for a family relationship of a son to a father. The Bible, moreover, teaches that, by nature, we are not always keen on this relationship. There is within us a tendency to want to keep our hands on the controls of our lives. It is this obsession with keeping our hands on the controls and getting our own way, regardless of what God has said, which is the basis of what the Bible calls sin. It is an all-pervasive tendency and, according to the Christian view, must be dealt with by God if man is to live in the way that God intended.

The Christian view of man is neither optimistic nor pessimistic; it is realistic. It asserts that man *is* made in the image of God. This truth is set out clearly in Genesis, taken up in the Psalms, and reasserted in I Corinthians 11:7 (KJV), where Paul affirms that man "is [not was] the image" of God, and by James, who tells us that our fellow men are "made in God's likeness" or image (James 3:9, NIV).

Scripture is quite clear that the first man, though made in the divine image, through disobedience marred that image; that Christ, the second Adam, gave a perfect obedience to God; that his obedience led him to death; and that he died for our disobedience. In Christ, the image is potentially restored and we can begin to regain the dominion over our sin and selfishness lost in the fall. In Christ, therefore, man may begin to retrieve his image which, in part, means to fulfil his role as God's vice-regent upon earth. He may begin again to exercise the lordship and custodianship of creation given to him in Genesis, while acknowledging, as Heb. 2:8–9 reminds us, that "we do not yet see everything in subjection to him [man] but we see Jesus, who for a little while was made lower than the angels, crowned with glory and honour."

This is not the place to develop in any fullness what is meant by man in the image of God created, marred and renewed, but we must pause long enough to draw out some of its implications for the practice of psychology. No Christian, with a biblical view of man, could ever be party to or condone an approach to his fellow man which suggests that he is a thing to be manipulated, rather than a person to be respected and loved and with a dignity which is his both in view of creation and redemption. Yet a Christian assessment of man will be sober and realistic. He is not surprised when research in social psychology underlines the depths to which men can stoop in treating other men. He is not surprised when he faces the results of research in the psychology of religion, indicating the deviousness to which man can go in deceiving himself, even as regards his most cherished beliefs, be they religious or otherwise. He is not surprised to know that man can delude himself even about things he claims to be the most serious in his life.

Certainly the Christian psychologist will face the reality of all that he learns about man doubly motivated wherever his skill is relevant to share the challenge of helping man at every point. As a psychologist, he will want to direct his particular training towards the solution of specific problems. As a Christian, he will see his work as one way of expressing his love for his brother and of fulfilling Christ's commands. At the same time he will be under no illusion that man's basic spiritual problem, which stems from a deep underlying attitude of rebellion against God and his claims upon men, can be dealt with by psychological techniques alone, be they ever so sophisticated. To believe that would be to perpetuate the unfounded optimism which was so current towards the end of the last century, and which has been revived in recent years by men such as Teilhard de Chardin, with his belief in man's continuing ascent to perfection. Whatever else Freud may have taught us, and however misleading he may have been in some of his theories, Professor George Miller was surely right when, in assessing Freud's contribution, he pointed out that "Freud struggled to see man as he is, not as he ought to be or as Freud would have liked to imagine him" and that after Freud, "the old faith in the inevitability of human progress, through man's constant growth of knowledge and understanding, sounded like an innocent myth concocted to amuse little children."[15]

The Christian can accept without fear and without despair what the psychology of religion may tell him about the self-deceptiveness possible even in the use to which he seeks to put his religious beliefs, whether it be of escapism, excessive dogmatism or whatever. He does not have to become unduly defensive, but can face up to new insights into his own shortcomings which the results of psychological research may reveal. Neither will he see social psychology as a rival to what the Christian church is doing and teaching. He will not see his faith threatened because psychological knowledge may be used to alleviate the more harmful consequences of sin. He believes that ultimately the root problem of sin can be dealt with only by God acting in Christ, nevertheless, as a Christian psychologist, he will accept the challenge to bend all his energies to try to find a remedy for the antisocial behaviors which are the symptoms of our condition as sinners. In this way, fulfilling the command to love his brother, he can to some extent help to lessen the personal and social hurt which results from such behavior.

The Christian can never be satisfied with tackling these problems only at what might be called the horizontal level. Christianity, rightly understood, must by its very nature bring in an entirely new dimension, a dimension desperately needed in the pessimistic world in which we live today. This dimension is the hope that comes as one recognizes that man is a creature belonging to God, made by God, redeemed by God, and still loved by God. It is not enough to devote our energies to obeying the command to love our brothers and to do so with all the insight and effectiveness which may be added by a proper use of the fruits of psychological research. As Christians we are constrained to spell out the message that despite all our shortcomings God loves us and offers us life in all its fullness through a personal relationship with Him. As Christians, we must insist that, when scientific psychologists have spoken their last word about what really makes man tick, there remains something even more fundamental to be said. This is that man was made by God, in his own image, and for the purposes of God. Without this dimension, the pessimism abroad today and found even among some scientists is understandable. The Christian has no part in this pessimism, for he knows that "all things work together for good for those who love God and are called according to his purpose" (Rom. 8:28, KJV) and that "the One who started the good work in you will bring it to completion by the Day of Christ Jesus" (Phil. 1:6, NEB).

NOTES

1. Michael Polanyi, *Personal Knowledge* (London: Routledge and Kegan Paul, 1958).
2. Jerome S. Bruner, "Freud and the Image of Man," *Partisan Review* 23 (Summer 1956): 343, quoted in G. A. Miller, *Psychology: The Science of Mental Life* (London: Hutchinson, 1964).
3. P. Klein, *Fact and Fantasy in Freudian Theory* (London: Methuen, 1972), p. 346.
4. Hans J. Eysenck and G. W. Wilson, eds., *The Experimental Study of Freudian Theories* (London: Methuen, 1973).
5. H. J. Eysenck, "The Experimental Study of Freudian Concepts," *Bulletin of the British Psychological Society* 25 (1972): 261–267.
6. Orval H. Mowrer, *The Crisis in Psychiatry and Religion* (New York: Van Nostrand, 1961).
7. Perry London, *Behavior Control* (New York, Harper & Row, 1969), p. 95.
8. Konrad Lorenz, *On Aggression* (New York, Harcourt, Brace and World, 1966).
9. Ashley Montagu, ed., *Man and Aggression* (London: Oxford University Press, 1968).
10. Montagu, *op. cit.,* p. 26.
11. Donald M. MacKay, "The Bankruptcy of Determinism," *The New Scientist* 47 (2 July 1970): 24–26.
12. Donald M. MacKay, *Aristotelian Society Supplement* 32 (1958): 105–122.
13. William Sargant, *Battle for the Mind* (London: Heinemann, 1957); *The Mind Possessed* (London: Heinemann, 1973). Cf. also "The Physiology of Faith," *British Journal of Psychiatry* 115 (1969): 505–518.
14. Sigmund Freud, *The Future of an Illusion* (London: Hogarth Press, 1934).
15. G. A. Miller, *Psychology: The Science of Mental Life* (London: Hutchinson, 1964), pp. 246 ff.

XI

The Spiritual Dimensions of Science

WALTER R. THORSON

In its methods of study and in its deliberate limitation of focus to mechanism rather than purpose, natural science is that reflective activity of man which seems specifically not concerned with God and therefore should be most lacking in positive spiritual elements. It may therefore be surprising that anyone should argue, as I shall do in this essay, that the scientific enterprise has certain essentially spiritual features and some very important positive spiritual lessons for the Christian understanding, which for the most part the church has not yet appreciated.

Science is concerned with truth, though it is truth of a peculiar and

Walter R. Thorson is Professor of Chemistry at the University of Alberta, Edmonton, Canada. He received his B.S. and Ph.D. from California Institute of Technology. He was a faculty member for ten years at Massachusetts Institute of Technology in Cambridge, Massachusetts, prior to going to Canada in 1968. His professional interest is in both physics and chemistry, primarily the theory of atomic and molecular collision processes. He maintains a lively interest in philosophy, theology, and Christian apologetics, seeking as a practicing Christian to unify and clarify perceptions of God and his creation. He has been quite active in university Christian communities, including Inter-Varsity Christian Fellowship, and has lectured and taught summer courses on subjects relating to science and philosophy at Regent College in Vancouver, British Columbia. His primary philosophical interest is epistemology.

limited sort; Can we learn anything about the nature of truth in general from a sound understanding of scientific truth? Science is an activity of man which is rooted in man's perception of his role and destiny in creation; If that perception is a biblical one, how does it affect our understanding of the Christian faith? Lastly, science is concerned with matter and has tremendously enhanced our appreciation of the integrity of the material world; how might that influence a Christian understanding of the relation of spiritual and material realities? These are the questions we need to answer.

The church traditionally has not found it easy to look on science as even a neutral enterprise. There is a very subtle boundary between the remarkable independence, boldness, and critical thinking that marks the scientific mentality in action, and the rebellious pride pictured in the biblical stories of Cain and his culture or of the tower of Babel; and for most people, that boundary is insignificant, crossed without comprehension. Enterprises like Project Babel, because they are conceived in pride and executed in alienation, will eventually come to nothing in themselves. In bearing witness to that fact, the church is only being faithful to the Word of God, and a certain amount of misguided zeal in that witness is as humanly understandable as it is humanly mistaken. From a biblical perspective it's clear that the main significance of science and technology to modern man is to afford him one more bulwark in the city of his defiant independence of God, and one more idol which cannot really deliver him. No one, therefore, should misunderstand this essay as a humanist proposal for salvation through cultural evolution in the manner of Julian Huxley[1] or even of Harvey Cox.[2]

Nevertheless, the church has been much too suspicious of the scientific enterprise itself, and on the whole has either ignored its positive significance or even identified it with rebellion against God. When creative and critical thinking challenges our traditions, it is easier to dismiss it as sinful pride than it is to make the painful reassessments which honesty and humility of mind demand. This has been the worst aspect of the warfare between science and theology. *Hubris,* the destructive pride that alienates the mind from God, has been much too common in *both* camps. Since a rotten tree never bears good fruit, and since the church has been willing enough to accept the good fruit of the scientific revolution, the inconsistency of its continued hostility to the ideals of that revolution has become increasingly evident to everyone and is one reason for the church's lack of intellectual authority today.

Nor is it enough for the church to adopt a merely neutral view of the enterprise which has so altered the last few centuries. Dietrich Bonhoeffer spoke of "man come of age."[3] I'm not sure what Bonhoeffer really meant by that. I suspect it wasn't nearly as optimistic a view as most of his liberal interpreters have since made out. It's an unfortunate expression because it suggests a false idea of completeness and, like the expression "adult entertainment," a false idea of moral progress. But it does convey one very important truth: for better or for worse, man's cultural consciousness is in some ways much older than it was (say, in 1500). If you like, let's say that the little monster has become a teenager. But I want to insist that in spite of all the new dangers it has created, the scientific enterprise has really been a very healthy and creative element in this change. It therefore seems to me that a major purpose for a book like this one is not simply to alert the church to all the new devilry the other side is up to, but to stimulate a truly Christian appreciation of the new insights and understanding, as well as of the enormous new dangers, which the scientific revolution has created for mankind. Such an appreciation is long overdue and is a necessary part of our rediscovery of the fact that Jesus Christ, not the prince of this world, is the Lord of history.

THE END OF THE AGE OF SCIENCE

The development of a mature Christian appraisal of science and the scientific enterprise is made more urgent because we are near the end of an age—the age of science. We are all aware that we are in a period of immense change, and that this is more than the gradual change common to all times and conditions. Such revolutionary periods do occur in history; more important changes occurred in Europe between 1500 and 1600 A.D. than for the thousand years previous. In the three or four centuries since, the West has been working out the concrete manifestations of those changes, especially and most extensively, those changes implied by the scientific revolution—and the impact has been world-wide. Is this development reaching a new stage? There are some unmistakable signs that it is. In the last few decades, society has experienced the fusion of physical science and technology. Further development of knowledge, both in depth and in detail, may occur, but it will be, in the main, technologically motivated and directed. From the purely technological viewpoint, the fusions still to be achieved are with biological, and perhaps even psychological, "science," fusions which would lead to the realization of all life and of man himself as a tool. This horrible vision of the future is only one possibility: either the complete technological manipulation of man will be attempted (and perhaps succeed in part), or massive resistance, conflict, and upheaval will prevent it. In either case, an age is passing. People talk nowadays about future shock, about emerging technological control of economics, politics, and social structure on an unprecedented scale, of existence "beyond freedom and dignity." To this there is antithetical response in "counterculture"—men and women seeking refuge from manipulative technique; but for the most part this response is also anti-Christian. On the one hand, people are again adopting irrational, superstitious, and magical views of reality; on the other, they attempt to answer the *objectively real* questions of religion with a pure subjective existentialism or the identity-dissolving religious thought of the Far East. Perhaps the most disturbing and powerful impulse of counterculture, most easily manifest in action, is the will to destroy as an end in itself, which has become explicit in the emergence of Satanism.

In response to this situation, many Christians have come to think the return of Jesus Christ is very near. There is much real evidence to support this view. In many respects, our situation is without precedent in history, and in these respects it is painted with remarkable accuracy by apocalyptic prophecies in Scripture.[4] While the Christian response is always "our Lord, come," this immediate expectation could be mistaken. It is not ours "to know the times or seasons which the Father has fixed by His own authority" (Acts 1:7, RSV). Meanwhile, He remains the Lord of history.

In any case an age is passing. I am not a futurologist, Christian or otherwise, and this is not an essay about the future. It is, rather, a reflection upon the significance of the immediate past. In a very special and yet a fundamental sense, *the age that is passing is the age of science.* There are several reasons for this.

In the first place, science can no longer be innocent. I have mentioned the fusion of science with technology. In the long run, it is the philosophical meaning of this fusion, and not its technological impact, that is most important. Having finally understood that scientific truth is a source of power, man has made the crucial decision that from now on the will to power and the uses of power should dictate the relevance and value of that truth. Because of that decision, "pure" science, the science of the past four hundred years, will begin to be altered in subtle ways and will eventually disappear. In recent years, the scientific community has been made aware of this change through economic pressure from government and industry (who wish to determine in advance the goals of knowledge), and we have started to talk (rather ineffectually) about it; but the real decision was made twenty years ago when that same community compromised its innocence by accepting enormous increases in financial support from the society, without any concern for why the society was giving it. This loss of innocence comes home to me personally. It is increasingly difficult to speak about the ideals of pure science and their spiritual dimensions —as in fact I am trying to do in this essay. I am certain to be interrupted by someone who will say, with genuine moral concern, that I have no right to talk about such abstract irrelevancies or, for that matter, even to carry on my work, unless I am prepared to evaluate the results morally. The traditional answer to this view has always been that truth pursued for its own sake is good, in and of itself, and that the decision regarding the ends to which we shall put knowledge of truth is a separate moral question. I believe this is fundamentally the correct answer—or rather, *it was the correct answer. The fusion of science and technology means that, increasingly, the moral decisions as to the uses of truth will be made pre-emptively, before the truth itself is even sought; we shall seek only the truth which fits our purposes.*

But science which is no longer innocent cannot remain pure science either. This is not mere metaphor. When scientists talk about "pure" science, they are not referring to innocence in the moral sense I have described above, they are talking about intellectual motivation— "truth for its own sake". The fact that moral innocence and intellectual purity are *necessarily* connected is an illustration of *the intrinsic nature of divine judgment.* Man assumes, from a position of very incomplete knowledge, that he can anticipate the range of possible discovery—and therefore that he can allow the utilitarian motive to decide which specific knowledge in that range is "relevant." But that stance is the essence of technology, not of science. Here I intend no necessary criticism of technology, but it is not at all the same thing as science. The pure scientists are themselves extremely concerned about the impact that the utilitarian approach is having on the character of scientific work, and they feel a deep frustration that this concern is apparently not understood outside their own ranks and that it is regarded as an abstract and academic issue by the elite of the technological power structure in society. Nowadays I can hardly go to a scientific meeting without hearing a good deal of public expression of this frustration.

More subtle than these external pressures, and less appreciated by the scientific community, is the internal pressure exerted on intellectual climate by the existence of short-term, absurdly superficial yardsticks of achievement generated by money and the program-production orientation of "big science." Few among my generation and that of my teachers realize how extreme the pressures and how severe the consequences of "not succeeding" have become for young scientists. It takes tremendous courage to work on fundamental problems when "results"—and plenty of them—are the major token of value. By and large, we have failed to realize that by demanding "productivity" on a short-term basis, we shall get what we demand, that is, a large volume of uncreative and poorly disciplined students. Furthermore, the mechanism for unchecked growth of science of such low quality is built in, since teachers tend to produce students who share their perceptions and values regarding scientific research and its purpose. Like any cultural or artistic tradition, the Western tradition of science is extremely fragile.[5] It will eventually die out unless the inner integrity of the enterprise is communicated to succeeding generations of craftpeople.

A second factor which will contribute to the death of science is the collective movement of our culture toward new religious and philosophical syntheses. The explicit counterculture is only a surface phenomenon of a movement which actually permeates the thought of the whole society. As far as the future of the scientific tradition is concerned, the most important motif of the age of Aquarius is the devaluation of objective truth, the denial of its human relevance, and, ultimately, the denial of its reality. Fundamentally, this movement must be understood in philosophical and, really, in religious terms, but it is equally important to understand that most of its manifestations are *not* explicitly philosophical or religious. Systematic analysis of the new synthesis is beyond my scope here, and I will restrict myself to a few comments and observations.

Truth of any kind is significant for man precisely because he is an agent in the world. He can make choices which change not only himself but also the material form of the world (our culture is not yet so completely drenched in Oriental mysticism that we could suppose that such changes are only illusions). When we say that *truth is objective,* we mean that it stands outside man, has an existence not created by his will, and by that existence demands, once it is discovered, his acknowledgment and ultimately his responsible "obedience." Truth also has *authority.* This has two aspects. The first is *restrictive authority,* that is, the existence of truth rules out some of the hypothetical alternatives created by the imagination, and teaches man that his will and choice must be disciplined by consistency with what *is;* the second aspect is *delegated authority,* that is, by making choices enlightened by his knowledge, man brings about changes in himself and the world that really increase his own freedom and power. One might even say that in this process truth, working through man as a conscious agent, has the capacity to shape the future. I use the word *truth* here in the most naive and direct manner possible. The theological tone of my language is also quite deliberate. I really believe that all truth and authority come from God, and therefore I believe that the truth we can learn about in the scientific enterprise is a part of one "given" fabric of reality.

I am glad to be able to remind readers of the writings of Francis Shaeffer,[6] Hans Rookmaaker,[7] and others who have interpreted the cultural development of the West, especially in philosophy, literature, and the arts, as an outgrowth of man's increasing apostasy and rebellion against the objective reality of God. Stated briefly, Shaeffer's thesis is that by denying the objective reality of God and the possibility of knowledge of Him, man has chosen a course which has also progressively emptied the natural world, and finally his own existence, of objective meaning. The logical end of that course is pure subjective existentialism, which denies that any meaning exists other than that chosen and willed by the ego. Sartre has stated it well: "There exists no human nature—since there exists no God to conceive it."[8] *The basic theme—that the progression to pure subjectivity is the inevitable result of denying the possibility of a divinely "given" authority—is quite correct.* This is relevant to the death of science: at some point in such a progressive development, the principles and practice of science must become unacceptably alien to an existentially based mentality.

There is evidence that this point has been reached or will soon be reached, not merely in some academic or intellectual levels of the society, *but in mass culture.* What are the obvious points of friction? Science is a tradition with a concept of history and progressive development; it insists that the objective truths acquired from the past do have functional authority in the present, even though it is prepared to perform the ritual of their repeated verification as part of the education process. It demands of its disciples the constant immersion of their thinking in the *practice* of restricting the human will and its choices according to what is already known and believed to be true, even while it affirms the *principle* that all true knowledge will remain testable. There is hardly anything more authoritarian—even in the valid sense of that word—than a basic textbook in physical science. The scientific enterprise is committed to the notion that knowledge has explicit and extensive structure, with enormous complexity of detail, and therefore demands rigorous intellectual discipline as a credential. No one can seriously "get into" science without tremendous personal commitment to its philosophical ideas. In short, *science is definitely not "cool":* it is not received by, nor understandable to, the uncommitted mind, the passive mind, the mind for which reality is only immediate, unplanned, and unreflected experience. I am familiar with the experience of being considered a religious fanatic in, not one, but two contexts: that of a Christian, in relation to the non-Christian mind, and that of a scientist, in relation to the deliberately (or even passively) unscientific mind. Nearly every scientist has known the latter experience. The scientific enterprise is becoming too intellectually puritanical, too "religious" in the way of the old religion, for the new cool culture. The pure scientists realize that this is happening, but most fail to recognize its cultural depth, just as evangelicals often fail to realize the depth of contemporary culture's estrangement from biblical ideas of God, man, and salvation. I have sat in on many discussions of pure scientists concerned with encouraging more interest in science by young people; the specific concerns expressed, and the conception of the job to be done and methods to be used, reminded me very much of the endless and mostly ineffectual attempts to improve techniques of evangelism that go on in evangelical churches.

One must keep in mind that most of this alienation is not expressed in philosophically explicit terms. There are, of course, the surface manifestations in counterculture. We do have increasing numbers of incense after-burners and inner spacemen; we do have more people who deliberately refuse objective reality as an illusion, or regard the questions it poses as a kind of nonsense. One of the curious features of the growth of Far Eastern religion[9] in our culture is the popularity of those forms which introduce it as *technique.* This is true whether one considers physiological or biological technique (the use of drugs, incense, yoga), psychological technique (as in transcendental meditation and related programs), or intellectual technique (as in the forms of Zen which deliberately reflect questions about reality back into the existential consciousness). To the naive, it might be thought that people committed to and involved with life-as-technique would also be those most committed to "objectivity" and therefore least vulnerable to the basic thrust of Far Eastern religion. But this is not so, and it illustrates the fundamental difference between science and technology. Technology was never alien to Far Eastern thought, because *technology and technique as such never raise the mechanistic problems of the real world to the level of intrinsic intellectual significance;* their concern is pragmatic, not rational.

The resurgence of superstition and magic, growing interest in the occult and the demonic, is another aspect of explicit countercultural rejection of the validity of science, though of course it involves far more than that. Superstition and magic never really died out in Western culture, even when the idolatry of science was at flood tide. Indeed, for most people, science was only a new sort of magic; they could never share in the scientist's enthusiasm to see "how it is all put together." Magic is pure technique, divorced from reason. Its concern is with power and the will to power, not with reflective understanding of an objective, faithfully consistent reality. In fact it denies that such understanding has relevance, and expects caprice, not order, in the world. The attitude of the magic and occult movement in our culture, therefore, is *not to deny the results of science, but rather to downplay and devalue their intellectual and philosophical significance in relation to reality.* The style of its expression is to pour scorn on the tradition of science as mere child's play in comparison with the real secrets of power known only to the initiated. If magic and the practice of the occult *were* only humbug, such hostile attitudes could have no impact on the vitality of science as a tradition. Unfortunately, the culture has again become aware of the reality of demonic power, a reality to which science *as such* can make no response. For those who have perceived the power of darkness which is possible, and is suggested so deliberately in movies like *The Exorcist,* of what importance is it that a scientific explanation of the phenomena involved could be given? The *meaning* is obviously something else.

It is just here that a powerful temptation exists for the Christian. The Christian knows that demonic power is real. His response to it is not mere disbelief; he does not have to explain it away. But he is very likely to fall into the trap of giving it an authority and a reality which it does not actually possess. He is liable to accept *the magical view of the world* (even though he rejects magic on moral grounds) and thereby devalue and discard the image of the world as a consistent, orderly reality—the great treasure of the scientific enterprise. He is the more likely to do this if he thinks of science as a tradition hostile to Christianity. This is a terrible and tragic error, not only for the future of science but for the health of mankind. To this temptation, the New Testament critique of magic and the demonic offers a powerful antidote; it is in complete harmony with, and encourages, the scientific understanding of the world. "An idol", says St. Paul, "has no real existence. . . . For us there is one God, the Father, from whom are all things and for whom we exist, and one Lord, Jesus Christ, through whom are all things and through whom we exist" (1 Cor. 8:4–6 RSV). And then on the same topic (the devotion and worship of pagan idols) he says two chapters later: "Do I imply then that food offered to idols is anything, or that an idol is anything? *No, I imply that what pagans sacrifice they offer to demons and not to God"* (1 Cor. 10:19–20, RSV). The relevant exegesis is clear. The alleged secrets of magic and the occult have no real existence. Everything real, *everything that can be objectively known,* derives its existence from God and

His purposes—purposes expressed in creation through our Lord Jesus Christ. Demonic power comes into the world in *the intentions of the human will,* and *in the perceptions of the world* which the human mind receives under the influence of those intentions. Demonic power is not material, but spiritual; it can be realized or made actual in the world only through the deliberate acquiescence, or the enslavement, of the human will in the Satanic one, and the altered perception of the world and its phenomena which man makes possible by choosing to believe a lie. As a Christian, I do not deny the reality of demonic power; but I do deny more heartily than any mere materialist that there is any objective reality or truth in magic or the occult.

Unfortunately, our culture is moving the other way: back to superstition and magic, back to irrationality, in the end, back to fear and darkness. Not all the leaders of this trend are dressed as black sorcerers and Satanists. Some masquerade as rational thinkers, analyzing the evils of the objective approach to reality, discovering that the biblical idea of nature and man's place in it is the source of our environmental problems. Theodore Roszak's incredibly naive recommendation that we deliberately return to a pagan mystical participation in nature in order to avoid the evils of technology is typical of such thinking.[10] It *is* naive for reasons I have already indicated. Roszak has evidently never understood the difference between science and technology, or between a realistic epistemology of objective knowledge and the superficial myths of positivism. He supposes that if we deliberately devalue or suppress the ideas of reality, truth, and knowledge relevant to the scientific enterprise, then we would somehow avoid enslavement by technology. This is an attractive and ancient lie: ignore one clear truth for the sake of a greater truth. With the death of science, technology and the manipulative society will not disappear. Instead they will acquire a dark and cruel quality, since there will be no need even to pay lip service to the ideal of objective truth.

These and other explicit countercultural rejections of the concept of objective reality are important and dangerous, but since they are openly hostile to science, their effect on it is limited. The really serious threat to the scientific enterprise is less explicit and much more widespread. The survival of the scientific tradition requires that its ideals and practice be passed on to succeeding generations. *But science is not "cool." It is not received by the passive mind, the uncommitted, undisci-*

plined mind, the mind which has known reality only as immediate experience without structure or reflection. Increasingly, the cool mind is the sort of mind we encounter in the university classroom.

I must emphasize as strongly as possible that *we must understand the phenomenon of the cool youth culture in religious and philosophical terms.* It is a serious blunder to appraise it as a result of educational technique, or as a superficial behavior pattern induced by prolonged exposure to the cool media of cinema and television. Certainly, the cool media create an image of reality, an emphasis on immediate existential impression, which must be destroyed or superseded if there is to be structured learning. Certainly, it is true that sloppy, unstructured, undisciplined modes of "education"—such as oral, rather than written, French; *gestalt*-based, rather than structure-based, reading instruction; rootless "values and issues" social studies, rather than factual history—leave students ignorant, unsure of what they know, and bored. But the problem is deeper. Young people acquire an overall perception of the nature of reality in the joint indiscipline of home and school; *but this is fused into a total synthesis, a complete lifestyle, in the religion of the pop culture.* This culture and the music and art forms it employs have an increasingly powerful hold on young people, precisely at that age when their attention and energy should be turning to the rich and complex historical and cultural traditions of the West. The message of pop culture is almost pure existentialism. The "cool" person takes life as it comes; nothing deserves commitment except the feeling of the moment. This stance rejects *even in principle* any idea of intellectual or spiritual authority, because such an authority presupposes an objective truth as standard. The age span affected by the pop culture is growing—at both ends. More and more young people are unable to understand or to endure the demands of serious study in university. Objective evidence of the changes produced by pop culture can be found in deteriorating performance levels in the basic skills of literacy, coherent expression, arithmetic and logic. I can illustrate the impact of these changes by a few examples drawn from my own experience:

a. "Oh, I don't want to *understand* it; just show me how to *do* it so I can pass the exam." (a freshman chemistry student's remark to a lecturer attempting to explain key concepts). What idea of knowledge is implied here?

b. Student in professor's office seeking help (and hence relatively serious about his work): "I can't understand Chapter 15." Professor: "How do you know? Have you done the problems?" Student: "No; I just can't understand them." Professor: "Have you *tried* any of the problems?" Student: "No; I can't understand them." Unless he could understand the problem, and its answer, in a single intuitive perception, this student felt that there was no point in making the emotional commitment, running the risk of error, and enduring the discipline of putting even a single mark down on paper. Such people cannot become scientists—or serious scholars in any discipline.

c. Last year I talked with a student who was doing poor work but who showed evidence of remarkable ability. He admitted that he knew he was capable of much higher achievement and that the problem was his failure to commit himself to the required discipline. His reason for that failure surprised me by its clarity. Although he allowed that he found the distractions of wine, women, and song pleasant, his fundamental belief was that a conscious decision to alter the pattern of his experience—and his character—by rational choice, would be artificial, and "against the way life is supposed to be." As far as I can tell, he had acquired this ethos from the pop culture, not directly from existentialist philosophy. This student was remarkable in that he had understood his feelings and could describe them in coherent sentences; for every one like him there are a hundred others who feel the same way and *act it out* without ever analyzing it. Is this really so surprising, when we remember that this is a generation which has grown up listening to music, often of great artistry, which describes all authority and discipline as absurd and futile?[11]

I should like to close this discussion with an observation which is consistent with the arguments I have advanced and also points a useful moral. I have observed that, in the great majority of cases, Western students who are attracted to science, and are able to excel at it, come from family and cultural backgrounds of a specific type. They have been subjected to a strong emphasis on the value of personal discipline, hard work, and moral responsibility (qualities that make up the much maligned and fast-disappearing "Protestant ethic"); and they have usually been exposed to an idealistic tradition and a strong commitment to the objectivity of truth and goodness, usually embedded in a matrix of religious tradition. The religion may be Judaism or any of the forms of Christianity. In many cases, students may be in process of *rejecting* the specifically religious elements in their background; but the interest in science is retained because they have not rejected the idea of an ordered universe acquired from that background. Since God is in heaven, the world is rational. What one almost never finds are students with a consciously existentialist lifestyle—no matter what philosophy they expound. The moral is clear: How will the scientific enterprise survive if most future scientists have to come from such backgrounds? As mass culture (and new generations of parents) drift away from the concept of an objective truth, how explicitly religious would a background need to be (in the Judeo-Christian sense) to produce scientifically minded young people? If the church can overcome its traditional hostility to science, Christians could play an important role in the future preservation not only of philosophical ideals but also the scientific enterprise itself by practicing pure science as a serious Christian vocation. It would not be the first time the church has preserved the treasures of an earlier age.

I myself am inclined to think that in the long run the scientific enterprise may not survive. I note the relevant irony in the biblical story of Project Babel: God did not destroy what they had built. Their language became confused, there was a breakdown in communication and in their understanding of what they were doing; *so they stopped building.*

I'm aware that this view of the future of science may seem visionary and perhaps unduly pessimistic. Christians are not the only pessimists on this subject; morale in pure science is low these days. I could be wrong. The future has an enormous capacity for surprise. I suppose I feel a bit like the weather forecaster. I would rather warn of a coming disaster and be proved wrong by events than say nothing.

SPIRITUAL DIMENSIONS OF SCIENCE

In the foregoing discussion of contemporary cultural change and its potential threat to the scientific tradition, I have tried, first, to create some appreciation for the extreme fragility of science. It is no accident that science arose when and where it did, and it is a mistake to assume that science will survive regardless of cultural change. Second, I have tried to show that the cultural forces and ideas which threaten the survival of science are precisely the same forces and ideas which are opposed to Christianity and the biblical ideas of God, man, and the world. The church has nothing to gain, and a great deal to lose, by the death of the scientific tradition. (This fact needs strong emphasis. Far too many Christian intellectuals seem to welcome the new cultural synthesis because it rejects science; they seem foolishly relieved that they need no longer contend with the complicated issues which revolve around science and the problem of objective knowledge.) Last, I have stressed the determining role played by philosophical and religious beliefs in either sustaining or destroying the scientific enterprise. If the age of science comes to an end, it will really be because people collectively have not cherished and sustained that practicing faith in the reality and authority of truth which makes science possible.

My aim in making these points was not simply to show the fundamental sympathy between the scientific tradition and Christian thought, nor was it simply to suggest apologetic arguments of the sort that show how the truly valuable traditions of our culture go back to Christian and biblical roots—though many such arguments are valid and are worth making. I think that the scientific revolution, and the new kind of thinking it encourages, should properly be understood as a new expression of Christian thought, not as an irrelevant and divergent secularism. Otherwise, I do not believe we can theologically understand the astonishing success of the enterprise. A bad tree does not produce good fruit, nor a wrong attitude to truth, knowledge. There must be "spiritual dimensions" to the whole business.

Now, there are two interpretations of the expression "spiritual dimensions of science" which I certainly do *not* intend at all, and to avoid misunderstanding I should specifically exclude them here. In the first place, I certainly do *not* mean that the scientific enterprise —or any other creative cultural enterprise of man, whether in Adam *or* in Christ—is in any sense a vehicle or means of salvation for man. God's saving power is revealed in Jesus Christ personally. It is not to be found in the church as such, nor in "Christendom," nor in secular culture affected by Christian belief or Christian hope. This is not merely an evangelical manifesto; it is the clear teaching of the Word of God. The tendency to replace the gospel of Christ by a purely human "salvation" is the characteristic mark of secularism and humanism.

Nor, second, do I mean that there is some special "spiritual" quality to human experience in science itself, which would set it apart in principle from other human activities. We do not necessarily get closer to God by thinking about things scientific—or things theological—than we would be washing pots and pans like Brother Lawrence.

By "the spiritual dimensions of science," I mean that there are serious implications—including theological ones—of the scientific tradition for Christian understanding. Assuming, as I have suggested, that the scientific enterprise really is a valid new development in Christian thought, and not something which diverges from it, what are the lessons we can learn and the problems we have to consider? Because of the scientific revolution, we can have an appreciation of some aspects of creation and our own identity that did not exist, and could not have existed, for the medieval mind. There is a spiritual authenticity to science that medieval theology either ignored or denied would be even possible. In view of the evident success of science, the church now concedes the legitimacy of the enterprise *itself;* but it has never taken the idea of science seriously at a *philosophical* level, and *therefore it remains medieval at heart.* The inadequacies and ambivalences resulting from that medieval outlook create difficulties in framing a proper Christian response to non-Christian ideas of the world, and make us strangely silent at a time when the world has become acutely conscious of its own intellectual chaos; *silent, because we ourselves have not understood things properly.*

In this short essay I could not hope to give an adequate critique of this medievalism of contemporary Christian thought, much less formulate an adequate alternative to it. What I can do is sketch the outlines of the problem as I see it, and suggest some useful avenues for constructive thought. I have called this essay "the spiritual dimensions of science" because I am convinced that an important key to our understanding must come from thinking through the philosophical and theological implications of the revolution which shattered the medieval world. I want first to look at medievalism itself, and suggest why the new attitudes which so clearly expressed themselves in the scientific revolution were a necessary critique and a proper response to the inadequacies of medieval thinking: this is the *historical dimen-*

sion. Second, I want to look at the intellectual problem of the philosophy of science to ask whether it has any useful bearing on the Christian conception of truth and knowledge, and I want to suggest, with some qualifications, that it does: this is the *philosophical,* or *epistemological, dimension.* Finally, very briefly, and very much more tentatively and speculatively, I want to record some general impressions I have formed as a physical scientist and a Christian about the enormous spiritual significance of the material world: I call this the *metaphysical dimension.*

The Historical Dimension.   "The Kingdom of Heaven," Jesus said to His disciples, "is like a grain of mustard seed; it is the smallest of all seeds, but when it is planted in the earth, it sprouts and becomes a large tree, big enough that the birds of the air roost in its branches" . (Matt. 13:31–32, RSV). Of all the explanations of this parable of Jesus, the one I like best is the one I first heard as a child: this is a picture of the cultural history of Christianity; the mustard seed depicts the characteristic small beginnings of the Christian community—it is nothing in the world's sight; the bush or tree is the institution and the culture it creates by its growth; and the birds of the air symbolize all the cultural dependencies it may shelter, at best incidental to God's real purpose, perhaps at worst alien or even hostile to it. Of course, the tradition of my evangelical upbringing suggested that the Lord implied a negative judgment, even of Christian culture, in this parable: the overgrown mustard bush, and surely the birds roosting in it, are undesirable results. But I really think Jesus deliberately left this value judgment *unresolved,* even though He equally deliberately suggests by the story the possibility of alien or evil cultural influences. *He was describing what always happens,* and leaving the assessment of good and evil open to us. And it is this very fact which itself provides the essential critique of the entirely negative view of Christian culture: even the most sincerely evangelical and biblical community keeps sprouting up into some form of culture and some sort of institutions, which depend on the climate and the soil in which that seed roots. It is no use, then, pretending that we draw nothing from past or present culture; nor can we create or recover an exclusively biblical culture *merely* by rejecting what we currently perceive as alien or negative in culture. The mustard bush always grows up anyway.

The relevance of this to our present topic is that by a purely negative appraisal of cultural development since 1500, or by ignoring it, evangelical thought does not so much recover a truly biblical cultural form, as it does react backward to an earlier cultural basis that has already been found wanting in certain crucial respects, namely, the pattern of medieval thought. In addition, since by doing this the church fails to understand contemporary life in a balanced way, it is made more vulnerable to the great dangers of the present age—its ignorant materialism, its obsession with technique, and its obsession with subjective feelings.

The general outline of a negative criticism of modern culture is already familiar, and I have referred to it earlier. In this analysis, modern man is seen as an apostate and the entire cultural development as an expression of his apostasy. The line of development can be summarized briefly as follows: Having rejected the authority of divine revelation, man abandons belief in an objectively real God, and begins to regard religious knowledge as subjective. His attention then turns to himself as the center of thought and action in the world, and to the secular world as the only valid *object* of his creative thought; this is the humanism of the Renaissance. As a part of this shift he is then committed to his own *autonomy,* that is, to himself as a self-originated authority, as the starting point for knowing all truth and discovering all meaning. But man's project to do this turns sour as he finds that his objective knowledge of the world as machine provides him no identity other than that of an animal or even merely that of a machine. The more he affirms the picture of the world without God and denies the necessity of the *divine* image, the more he destroys the possibility of finding *any* image for himself in his experience of the world. This produces an increasing despair and a retreat into pure subjectivism, which manifests itself in his art and his philosophy, and in his deliberate moral debasement of himself. The description has been very fully drawn by Francis Shaeffer and many others. For Shaeffer, the Christian response to contemporary culture is seen entirely as *antithesis,* that is, a denial of all its conclusions and a deliberate return to the intellectual (and spiritual) framework which was abandoned at the outset.[12]

I stated earlier that, as a critique of apostasy and its causes and as an account of the results of apostasy in culture, this negative appraisal is in main valid and very important. But I do not think it is the whole story, nor do I think that antithesis *alone* constitutes an adequate response to the problem.

It seems to me that the world view which is idealized and aimed at by the message of antithesis alone—whether consciously or not—is in some ways not so much *biblical* as it is *medieval*. My point is only underscored if someone replies, as a great many evangelicals do, by asking in what respects the medieval position is not biblical, for this shows clearly that the difference between them is not appreciated. I notice a great enthusiasm lately for the medieval cultural and artistic synthesis among Christian intellectuals, and while this movement has very vital elements, especially in its appreciation of symbolism, the medieval view as a synthesis is deficient in fundamental respects. The breakup of that synthesis in 1500 was the result not simply of apostasy, but also of the failure of medieval thought to give a satisfactory account of reality.

The inadequacy of medieval thought is a complex problem for the Christian, who recognizes its biblical symbolism. However, the problem is focused very clearly by the possibility and the actual rise of science, which is the significant positive achievement of the modern age and indeed has been its one great sustaining impulse. This impulse was able to sustain culture for four centuries after the collapse of medieval synthesis, *because it is really a biblical impulse.* The purely negative critique of modern culture, critique by antithesis, is strangely silent on the subject of science and the meaning of the scientific enterprise; this silence is the most eloquent evidence possible that it is a critique with essentially medieval roots.

In case you have forgotten it, or taken it for granted, I should like to depict for you the magnitude of the achievement of science. In doing so, I feel a bit like the apostle Paul, who begged leave of his Corinthian readers to speak as a fool. I also confess the limitation of my perspective as a physical scientist; knowing the limits of my field as well as its potentialities, I have encountered far less often than others the arrogance and unwarranted claims of scientism masquerading as science, and this makes my outlook a rosier one.

In the recent past, we have been able to add splendid full-color views of the landscape of Mars to the extraordinary picture book which already contains views of men walking and even pleasure-driving on the moon, and, most stunning of all, an incredibly beautiful look at our own home seen from outside, a look generations before us dreamed of having. We have not only fulfilled the dream of Copernicus and Kepler; *we have manifested the astonishing reality of the truth it contained.* With those pictures we can also remember the awed reaction of man, whether he heard again the word of God speaking, or the optimistic humanism of Neil Armstrong speaking the word of man: man understanding his *humanity,* grasping for a fleeting instant one tiny glimpse of the meaning of the *imago Dei,* and that only a fragment—for "we see not yet all things put under him" (Heb. 2:8, KJV). No Christian can worship the greatness of man at that or any other moment; but no Christian can refrain from astonishment at the purpose of the Maker, seen in the majestic size of the ruin which is Adam. Surely the gifts and calling of God are irrevocable.

And this glossy picture book is only the easiest one to read; there is a whole library. I think of the healing power of modern medicine, and I remember Pasteur, Fleming, and thousands of others doing their painstaking chemistry, or I think of a colleague even now struggling to design molecules which will fool cancer cells into starving themselves. I think of all the wonderful machines, clumsy at first, but finally simple and beautiful: the jet plane and the high-speed computer, the telescope and the laser, each one the manifest embodiment of the authority that truth gives to those who obey it. I think lastly of a book with far fewer readers, which depicts the elegance and beauty of the fundamental mathematics and physics of the world, but which I have had the privilege of looking at; I wish words would permit me to tell what I have seen there to you who cannot read it, for in that book it is not man's authority but the beauty and majesty of truth alone which is celebrated.

I suspect, however, that even now my speech as a fool is going to be cut short by two professedly Christian criticisms. The first one is more familiar to us, and lately we have been learning to dismiss it and the attitude behind it as mistaken, though we do not often know why. This is the attitude which has always regarded the whole enterprise of science as an impious blasphemy, a conspiracy of rebels against God. When it was able, this attitude opposed science by persecution, suppression of ideas, and forced recantations. More recently, it has been confined to saying loudly that "God will never allow it to succeed," and then having to eat crow when it *did* succeed. This is the same attitude which is always warning us that "the findings of true science must always agree with the Bible"—of course, meaning always its own traditional interpretation of the Bible. For whatever reasons, perhaps including simply its poor batting average, we are not inclined to take this criticism very seriously nowadays. We have generally agreed that science is a legitimate human enterprise; otherwise we could not face the inconsistency of enjoying its benefits.

The second criticism is more subtle and much more widely believed, and it is the one which really concerns me when I talk about medieval thinking in the church. It is the sort of criticism which begins by saying (of scientific truth), "Oh well, *that kind of truth* . . . isn't really very important" or "isn't real truth." *That view is essentially a medieval one.* For whom, and for what purpose, is *any* truth "important"? In relation to what activity is the reality of truth demonstrated, and how is that to be manifested? I hope I have already made it amply clear that the truth accessible to man in science is not a *saving* truth; after all, that is not its purpose. In the section to follow on the epistemological dimension, I shall take a more detailed look at the problem of truth and knowledge, especially the issue of "*real* truth" (vs. "relative truth"). Here, I am concerned with an historical perspective, and the essential point about this criticism historically is the value it teaches men to place on scientific activity, which is—let's face it—a very small value indeed. It is all very easy for us to talk condescendingly about science, surrounded as we are by its concrete achievements. Assuming a twelfth-century person could glimpse the scientific mastery of the modern world, I'm sure he would not be as quick as we are to dismiss our knowledge as "unimportant." He would have a different problem: he would be tempted to think us either angels or black sorcerers. Conversely, I think we would discover our greatest difficulty in making him understand that there is such a thing as a true scientific explanation of what we call natural phenomena. And, if we want him to understand that, we had better be very careful not to indulge in sophistries regarding whether such knowledge is "*real* truth," because for him and his age the main obstacle to the discovery of science was precisely the decision they had made in advance that such knowledge is *not* "really true."

For medieval man, we recognize that the experience of the world as a direct symbol of spiritual realities was the dominant theme, influencing all his culture and indeed his very language and perceptions. This account of medieval thought and life is so familiar and so well described elsewhere[13] that it needs no development here. The over-arching meaning of the whole was the Christian drama of God's salvation of mankind, and all history was the playing out of that drama in the lives of men as individuals and collectively in the integrated community of salvation—the City of God.

The essential weakness of the medieval world view is its failure to appreciate the authenticity—the genuine depth and integrity—of creation. As Christians we recognize the profound truth in the medieval understanding of the world as symbol of a spiritual meaning; but we should also recognize that medieval man had made far too cheap an estimate of the stage scenery and far too simple a resumé of the plot line of the drama. The medieval world view always makes me feel that the world could really be made of papier-maché; the construction is artificial, lacks depth or inner consistency, and has a fabric quite unrelated to the drama itself. The great theological discovery implied by the scientific revolution is that God did not make a papier-maché, throw-away universe, but a real one, having its own integrity. Therefore, the dominion which God gave to man in Adam and redeemed in Christ is really *infinite,* within its own consistent terms as a creation. Medieval thought seems to have missed this idea completely, and in my opinion the church has really not considered it thoroughly, either.

In the Middle Ages, a very specific phrase was used by philosophers and theologians to characterize all scientific or mechanistic explanations of natural phenomena: "saving the appearances," or "saving the phenomena." This turns out to be an *a priori* value judgment or truth judgment on the meaning of science, which is the same judgment as the criticism of science I mentioned earlier, that is, that scientific truth is "not important" or is "not *real* truth."

A useful illustration is provided by ancient astronomy and medieval attitudes to it. The Babylonians, who attributed astrological significance to the heavenly bodies, developed very elaborate and accurate empirical schemes for predicting their apparent motions. These schemes were later comprehended in the integrated cosmology of the Ptolemaic system, with its geocentric system of crystal spheres. Now, *we* would probably *not* wish to call Babylonian astronomy a *science,* even though it had very accurate predictive power; in a word, we consider their astrology to be nonsense.[14] We recognize in the Ptolemaic system a certain amount of rational ordering, enough that we might call it a *scientific theory;* but of course we take the view that, successful as it was, it is in fact *not true*— that is, it does not describe the actual state of affairs. On the other hand, we praise the Copernican theory as the first step toward "the truth." *But medieval thinking was not like ours; it did not consider that any scientific explanation might be entertained as "true"* (in the actual sense in which I have just used it for modern thought). *Scientific explanations only "saved the phenomena,"* that is, they were regarded merely as computational devices for predicting the observations, just as we should regard the Babylonian prediction schemes, and they could have no *real* meaning. Medieval thought always assumed that the *real* explanation is that God causes phenomena to happen; they believed that any real understanding would always be intrinsically and directly theological. But they meant this in a trivial and naive sense (and even speculated metaphysically about it). Perhaps the meaning of my comment about a papier-maché universe becomes clearer now, for surely our criticism of their thinking is not that we deny that God "causes things to happen," but that we realize His agency is not trivial, like that of the puppeteer or stagehand; the creation has its own given authenticity.

Indeed, what was truly revolutionary about Copernicus was not his specific model of the universe, most features of which were proposed much earlier; but the fact that Copernicus insisted that his model was or could be *actually true,* and clearly rejected for the first time the medieval doctrine that all scientific theories merely save the appearances. It is hard for us to grasp the crucial psychological importance of this change for science. Destruction of the medieval doctrine made it possible to take the scientific enterprise seriously and opened the way for the scientific revolution. Yet when people argue that the truth known by science is "not important," or "not real truth," to some degree they are reaffirming that science only saves the appearances, and that is a medieval thought pattern. The whole problem of creation and its dependence on God is much richer than that, and we cannot understand it by retreating to a medieval frame of mind.

In a very thought-provoking book, Reijer Hooykaas has discussed the historical roots of the scientific revolution and its relation to religious and philosophical belief. He shows that an astonishing proportion of the early scientists were convinced and serious Christians who thought deeply about the theological significance of science, and he suggests that it is no accident that they also were the pioneers of modern science itself. His discussion provides a further critique of the inadequacy of some medieval thinking—and, by implication, of some current evangelical ideas. This critique arises out of a discussion of the relevance of the dispute between rationalist and nominalist philosophies to the rise of science. For more complete discussion readers are urged to refer to Professor Hooykaas's work.[15]

The medieval controversy between rationalism and nominalism is very complex, and can here be treated in only summary form. In general, the *rationalists* believed in the *a priori necessity of rational order* and the "absolute truth of reason." They, therefore, tended to emphasize the fundamental role of reason, particularly deductive Aristotelian logic expressed in syllogisms, in arriving at truth. The more extreme rationalists even argued that God Himself was *bound* to act according to the principles of reason, not by His sovereign choice, but as a matter of necessity (though most rationalists felt uncomfortable with this position and preferred to admit that God is the source of reason, just as he is the source of goodness). The *nominalists,* on the other hand, insisted that there is *no necessary rational order in the universe;* it is all as it happens to be, that is, *contingent.* They argued that the forms reason gives to our experience of the world are conveniences which at best happen to agree with reality and at worst are only constructions of our minds. More extreme forms of nominalism deny that any logical classes or categories really exist, saying instead that we experience everything real, not as instances of necessary logical categories, but as individual and specific entities. More generally, nominalists did acknowledge the *validity* of reason, but they saw it as a *contingent* validity derived from the sovereign will of God. They considered the rationalist belief in the *a priori necessity of reason* an impious blasphemy, since it placed reason above God.

This is of course only a sketch of a controversy which has many ramifications in modern thought, and there are philosophical and theological weaknesses in both the nominalist and rationalist positions. The relevant issue for us, however, is not the controversy in full, but its significance for the rise of science. We want to know what nominalism and rationalism meant or implied for the thinking of the early scientists. By careful historical study, Professor Hooykaas has convincingly argued that, with one or two exceptions (notably, Descartes), the early scientists, the pioneers of the scientific revolution, all worked within the nominalist tradition, in most cases consciously so.

Why did *nominalism* seem to these Christian men to encourage science, and rationalism to be opposed to it? Professor Hooykaas's study suggests several reasons. First, these early scientists emphasized their appreciation of the intellectual humility and openness of the nominalist view—and contrasted it with the arrogance of rationalism as they had encountered it. They stressed the idea that rationalism fosters pride and an overconfident dogmatism, and they never tired of pointing out that this produces both error and a closed mind. Francis Bacon epitomized this attitude when he insisted that if a man wishes to know reality, he must abandon the dogmatic confidence of his pride in reason alone and sit down humbly before the revelation of God, whether that were the book of Scripture or the book of nature. This parallel between scientific and religious knowledge, both of which are to be acquired by "reading the revelation of God," and not by *a priori* reason, is a favorite and important emphasis of the early scientists. The parallel has been deliberately ignored by secular accounts of the scientific revolution, which identify *empiricism* (i.e., sense experience) as the important ingredient. Professor Hooykaas shows us that for the early scientists the relevant issue is not empiricism *per se,* but the nominalist tradition, which emphasized contact with reality itself as the only source of truth. These early thinkers thought of themselves as "empiricists" with respect to Scripture as well as with respect to creation. It is an attitude we need to examine deeply if we claim to believe in revelation.

The second attitude which appears to have been fostered by this nominalism of early scientists entails, not a complete rejection of the validity of reason, but its acceptance as a useful tool of the human mind. As I mentioned, earlier thrusts of nominalism had sometimes denied all validity to abstract reasoning; this new nominalism retains reason, but gives it *a human place,* not a divine one. It is a useful skill, like our perceptive skills, but it must not be made into an absolute, and it must be educated by constant encounter with reality. The importance and fruitfulness of this attitude cannot possibly be over-estimated.

Third, and partly as a result of the first two attitudes, *this nominalism creates or heightens the distinction between truth as an objective reality, existing independently and outside myself, and my knowledge of the truth, which involves the interpretation, by my reason, of my experience of that reality.* This was important for the early scientists, who were keenly aware that they had much to learn before they could competently think the Creator's thoughts after Him. They clearly saw that the main mistake of rationalist thought is to confuse the rational representation of truth with truth itself, and they understood that this mistake fosters dogmatism and pride.

In the next section I shall describe in more detail the problem of knowledge as a philosophical and theological problem. Here I am raising a more general question, which concerns us as people, rather than as philosophers or theologians. We have seen that the early scientists explained their empirical approach to nature by comparing it to a certain attitude which they thought a Christian should have toward Scripture as the revelation of God. *Perhaps we now need to think about the parallel in reverse.* The early scientists recognized that the sterility and error of previous "natural philosophy" was in large part due to rationalism and the attitudes rationalism encourages. Is it the case that to some extent Christian thinking is still instinctively rationalistic in the medieval sense? Many times in the history of conflict between theology and science, we have later realized that the problem was not created by Scripture itself, but by the interpretation of Scripture within some traditional *system* having certain *a priori* rational ideas built into it. In effect, the fullness of Scripture had been confined and shaped to the limits of that system. For example, the doctors of the Roman church argued that Galileo was wrong to believe the Copernican theory because, they said, it contradicted Scripture (in particular, Eccles. 1:4). We cannot doubt the sincerity of their thinking, *within their system,* but today we can easily see that their system was more a product of their minds than of either Scripture or the creation, and the main thing that prevented them from learning this was the arrogance of dogmatic rationalism. Is the same pattern perhaps being repeated in some present-day conflicts? If so, the reason will be the same, namely, that we are being more dogmatic and rationalistic about our *system of interpretation* of God's revelation than is warranted by the human condition of ignorance. What does it *really* mean to "sit down humbly before the revelation in Scripture"? I am afraid that for many people it means only a blind and unquestioning acceptance of some traditional system. Rationalism and rationalistic systems are characteristically *closed;* they deny the possibility of ignorance or of an open question. We cannot ever avoid the possibility that our understanding of God's Word is colored by our culture and may be mistaken in some points; but we can and should avoid the folly of medieval rationalism, which leads us to refuse the opportunity of developing and correcting our understanding.

Happily, there are signs that in actual practice the church *is* learning the habit of sitting down humbly before the Word of God. In the last few decades Christian people seem less eager to be dogmatic on every issue. They are more open to discussion, less fearful of disagreement where there is love, readier to admit they do not have the answer to a problem and to leave it unresolved before God and each other. They are not afraid to be wrong and not afraid to ask questions. They have come to understand that "defense of the truth" may not necessarily be identical to "defense of our position." God has become intellectually bigger to them, just as their understanding of the physical universe has outgrown the papier-maché medieval picture. This is good. Our confidence may be increased and our anxiety lessened when we can recognize that this new attitude of intellectual openness is the very same attitude which proved so fruitful in the scientific enterprise. In that sense, the church *has* actually begun to learn some lessons from the history of science.

The Epistemological Dimension.   *Epistemology* is the philosophy of knowledge and knowing. Its development in Western thought is closely connected with the rise and development of the scientific enterprise and with the disintegration of the medieval system. For modern man, who has no knowledge of God to speak of, the statement "I know . . ." is automatically centered on objects in the creation around him, or upon himself as the knower. The Christian claims to *know* more; if faithful to the language of the Word of God, he not only says "I *believe* in (and on) God," but also says "I know . . . ," in relation to God Himself and to those truths He has revealed in Jesus Christ. This states the problem directly, because we all know that the immediate reply of the non-Christian is to try to correct our language: "Don't you really mean to say 'I believe'?" If we agree with him about that, we will have made an important mistake in our thinking. He understands that to say "*I believe*" is to say something personal—no matter how significant—about myself; but to say "*I know*" is to say that there is a reality outside myself that does not depend on me to be what it is—and that it can also be known by someone else. Since Christians *do* mean to say just such things about the object of Christian faith, they are not correct to settle merely for "I believe." But then we shall have to give some serious thought to truth, knowing, and believing. We must try to understand the situation adequately for ourselves and we must try to present a reasonable explanation of it to others. As I understand it and will discuss it here, the job of a Christian epistemology is to justify the use of the statement "*I know . . . ,*" which retains the idea of this crucial "*otherness,*" or objectivity,[16] of the objects—whether we speak of created things *or of God*— yet retains in a biblical way the essential role of faith-in-knowledge.

This conception of the problem of knowing is of course not new, but perennially recurrent wherever real knowledge exists. I regard it as the central and authentic conception. Its source is biblical, and though *both* medieval ideas of knowing *and* the epistemological tradition of modern philosophy spring from it, the evolution of each has been in large part unfaithful to and divergent from it. As we are all aware, modern philosophy has schizophrenically attempted to remove faith from knowledge (positivism) and knowledge from faith (existentialism);[17] but medieval rationalism was equally divergent in its attempt to identify the divine truth with a rationalistic logical system that reduced faith to mere intellectual dogmatism and made knowledge founded on human reason into an absolute. Nevertheless, from time to time the correct perception of the epistemological problem recurs, which recognizes that all knowing involves, and is sustained by, faith. We already noted the attitudes of the early scientists toward Christian and scientific knowledge. A more recent expression can be found in the work[18] of the late Professor C. A. Coulson, a man beloved by those of us who knew him, whether as Christian or scientist.

My aim here is to make some remarks on this problem of a Christian epistemology, and to sketch some important features which an adequate solution should possess. The actual development of such a solution is an enormous task, to which serious Christian scholars should commit themselves. As I have implied by the title of this essay, I believe that the scientific revolution and epistemological experience acquired from the scientific enterprise have a vital relevance to that task. As the scientific tradition and scientific knowledge grew, so did philosophical interest in the problem of truth and man's relation to it. It is significant (as well as amusing) that it is the very culture which has been so productive of real knowledge of this sort that is also uniquely obsessed with the problem of doubt and the problem of the existence of objective truth. The obvious fact that we do possess scientific knowledge, and the ability to discover it, is precisely what creates our puzzled interest in epistemology. Therefore, many of the problems raised by philosophy regarding scientific knowledge are legitimate ones, whose *proper* solution or discussion is relevant and worthwhile to Christian thought.

We have already noted that the rise of science involved a devastating critique of medieval rationalism and that this critique was essentially concerned with the problem of knowing truth. It was a consistent and practical critique because the early scientists were not interested in philosophical debate as an end in itself, but in the actual discovery of scientific truth, and they *manifested* the consistent validity of their epistemological ideas by practicing them. Earlier, I mentioned three general attitudes or ideas they held which I regard as essentially correct and extremely important to a Christian epistemology:

1. They believed the same general principles are applicable to our knowing truth, whether the source of that knowledge is creation or divine revelation. Their empirical attitude to natural phenomena was of a piece with the openness to the revelation of Scripture which marked the Reformation, and they emphasized the parallel. By implication, they equally rejected the approach of medieval rationalism to *either* kind of knowing.

2. They emphasized the distinction between *truth* as an objective reality other than and "outside" human knowers, and *knowledge,* which is the creature of the knower. The absolute claims of rational-

ism regarding theology were rejected by the later nominalists as blasphemous, undoubtedly in view of the clear witness to divine sovereignty in Scripture; once it was realized that the creation possesses inner integrity and authenticity given to it by God, the same attitude generated the empirical humility of science: what matters is not what I suppose, merely, but what creation manifests in actuality.

3. They recognized the importance of human reasoning as a *useful tool* rather than as an *a priori*, necessary absolute. This permits the correction of reasoning (as hypothetical) by comparison with *truth* (seen as the actual). Logical consistency and completeness then become useful, and even very important, characteristics of *knowledge*, but can no longer be mistaken for sufficient evidence of reality itself. Further philosophical development of this view would lead to a "psychological" appreciation of reason as a kind of epistemological extension of human perceptual skills. This is in fact the appraisal Michael Polanyi gives of the role of rationality.

Though modern philosophy arose with the developing scientific tradition, and many of its epistemological questions are interesting and important, I believe its central idea of the epistemological problem is mistaken, and is the origin of that schizophrenia of positivism and existentialism to which I have already referred. *This mistaken idea is that there is such a thing as knowledge without faith,* knowledge which entails no commitment.

Descartes is usually regarded as the first modern philosopher. He introduced this mistaken view of knowledge in an open fashion. He explicitly rejected the validity of revelation as a basis for knowledge, and proposed instead that all knowledge must be established by the knower himself. It is of the greatest significance that he was a rationalist; indeed, his thinking is really a modern continuation of the attitude implicit in medieval rationalism. This rationalism permitted him to suppose that rational knowledge and truth are the same thing; therefore he thought that the nature of all reality could be deduced by human reason, through isolating "clear and distinct ideas." Descartes proposed to start all his reasoning from the self-consciousness of the human mind: "Cogito, ergo sum—I think; therefore I am." From this, he proposed to establish *beyond doubt* the existence of all reality—including the existence of God. He would have need of neither a revelation of God *nor* a created physical universe.

What is most important about Descartes for the tradition of modern philosophy is not the folly of his rationalism, the inadequacy of which is now generally clear—with respect to creation, at least. *It is the folly of the claim to epistemological autonomy* which is implied in the cogito—that knowledge and truth must be anchored and secured from the self. "Cogito, ergo sum" is not a statement of objective knowledge, nor the result of any possible observation. It is existential awareness that whenever I do anything in relation to the world—such as thinking—I cannot avoid believing in myself in order to do so, and then acting in the framework of that commitment. This is indeed our experience; but what are the consequences of using it as a starting point for philosophy?

(1) Since Descartes asserts that subjective existential consciousness is the basis for knowledge of all reality, he is really the father of existentialism (Sartre clearly recognizes this, and call himself a Cartesian).[19] (2) Objective reality is not identified on its own terms, but as *"that which is known by me."* This places a focal emphasis on the *explicit, formal structure* of my knowledge, which is my own creature, and ignores the distinction between that and the reality which is the object of knowledge; knowledge is mistaken for *truth.* This emphasis is not congenial merely to Cartesian rationalism; even when rationalism is replaced by empiricism, *the same preoccupation with explicit formalism and logical structure of knowledge* can (and did) continue in modern philosophy. (3) The Cartesian program avoids the question of *my relation to the other which is known.* As Michael Polanyi shows, even in the case of science, that relation involves acts of deliberate commitment, trust, and faith; it is not a question of proof beyond doubt. Descartes explicitly rejects the epistemological identifications "I am he who trusts" or "I am he who believes," in favor of "I am he who knows . . . reality outside myself." Had he allowed these, he would no longer have possessed grounds for denying that revelation could be a valid source of knowledge. (4) Since there is really *no necessary or logical relation* between existential ego or its thoughts, and any objective reality, a complete cleavage can be created between those who, like Sartre, radically affirm the self but deny the necessity of responsibility to, or meaning in, an objective reality other than self, and the positivists like A. J. Ayer[20] *who attempt to prove that knowledge exists as an*

object which requires no belief by the knower, and even argue that
there *is* no "knower" because self-consciousness is an illusion. Only
the admission of a commitment relation between the subject who
knows, and the *other* which is known, can bridge that gap; this,
Descartes—and much of the modern epistemological tradition since
Descartes—steadfastly refuse to face.

I claim, then, that philosophical objectivism—the tradition which
culminates in the many varieties of positivism and analytic philosophy
—remains spiritually *Cartesian,* even though it was abandoned rationalism and the Cartesian *cogito* as technically untenable. The task
which Descartes sets for philosophy is that of creating and guarantee-
ing knowledge beyond doubt, knowledge as *object-in-itself.* Objectivism's long search for "objectivity," defined as *impersonal knowledge
from the machine of scientific methodology,* is really the continuing
attempt to perform that impossible task. There is no knowledge beyond possible doubt. The refusal to acknowledge personal participation, and the insistence upon an explicit, external formalism devoid
of personal commitment, is really the refusal to admit the necessity
of faith by the knower in reality outside himself; that is too religious
an act for autonomous man, Cain the epistemologist (Gen. 4:8–24).[21]
Indeed, in theological terms the whole thing is childishly simple. The
essence of Descartes's program is autonomy for the human mind; the
Cartesian self is a self-proclaimed God, epistemologically speaking;
and the existential task which is set by Descartes, and accepted by
much of modern philosophy, is the creation of a world from that self
as origin, a world where no faith is ever required. The present rather
sterile and confused state of analytic philosophy, preoccupied since
Wittgenstein with *disputes about words,* could quite fairly be carica-
tured as the resultant milling around at the dead end of the route:
Whatever became of objective reality?

To philosophically trained readers I must apologize for what surely
seems a glib and superficial dismissal of four hundred years of philosophy! However, I do not quite intend that. Many of the lessons learned
en route are valuable and instructive, and of course some philosophy
has a high degree of intellectual integrity. After all, modern philosophy does seem to have reached the correct conclusion, namely, that
the Cartesian program of proof beyond doubt, or knowledge without
faith, cannot be achieved. But I do maintain that a serious critique of

modern philosophy along the lines suggested here is possible, and that it will lead to the conclusions indicated.

Two philosophical studies which bear out some of the ideas suggested here, and which have had a significant formative influence upon them, are John MacMurray's *The Self As Agent,* which examines the problem of knowing and self and gives a good, clear account of the role of Descartes in shaping modern philosophy; and Michael Polanyi's *Personal Knowledge,* which shows the inescapable personal participation and personal commitment even in that least personal of activities, science. (These books are on the list of suggested reading at the end of the volume.) Some discussion of positivism on Polanyi's lines, and a critique of modern existentialism in Protestant theology, is to be found in my article cited earlier (see note 17).

In *Personal Knowledge,* Professor Polanyi shows very convincingly through a close study of science as practiced that all human knowledge—even scientific knowledge—is personal. It involves tacit, inescapable, personal participation by the knower. "Objectivity," whatever it is, does not mean *impersonality;* the impersonal validation of anything is impossible. He shows how positivist philosophy conceals or ignores personal participation by its use of deceptive and misleading language, and by its focal attention to explicit formalisms while ignoring the inarticulate and tacit elements in thinking. From the positivist viewpoint—or the Cartesian viewpoint—Polanyi's achievement is destructive, since he insists that all knowledge is sustained by personal participation and acts of personal *commitment* to what is believed by the knower to be true. In short, there is no knowing without believing (note that this does *not* necessarily mean believing *is* knowing).

Suppose, however, that we really abandon the Cartesian position and return to a more authentic conception of epistemology. We accept the importance of the distinction between truth and knowledge; we recognize knowledge as the creature of knowers; we see reason and rationality as a tool to be used skilfully. Then Polanyi's epistemological study has a positive purpose as well. He tries to construct an epistemology of personal knowledge which can legitimately end by claiming that knowledge of objective reality *does* exist. The important point is that he does this by denying the possibility of knowledge beyond doubt or risk and returning to the position of knowledge-held-in-faith, which I believe to be the only proper stance for epistemology.

In that stance, epistemology becomes a study of how human knowers acquire and use their knowledge, and not a purely formal exercise in logic. It is an epistemology of *discovery* and *application,* not a merely structural description. It is a "psychological" epistemology, as I suggested earlier. The impressive and creative achievements of abstract thought are to be understood as *conceptual* extensions of perceptual skills which man shares with other animals. Reason, with its remarkable capacity to anticipate reality, is nevertheless a conceptual tool which man has acquired on the basis of his ability to create language as the vehicle of abstract thought and communication. We could believe that, as a tool, reason is remarkably appropriate for knowing reality (and indeed we ought so to believe, in view of the astonishing success of science); we might, as Christians do, attribute that capacity to the *imago Dei;* but all the same, it is a creaturely gift, limited and fallible. In this sense, Polanyi is clearly in the nominalist tradition identified by Hooykaas,[22] and his epistemological stance is fundamentally the "naive" one of the early scientists.

According to Professor Polanyi then, my knowledge is a conceptual tool, a framework to which I commit my thinking. As with any tool, it and my commitment to it are directed toward an end I believe appropriate. To employ it as a tool, I do not examine it focally, but *indwell* it, "pour myself into it" psychologically, strive to see the world in the perspective it creates—just as when I use a hammer properly it becomes a psychological extension of myself, assumed for the focal purpose of hammering. I commit myself to my knowledge because *I believe* it is an appropriate tool in relation to the objective reality upon which it is focused; but this commitment is not an absolute and dogmatic one. On the contrary, my commitment is made in the belief and expectation that if my *knowledge* is not appropriate to the reality toward which it is focused, then *that other,* the reality itself, will manifest that inappropriateness by surprising outcomes which challenge my mistaken conceptions; on the other hand, if it is appropriate, this will also be manifest in the continuous growth of new perceptions, anticipations, and confirmations in the same outcomes. *But this amounts to an absolute commitment, not to my knowledge as such, but to the integrity and consistency of that reality which is in the Other* (cf. Heb. ii: 1–2, 6). I am acting in the faith that truth will manifest itself in this relation of humble and yet responsible commitment, in which my knowledge is never made absolute but is subject to alteration on the basis of its continuing adequacy to account for the manifest expressions of reality.

This picture of knowledge abandons the idea of a self-sustained absolute: there is no knowledge which in principle lies beyond doubt. Suppose Q to be a proposition—and hence a part of my knowledge —which refers to an objective reality. The statement "Q is true" is *not* distinguishable from the statement "I believe Q," as far as my activity or *knowledge* is concerned (except as it indicates my belief is strong). Of course, when I say "Q is true," I am *appealing* to the reality, the truth itself of which "Q" *is* true; but there is not the least thing I can do in the world to make the truth of Q manifest that can go one whit beyond the consistent thought, speech, choices, and actions which accompany the genuine statement "I believe Q." It is not my belief which makes Q valid, but if, as I believe, "Q" *is* true, then the behavior expressing "I believe Q" will issue in manifest confirmations of Q by that *other,* that *reality,* in an unspecifiable, and hitherto unanticipated, variety of outcomes.

As a practicing research scientist, I find Polanyi's view of the epistemology of science extremely satisfying in its realism, and I commend it to nonscientists and scientists alike for serious consideration in detail, even as simply an epistemology of science. In this very brief sketch of the main issue, I have had to gloss over many important technical problems, such as problems of empirical methodology and judgment, verification versus falsification, the significance and construction of formalisms and the status of mathematics, and so on; useful thinking about these has been done in modern philosophy, and more needs doing.

But of course I intend far more than an epistemology of science, for it seems to me that we are placed in fundamentally the same situation in the knowledge of God, as indeed the early scientists also assumed. And here at last is the main point of all this discussion: the Christian epistemological understanding of *knowledge whose source is revelation* should and must outgrow the medieval view, which is really rationalistic at heart.

I know by experience that merely to suggest what I have just stated brings out a barrage of statements about "subjectivism," "absolute versus relative truth," and so forth. It seems to be a popular view among some evangelicals that because *the revelation of Scripture* (rather than *the creation*) is the source of our knowledge of God, therefore such knowledge is on a radically different epistemic footing: in some way, *as knowledge,* it is "more absolute" than the knowledge we can have of creation. A second belief which is usually coupled with this one is that the *truth* about God could be fully enclosed and frozen in a deductive set of propositions (presumably created by God Himself *as* propositions and embedded in Scripture). It seems to me that this is a mistake of a medieval rationalist sort, because (a) it confuses *truth* with my *knowledge,* and (b) it assumes that some system of rational knowledge—which involves my personal participation—could limit and contain the divine truth Himself. I believe that true knowledge about God can and should be expressed in propositions; knowledge about objective reality usually is, the more complete and detailed it becomes. I believe that the Scripture is a revelation of God; like Christ, it is the *Word of God* which brings eternal life. Concerning the truths of the Christian religion which are a part of my knowledge, I say "I know . . ." as well as "I believe. . . ." But I cannot engage in the folly of medieval rationalism, which supposes that I myself in my knowledge *possess* the absolute truth coextensive with a rational closed system. My relation to truth is always *to know in faith,* just as I know the given order of creation. Truth itself remains always what it is, in God Himself, or in the given created order He has made; it is no creature of my making, as my knowledge must always be.

I believe the church must take special care not to fall back into the medieval thought pattern. It was abandoned because it proved inadequate *even with respect to creation,* not merely because of man's apostasy. Nor will it do to split truth into "real truth" of revelation and "relative truth" of creation, for that leads to schizophrenia. In the negative critique of modern philosophy, the critique of antithesis alone, there are revealing hints of this medieval thinking. For example, it is usually said in such critique that the error of modern philosophy lay in its *abandonment of presuppositional reasoning* (which marked the medieval tradition). But it should be evident from what I have said above that the error did not lie merely in that purely logical formalism, but in the denial of the possibility of revelation and in the deliberate rejection of a genuine faith-in-knowledge epistemological position. Descartes indeed denied revelation; but long before he did so, it was the *rationalist medieval theologians,* with their absurd pretensions to absolute knowledge, God-in-a-rational-box, who rejected the vital necessity of participating faith. If we would sit down humbly to learn from God's book of Scripture, as we may learn from God's book of creation—then we would *know* the truth; and the truth would make us free.

The Metaphysical Dimension.   In recent years, I have come to believe that the physical universe—*matter itself*—is much more precious and important to God's purposes than is now commonly supposed. Previously, I had always assumed that the only importance of *things* to God lay in "spiritual meaning"; but that view now seems to me in some way inadequate, or incomplete. Some of the ideas suggested here are intended to provoke thought, rather than take any position, because I'm sure I don't understand the issue very well.

This change in my thinking has come about partly from reflecting on the attitudes toward material things expressed in Scripture and partly from the experience of scientific research. In addition, about two years after I had started to think about this topic, I ran across Owen Barfield's remarkable book, *Saving the Appearances: A Study in Idolatry* (see note 13). In that book, Barfield lucidly discusses this very same question, and I am immensely indebted to him for the stimulation and clarification it has provided, even though I am not sure that I fully understand him, or, assuming that I do, that I agree with all his conclusions. Upon one matter, which I cannot take space to discuss here, he is particularly helpful: In what ways can we speak of an immanent relation between God and the material world, without falling into the error of pantheist or pagan religions? Does not the Judeo-Christian doctrine of the transcendence of God automatically exclude the possibility of matter as such having any "meaning" in relation to God? I will restrict myself here to much more direct, and, perhaps, simpler questions.

Does matter really matter? Medieval thinking was preoccupied with the world as a symbol of spiritual realities. Because of that, people of that period could not appreciate the possibility of an *authentic* creation, one which could be understood on its own terms. Through scientific understanding of material things, people living in

modern culture—non-Christian and Christian alike—have their eyes
open to creation in a completely different way. Before them is a
glimpse of the whole incredible system of the universe, seemingly
infinite not only in its physical dimensions but also in potentialities
and, above all, in the integrity and consistency of its order. They have
learned that understanding material things *as* material things is a
valid understanding and that it provides man with enormous potential
for authority and dominion in the universe.

Yet, precisely because of this understanding of creation as an *object,*
a temptation arises for us which never existed for medieval thinkers.
It is the idea of the *merely* literal, *merely* material reality, the idea that
literal, material things exist *without* any other meaning. It is not my
intention here to argue against mere materialism as a total philosophy;
I take it for granted that it is absurd. What concerns me is the effect
of this temptation for Christians.

By thinking of "spiritual significance" as something *unrelated* to
matter *as* matter, Christians also are responding to the concept of
merely literal existence. That is why some Christians have difficulty
with the doctrines of Scripture, which always link physical, "literal"
reality to spiritual reality in a peculiarly inseparable way. They try to
distinguish what is *spiritual* from what is *"merely literal,"* assuming
that "only the spiritual is important." The converse, of course, is that
the "merely literal" is not important. But then this amounts to saying
that the whole incredible universe is just stage scenery, which might
as well be papier-maché. Note that such thinking devalues not only
the scientific understanding of creation, but the creation, too. It is a
disposable throwaway, a cheap trinket God once gave to Adam, but,
compared to spiritual things, not to be taken too seriously. This
reinforces an indifferent, or even a negative, attitude to matter and to
the body that the Creator called good. Ultimately this is gnostic, not
Christian, thinking.

The most important reason we cannot pretend that the scientific
understanding of the world is irrelevant is that it would make living
a lie. In terms of all that we think, choose, and do, we are the most
ardent believers in matter that ever existed. Scientific understanding
is concretely manifest in every responsible action of our lives. If we
believe that such "secular" lives can express the life of God, as Scripture says they should, then we should not discount the things of this

earth as meaningless. Rather we must recognize that the physical reaction in all its immensity and rich complexity is also the very fabric of spiritual reality here as well; God has made them inseparable in creation.

We have the witness of Scripture that this creation itself is precious to God and important to His purposes. It is an object of divine redeeming love, and will be liberated from its present bondage to decay (Rom. 8:18–25, RSV). In some way we do not fully comprehend, matter is involved in God's eternal plans, and was not created just to throw away. There is an intimate connection between this world and that to come—as close as seed is to the living plant (I Cor. 15:35–58, RSV) —*and that world will be embodied, too.*

I suppose most human beings experience moments when they have an overwhelming sense that the world is not commonplace or ordinary, but extraordinarily beautiful and "odd" in some surprising way; and I think Christian belief would suggest that these perceptions, however distorted, are perceptions that the world is *not* "merely literal," but *means* something. The pagans knew this experience, but they mistook the meaning and worshiped the world itself as divine. Now, if scientific understanding of the material world *were* really irrelevant to God's purposes with humans, then we should find that the study of science would either interfere with this sense of surprise of queerness, or perhaps even destroy it. But it is my experience that this is precisely what does *not* happen. On the contrary, the sense of some inevitable wholeness of incredible beauty in things is intensified, and made more persistent, the better one perceives the elegance and order of the physical world structure. There is also an intellectual side to it. According to positivist dogma, thinking about science would eventually scour away all the old metaphysical feelings we have about nature; but in fact modern physics and biology are increasingly full of philosophical questions that entail fantastic metaphysical loose ends, and scientists no longer ignore them as "meaningless."

Humans have a problem of perception. We do not yet see created things as they really are—that is, as angelic beings see them (Ezek. 1:18; Rev. 4:8; I Tim. 3:16). The prophet Isaiah heard the seraphim say concerning God that "the whole earth is full of His glory" (Isa. 6:3). We *shall* see like that, in the world to come—quite "literally." What that might be like is sometimes hinted in the biblical descriptions: the morning stars *singing together* for joy, the hills leaping with life, God seeing that what He had made was *good,* the heavens *declaring* the glory of God. To that perception, science in all its elegance and rationality is not *irrelevant.* It is simply *incomplete.*

NOTES

1. Julian Huxley, *Evolution in Action* (New York: Harper and Bros., 1953; Mentor, PB); *Religion Without Revelation* (New York: Harper and Bros., 1927; Mentor, PB).

2. Harvey Cox, *The Secular City* (New York: MacMillan Co., 1966).

3. Dietrich Bonhoeffer, *Letters and Papers from Prison* (New York: MacMillan Co., 1962), pp. 194–200.

4. Compare the oddly specific passage in Rev. 13:16–18 about the economic control of the beast using a number in forehead or hand, with the accelerating trend toward computer-based finance and identification. What could be more logical (or better secure control) than to place an invisible binary number on every person? (I only speculate, of course.)

5. The true fragility of science becomes evident when we look carefully at its epistemology. Cf. Michael Polanyi, *Personal Knowledge* (London: Routledge and Kegan Paul, 1958), pp. 49–63, 203–222.

6. Francis A. Shaeffer, *The God Who Is There* (Chicago: Inter-Varsity Press, 1968).

7. H. R. Rookmaaker, *Modern Act and the Death of a Culture* (London: Inter-Varsity Press, 1970).

8. Jean-Paul Satre, "Existentialism and Humanism," trans. P. Mairet (London: Methuen, 1948).

9. Karl Heim provides an interesting discussion of Far Eastern religions in terms of the subject–object polarity in his book *Christian Faith and Natural Science* (London: SCM Press Ltd., 1953), pp. 151–174.

10. T. Roszak, *The Making of a Counter Culture* (Garden City, N.J.: Doubleday & Co., Inc., Anchor Books, 1969).

11. An excellent example: the famous song "Penny Lane" by the Beatles.

12. Shaeffer, *op. cit.*

13. For an especially interesting account of medieval thought, see: Owen Barfield, *Saving the Appearances: A Study in Idolatry* (New York: Harcourt, Brace & World, 1965), pp. 1–92. Of course, Barfield's main point is not the one I make here. Indeed, his critique superficially appears to support the medieval outlook, though he is really trying to show that *scientism* is idolatry.

14. S. Toulmin, *Foresight and Understanding* (London: Hutchinson and Co., Ltd., 1961).

15. R. Hooykaas, *Religion and the Rise of Modern Science* (Edinburgh: Scottish Academic Press, 1972).

16. In this article, I use words like *objective, true, real* (and the corresponding nouns) in a *deliberately* naive way, to refer to this *otherness* of a valid object of knowledge. This policy is consistent with the view (to which I subscribe) that modern philosophy has tended to poison our language by giving artificial and improper meanings to these words. The task of debate with analytic philosophy as to their proper meaning is obviously a major part of a serious epistemology. It is equally obviously beyond our scope here.

17. A somewhat polemical exposition of this view is given in my article: "The Concept of Truth in the Natural Sciences," *Themelios: An International Journal for Theological Students* (Lausanne: International Fellowship of Evangelical Students, 1968) vol. 5, No. 2, pp. 27–39.

18. C. A. Coulson, *Science and Christian Belief* (Chapel Hill: University of North Carolina Press, 1955).

19. See the essay on Sartre in: William Barrett, *Irrational Man,* (Garden City, N.Y.: Doubleday & Co., Anchor Books, 1962).

20. A.J. Ayer, *Language, Truth and Logic* (London: Victor Gollancz, 1946).

21. The essence of Cain's lifestyle is the refusal of dependence upon God, though he lives in the earth God made and is actually still under God's protection. Cf. Jacques Ellul, *The Meaning of the City* (Grand Rapids, Michigan: William B. Eerdmans Publishing Co., 1970), pp. 1–9.

22. Hooykaas, *op. cit.*

XII

The Limits and Uses of Science

GORDON H. CLARK

Most Christians, when they think about science, have in mind some immediate apologetic interests. For example, mechanistic philosophy denies the occurrence of miracles and questions the value of prayer. Ordinary Christians then want an argument to justify prayer and miracles. Or, again, behaviorism has elaborated a theory of human nature that undermines the biblical concept of sin and has led many college students to gross immorality. Devout Christians naturally want some defense against Freud, Russell, and Dewey. And underlying behaviorism is the theory of evolution that derives all life from inanimate matter and human life from the lower animals. Once again

Gordon H. Clark is a distinguished evangelical philosopher and author of numerous books. Since 1974 he has been Professor of Philosophy at Covenant College, Lookout Mountain, Tennessee. From 1945–1973 he was chairman of the Department of Philosophy at Butler University, Indianapolis, Indiana. Prior to that he was Associate Professor of Philosophy at Wheaton College, Illinois. His books include (with T. V. Smith) *Readings in Ethics* (1931), *Selections from Hellenistic Philosophy* (1940), (with Martin, Clarke and Ruddick) *A History of Philosophy* (1941), *A Christian Philosophy of Education* (1946), *A Christian View of Men and Things* (1952), *Thales to Dewey* (1956), *Religion, Reason and Revelation* (1961), *Karl Barth's Theological Method* (1963), *The Philosophy of Science and Belief in God* (1964), and *Historiography: Secular and Religious* (1971).

we want to view man, not as mere sensory animal, but as a rational soul who looks forward to a life beyond the grave.

Though most Christians think about these matters in a haphazard sort of way, it is clear that physics, psychology, and zoology are technical subjects in which haphazard and desultory thought is of no value. Scholars must make these sciences their professional concern and devote their lives to their technical formulation. Some extremely devout students, however, viewing with concern the apostasy of the churches, the secularism of the populace, and the universal rise in crime, drug addiction, and terrorism, now question whether a life of scientific research is worthwhile or even permissible for a Christian. Adults midway through their careers pay little attention to this question, but for a small number of gifted students, science as a vocational alternative is a forced and momentous option. The present essay, though chiefly interested in the nature and philosophy of science as such, permits itself, because of some current developments, to begin with the personal problem.

Every student must choose a life work: the problem is a real one. But Christian students may face the alternative of preaching the gospel or doing physics. They are not likely to deny that the Bible approves of every method of making a living except those that are sinful. There are many occupations, and not every Christian, however sincere, is obligated to enter the ministry. Science is therefore a legitimate vocation.

On the other hand, in the present state of affairs, the world at large holds science in such high regard that some Christians have begun to question the value of preaching the gospel. They have begun to share in the idolatry of science. Since they are professing Christians, reared in evangelical homes, retaining an attachment to biblical views, these theologian-philosophers have picked out Gen. 1:28, coined the phrase "cultural mandate," and so emphasized subduing the earth for man's comfort, that the ministry has actually been downgraded. Some have gone so far as to suggest that the preaching of the gospel should cease until society has been reconstructed along socialistic lines and thus made ready to accept Christianity.

In prediluvian days this cultural mandate of Genesis was fulfilled by the development of agriculture, the domestication of animals, the invention of musical instruments, metallurgy, and the rudimentary arts of war. These were scientific advances—scientific, at least in the sense that science had to begin in this way—but they were made, so the record tells us, mainly by the ungodly line of Cain, rather than by the descendants of Seth. Later on, as noted in Exodus, Chapter 31, some of the godly line were skilled in art, if not in science.

Scripture thus approves of arts and sciences. But it does not approve of physical research to the exclusion of other worthy occupations. Approval admits of, and in this case requires, a recognition of degrees of importance. In fact, the Old Testament shows little interest in mathematics and physics, while it assigns a continuing role to the priests and Levites. And in the New Testament, if Paul had considered fulfillment of the cultural mandate a prerequisite for the execution of the "great commission," Christianity would never have gone beyond the boundaries of Palestine. All the less does the cultural mandate now need emphasis, because, with the special help of the ungodly line, it has been much more fully obeyed than the great commission.

It should also be noted that there is a large logical gap between the simple words of Genesis and some current proposals made under its aegis. If anyone appeals to Scripture for a cultural mandate, he must also show, for example, that the precise policies of CLAC (Christian Labor Association of Canada), the devaluation of currency, the requirement that small businesses with only four or five employees should make lengthy quarterly reports in quintuplicate, the law against elderly people with arthritis in their fingers that prevents them getting their indocin in easily opened bottles, and volumes of irritating regulations are deducible by valid syllogisms from, not Genesis, but other parts of the Bible. Otherwise, however, science is an indubitably legitimate occupation for a college graduate.

So much for personal concerns. Science is both legitimate and important, as well as real and pervasive. This judgment, however, raises the question, What is science? What is the nature and function of laboratory experimentation? Does it, by valid syllogisms, support a mechanistic world view, banish God from the universe, and reduce prayer to meditation on other subjects?

Such questions are indeed matters of apologetic interest, but the answers come only through through technical philosophic analysis. Unfortunately, a short essay such as this can cover only a little ground. Therefore behaviorism, evolution, and much else have to be omitted in order to concentrate on one subject—physics—in more depth. This limitation can be justified somewhat because biology depends on physics, and the varying views of basic science profoundly alter all the dependent disciplines. Therefore, after a brief description of a few historical developments, the analysis of laboratory procedure and of the formulation of physical laws will lead to the conclusions here proposed.

Since the historical survey must also be brief, there is no point in peering into the pre-Newtonian era. Using the work of Galileo and Kepler, Sir Isaac Newton laid down principles that guided scientific advance for two centuries. From 1686, or as soon thereafter as scientists could read the *Principia Mathematica,* to approximately 1900, all physics was based on certain definitions and basic laws, of which the following examples are especially important:

> Absolute, true, and mathematical time, of itself, and from its own nature, flows equably without relation to anything external. . . .
> Absolute space, in its own nature, without relation to anything external, remains always similar and immovable. . . .
> Absolute motion is the translation of a body from one absolute place into another. . . .
> Every body continues in its state of rest, or of uniform motion in a right line, unless it is compelled to change that state by forces impressed upon it.[1]

On these premises, Newton, with incredible genius and infinite patience, worked out his gravitational system in extensive detail. Yet, though his triumph was overwhelming, today his edifice lies in ruins. Nothing of it remains. But its development and its demise shed light on the nature and compass of science.

During Newton's lifetime Leibnitz argued that the *Principia* depended on a set of contradictions. But other scientists were not impressed by objections from such armchair philosophers; they steadily built up the Newtonian theory in its many subordinate laws. Then two centuries later, Ernest Mach, quite innocent of Leibnitzian scholarship, rediscovered Newton's logical blunder: the law of gravitation and the concepts of absolute time and motion cannot be combined. As Hans Reichenbach has written: "The famous correspondence between Leibnitz and Clarke . . . reads as though Leibnitz had taken his arguments from expositions of Einstein's theory. . . . This conception of relativity was carried on at a later time by Ernst Mach, [who argued] . . . that a relativity of rotational motion requires an extension of relativism to the concept of inertial force."[2]

The relevant technical material is available to anyone who wishes to read it. Here it must suffice to indicate only two of Newton's difficulties. First, the idea that an absolute time flows equably without relation to anything external is scientifically useless and philosophically impossible. The reason is as follows. When we measure the motion of an auto, we say it goes at fifty miles an hour, that is, a certain distance in a certain time. But if time itself flows equably past us, this motion could not be measured by time, as the motion of the auto is, but only by its relation to some "supertime." Now, if time can be measured in seconds, and a car by feet per second, at what speed is the equable flow of time? Seconds per what? The auto goes at *feet* per *second;* time goes at *seconds* per what? After providing this answer, one must proceed and ask whether this "supertime" also flows equably. And so on ad infinitum.

A second difficulty with Newtonian theory concerns the principle of motion in a straight line. An empirical method for identifying straight-line motion in absolute space is impossible. The scientist would need, in addition to the present location of the moving body, a fixed point in space toward which the body was moving. A fixed star would satisfy this requirement. But there are no fixed stars. Hence the concept of motion in a straight line is useless in science.

Note too that the law of gravitation conflicts with the observed distribution of the star population. Gravitation implies a center to the universe where there are more stars per cubic volume than elsewhere, with the star population gradually decreasing from the center to a distant area of complete emptiness. However, actual observation does not bear out this hypothesis.

At this point the nonscientific reader may want another reference to apologetics. Three can be given. First, the hypothesis of Newtonian mechanism, by which W. K. Clifford, Karl Pearson, and others denounced miracles, has no experimental proof. Scientists may, and some do, remain mechanists, but they have no scientific basis for doing so. Hence there is no valid scientific argument against miracles.

Second, if the majestic Newtonian system has crumbled, and if science must always be tentative, no future synthesis can be taken as true and final. Everyone knows that physics has undergone immense changes. But even some scientists find it difficult to grasp this immensity. For instance, in *The Limitations of Science* J. W. N. Sullivan tells an absorbing tale of the advancement and difficulties of contemporary science. But although he details the difficulties, sets forth the limitations, and verges on skepticism, he cannot quite bring himself to admit that science will always remain tentative.[3] Yet his own evidence is conclusive. So rapid and so extensive have been the changes in physics since the abolition of ether and the invention of wavicles that one may confidently affirm that, whereas Newtonianism lasted for two centuries, no theory today seems likely to last two decades. The arguments of this chapter refer to physics directly; but if physics is always tentative and never final, can the dependent sciences be superior? Clearly not. Therefore anti-Christian arguments based on science always depend on premises that will soon be discarded.

There is also a third point, or at least a confirmation of the second. The following analysis of laboratory procedure will show why no law of physics ever has been or ever can be a true description of natural processes.

On the assumption that the concepts of absolute space and time are discredited, and that the law of gravitation has fallen before the onslaught of relativity, it is pertinent to contrast the twentieth century view of science as tentative with the nineteenth century view that physics arrives at absolute truth. The general populace, even though dimly aware of the great scientific advances of this century, still retains the Newtonian optimism that science really discovers truth. On the opposite side, some professional scientists know so much up-to-date science, and so little history, that they doubt there ever was a theory of fixed truth in physics. There was such a theory, however. Its exponents are not straw men.[4]

Karl Pearson, in his *Grammar of Science,* taught that "the classification of facts and the formation of absolute judgments upon the basis of this classification—judgments independent of the idiosyncracies of the individual mind—essentially sum up the aim and method of modern science." That the absolute judgments of science extend to theology and ethics Pearson asserted explicitly: "The goal of science is clear —it is nothing short of the complete interpretation of the universe.

Science does much more than demand that it shall be left in undisturbed possession of what the theologian and metaphysician please to call its 'legitimate field.' It claims that the whole range of phenomena, mental as well as physical—the entire universe—is its field. It asserts that the scientific method is the sole gateway to the whole region of knowledge."[5]

Professor A. J. Carlson wrote: "What is the method of science? In essence it is this—the rejection *in toto* of all non-observational and non-experimental authority in the field of experience. . . . When no evidence is produced [in favor of a pronouncement] other than personal dicta, past and present 'revelations' in dreams, or the 'voice of God,' the scientist can pay no attention whatsoever, except to ask, How do they get that way?" Carlson then confidently asserts: "The scientist tries to rid himself of all faiths and beliefs. He either knows or he does not know. If he knows, there is no room for faith or belief. If he does not know, he has no right to faith or belief."[6]

Even Hans Reichenbach, who, as the earlier quotation shows, ought to know better, succumbs to excessive optimism. In his *Modern Philosophy of Science* he contrasts the perennial inability of philosophers to agree on anything with the common ground, universally recognized, which science has developed. A science teacher can teach "with the proud feeling of introducing his students into a realm of well-established truth." The results of science are "established with a superpersonal validity and universally accepted."[7]

Philipp Frank, on the other hand, more accurately represents the contemporary state of affairs: "It took a long time for the present day theory of motion to develop, and we do not know whether or not it is the right scheme for the future."[8]

At this point it is instructive to note how backward are many liberal theologians. Rudolf Bultmann, for instance, asserts in *Kerygma and Myth* that "now that the forces and laws of nature have [really] been discovered, we can no longer believe in spirits, whether good or evil."[9] If he were consistent, Bultmann should deny the existence of God, for God is a good spirit; but he seems to be not quite that consistent. And then in *Jesus Christ and Mythology* he borrows from Auguste Comte and asserts that although science may change in some details, its method of thinking will never change again.[10] He goes even further and seems to suggest that, whereas geocentric and heliocentric astronomy may continue to change, the (Newtonian?) laws of motion are immutable truths.

To support the previous assertion that physics can never discover or formulate a true description of natural processes, it is proper now to continue with a technical, albeit simple, analysis of laboratory methodology. What a scientist does, what he must do, prevents him from ever discovering the truth—the allegedly fixed, absolute truth of Clifford, Pearson, and Carlson, the unalterable law, final and irreplaceable.

After choosing a problem and starting an experiment pertinent to his hypothesis, the scientist soon takes a measurement. In fact one may say that every experiment reduces to measuring the length of a line. It may be the length of mercury in a tube, it may be a certain distance on a meter stick, or the distance between two points on a dial. This reading the scientist records. Then he repeats the experiment and makes a second reading. Why? One possible reason for the second reading is that his eyes may have blinked the first time. They may of course blink the second time too, but the scientist hopes that a large number of readings will minimize these defects. But there is also another reason for making a second or a twenty-second reading. It may be that the mercury or the steel dial is palpitating, constantly expanding and contracting in the universal flux. A metal bar may not expand uniformly at all temperatures, nor at all times, even within very narrow temperature limits. Worse yet (so far as truth in science is concerned), the very thing being measured may be vibrating as well. Can any experiment prove that a cubic centimeter of gold, water, or sulphur always maintains the same weight? The measurements always vary, and atomic weights are only averages. If these variations are haphazard, then fixed truth is impossible, not only because our eyes blink but also because the object itself is not fixed. Indeed, in recent years this latter view has been accepted by some scientists, as will shortly be explained.

Before discussing further the metaphysical indeterminism to which the last paragraph refers, let us consider whether the use of averages can cancel out the blinking of the eyes and so preserve the truth of physical laws. What the physicist does is to repeat an experiment many times and record a list of the divergent readings. Then he calculates their arithmetic mean. There are other averages he could use, but for no empirical reason the physicist prefers arithmetic means. There are other nonobservational factors that contribute to the physicist's findings. In fact the physicist's findings are not findings at all. They are formulations. Several factors in the formulation of a law are completely without observational evidence; but for the moment it is enough to note that the physicist chooses one type of average from among others.

Next, each reading is subtracted from the arithmetic mean, and a mean of these deviations is calculated. This second mean is attached to the first and is called the variable error. At this point the physicist has a long list of figures such as 17.03 + .0007. He then repeats the experiment a tedious number of times and obtains a long list of figures similar to the one above.

To formulate his law, the physicist now transfers these values to graph paper, where they appear as small rectangles. Through them he draws a curve, determines an algebraic equation that will yield a corresponding curve, and announces this to the world as a law of physics.

To simplify the argument, let us suppose that the averages result in three spots on the graph paper that look as if they can be joined by a straight line. The scientist may then announce that the law is $x = y$, or $x = Cy$. This could mean that the pressure on the bottom of a vessel increases and decreases with the height of the liquid, or that temperature varies with the length of a column of mercury. However, these small rectangles can also be joined by a sine curve, in fact by an infinite number of sine curves, and even by any one of an infinite number of other curves.

That three areas, or even three points on a straight line, can be points on a sine curve is most easily demonstrated visually by drawing a straight line through such a curve. More reconditely, the equation $y = A \sin (bx \times c)$ can always pass through three points determined by $x = Cy$. But the two equations are by no means the same law in physics.

The patient reader may permit or skip a more complex example. Suppose a series of experiments yields several values to be plotted slightly above the x axis. To the eye, they too may look like a straight line. But they could be the asymtotic end of a hyperbola. Or, to take an actual case, the values could be the asympotic end of the law of gravitation, which is not a hyperbola. But since these values are rectangular areas, they could be connected by the awkward equation

$$y = \frac{e^{-\frac{A}{x}}}{x} + \ln{(Bx)}\ e^{-Bx}$$

Or, to acknowledge that the laws of physics are chosen for aesthetic considerations, the same values can also be determined by the much prettier equation

$$y = \frac{e^{-\frac{A}{x}} - e^{-\frac{x}{A}}}{x}$$

To bring this into connection with gravitation, the last equation may be changed to

$$y = \frac{e^{-\frac{A}{x}} - e^{-\frac{x}{A}}}{x^2}$$

Here we have the crux of the controversy between collision or contact and action at a distance. Newton thought that two bodies approach each other, collide, and rebound. Action at a distance seemed to him a nonmechanical impossibility, about which he made his oft-quoted statement, *hypotheses non fingo* (I make no hypotheses). But there is no observational evidence that requires bodies to collide. The force of gravitation may increase until the distance between the two bodies is infinitesimal, at which point a force of repulsion sets in, and the curve swoops down from a high point on the y axis to an equally great minus quantity. Hence action at a distance as well as Newton's impressed forces are equally compatible with the empirical observations. Experimentation never discovers how nature works. Every law of physics is an equation and, if viewed as a description of natural processes, false. The law is indubitably unprovable; it may also be called false because, even aside from the theory of indeterminism, from a strictly mechanistic view, the chance of selecting the true description from among all the laws observation allows is one in infinity, or zero.

In a conversation concerning the nature of ultimate reality Chaim Tschernowitz quotes Einstein as saying: "We know nothing about it at all. Our knowledge is but the knowledge of school children. . . . We shall know a little more than we do now. But the real nature of things —that we shall never know, never."[11]

From this the further conclusion follows that science can never disprove the truth of Christianity. It can never prove or disprove any metaphysical or theological assertion.

Two instances of this negative conclusion are now to be explained; and then a statement must be made on the value or import of science, if it is always false.

The two instances of this negative conclusion aim to emphasize that no metaphysical or theological conclusion is possible. Though the argument has shown that science cannot assert mechanism, it equally follows that neither can science assert indeterminism. About 1930 Heisenberg convinced the world that if his experiments on particles used sufficient light to locate the object, its velocity could not be determined because the energy of the light itself affected the object. On the other hand, if the light were dim enough not to interfere with the velocity, the object could not be located. But from this admirable scientific work Heisenberg went on to conclude that mechanism is false and indeterminism is true. This inference is invalid.[12] The scientist's inability to construct an experiment that can determine both velocity and position surely gives no information on the still unknown laws of infinitesimal particles. Or, for that matter, the scientist's inability leaves uncertain whether nature is constructed of particles at all or whether it is a continuum. The result is zero, neither positive nor negative.

Some Christian apologetes, although recognizing that this result destroys all scientific arguments against miracles, may still defend scientific mechanism because the second law of thermodynamics seems to prove the doctrine of a creation in the finite past and disprove the doctrine of the eternity of the universe. However, if it is impossible accurately to measure a line, and if a series of areas on a graph furnish an infinite number of equations from which to choose, the second law of thermodynamics, along with all the others, becomes tentative and false.

Suppose a scientist for the brief moment of his life stands on the ocean shore watching the ebbing tide. The water level drops three feet in twelve hours, or in twelve billion years. He concludes that the tide cannot have been ebbing from eternity, for if that were so the water would have reached its lowest level billions of years before he came to watch it. Of course, that the tide rises as well as ebbs is philosophically impossible; or is it?

Now, the thermodynamic scientist has watched some energy systems, few in number, and at most for the period of only a few lifetimes. He has seen the ebb, and without ever having seen an incoming tide, has recorded some points on a graph. They look like a straight line; but a mathematician can as well connect them by that disturbing sine curve. The scientist lives in the age of ebb; in a future age the energy differences will again increase.

Perhaps a simplified and artificial example will make it clearer how a series of numbers can accommodate a large, even infinite, variety of equations. Let us suppose that the first point is at 3, the second point at 9, and the third point at 19.[13] Now, suppose the experimentation had ended with the number 9. Experimentation must always end somewhere, for otherwise no time would be left to formulate a law. If, then, the last experiment gave the number 9, the law could be, and, in view of the scientist's dislike for Rube Goldberg complications, would be $x = 3^n$. The first number is three, the second is three to the second power, and the third will be extrapolated on the graph and predicted as 27.

But in this example the experimentation did not stop at 9. The scientist went on to his third average of 19. Hence $x = 3^n$ is refuted. A new formula must be devised. Well, the scientist has an infinite number of choices, of which two are:

$$x = 2n^2 + 1 \quad \text{and} \quad x = \frac{n^3}{3} + \frac{1\ln}{3} - 1$$

This artificial example should convince everyone that in any scientific theorizing there are infinite possibilities for extrapolation. Every one of them describes the natural process equally well; that is, not one of them can be shown to be the true description. Hence every law of physics must be false, for science is always tentative.

The general public, including conservative theologians, and some scientists, may reject this essay's thesis in irrational disgust; but if they do not, they are sure to ask—and it is a legitimate question—If science is always false, what value can it possibly have? Science has done wonders. Even if the cure of cancer still eludes us, we have put men on the moon. How could false laws have produced such marvels?

The answer is that a law need not be true in order to be useful. Scientific laws now universally recognized as false have often enough been very useful. For example, no contemporary astronomer accepts the geocentric theory of Ptolemy. Nevertheless, even after Copernicus stole his thunder from the heliocentric system of Aristarchus and Plato, the Ptolemaic system was still able to predict the positions of the planets with greater accuracy than the Copernican theory could, and hence Ptolemy's laws were more useful for whatever such predictions are useful for.

Similarly, the theory that electromagnetic fields exist is now denied by at least some scientists; but no one denies that this false theory greatly advanced the utilization of electricity.

To relieve the distress of those who tire of physics, another example, and a most interesting one, can be taken from zoology, or veterinary medicine. Last century, milk fever in cows was a fearful disease with ninety percent fatality. After the Franco-Prussian war, Pasteur proposed the germ theory of disease and cured cases of anthrax and rabies. Thereupon a brilliant veterinarian argued to himself: germs cause disease, therefore if I inject an antiseptic into the cows' udders and kill the germs, the cows will get well. He did so, the cows recovered, he published his findings, and mortality rapidly dropped from ninety to thirty percent. Then he and others argued, this further proves the truth of the germ theory of disease.

But one day a cow phoned her vet to come pronto or she would die. He immediately hitched up his Lincoln Continental and at 60 mph (mud puddles per hedgerow) soon arrived on the scene. But then, when he opened his black satchel, he discovered that most unfortunately he had neglected to put in a supply of antiseptic. More fortunately, however, some cows still died, and since neither the cow nor the farmer could tell the difference, they would never know that he had injected distilled water instead of Lugol. To his surprise, the cow got well.

Being of a scientific mind, he continued to inject distilled water in other cows, with the result that as many or even more cows recovered.

He too published his findings; and other inquisitive veterinarians tried compressed air, with even better results. What then of the germ theory of disease? Distilled water and compressed air do not kill germs.† The point is that the germ theory, now proved false with respect to milk fever, nevertheless was very useful in curing cows. Hence the utility of science can be defended even while asserting its falsity.

Now, in conclusion: science is forever incapable of producing a valid argument against the existence of God, the occurence of miracle, including a supernatural revelation, and a life beyond the grave. The author[14] of the article on "Atheism" in *The Encyclopedia of Philosophy* bases his arguments on the problem of evil; other writers may attempt to prove atheism on other bases. This article concerns physics; and physics, with its derivatives of chemistry and biology, is totally, totally, incompetent, both positively and negatively, to make any metaphysical or theological pronouncement. Science is always false, but often useful.

NOTES

1. A. Motte, trans., and F. Cajori, ed., *Mathematical Principles of Natural Philosophy* (Berkeley: University of California Press, 1946).

2. Hans Reichenbach, "The Philosophical Significance of the Theory of Relativity," in Paul A. Schilpp, ed., *Albert Einstein, Philosopher-Scientist* (New York: Tudor Publishing Company, 1949), pp. 299 ff. Cf. also Reichenbach, *Die Bewegslehre bei Newton, Leibnitz und Huyghens* (Kantstudien, 1924), and *Philosophic Foundations of Quantum Mechanics,* 1944.

3. J. W. N. Sullivan, *The Limitations of Science* (New York: Viking Press, 1933; Newton, 1957). Cf. also Henri Poincaré, *Science et Methode* (Paris: Flammarion, 1927), and its two succeeding volumes.

4. W. K. Clifford, *The Common Sense of the Exact Sciences* (New York: Knopf, 1946); Karl Pearson, *Grammar of Science* (New York: Macmillan, 1911), pp. 14, 24; A. J. Carlson, "Science and the Supernatural," in *Science,* 73 (1931), pp. 217–225, reprinted in *The Scientific Monthly,* 59 (1944), pp. 85–95.

5. Karl Pearson, pp. 14, 24.

6. A. J. Carlson, *op. cit.*

---

†(The reader may check to see if milk fever is now cured by injections of calcium in the cow's neck.)

7. Hans Reichenbach, *Modern Philosophy of Science* (London: Routledge and Paul, 1959), pp. 136, 149.

8. Philipp Frank, *Philosophy of Science* (Engelwood Cliffs, N.J.: Prentice-Hall, 1962), p. 90.

9. Rudolf Bultmann, *Kerygma and Myth* (New York: Harper & Brothers, 1961), p. 4.

10. Rudolf Bultmann, *Jesus Christ and Mythology* (New York: Scribner, 1958), pp. 36–38.

11. *Reader's Digest* (August 1972), p. 28.

12. For a technical discussion see C. T. Ruddick, "On the Contingency of Natural Law," *The Monist* (July 1932), pp. 330–383.

13. Morris R. Cohen and Ernest Nagel furnish this example [*An Introduction to Logic and Scientific Method* (New York: Harcourt, Brace and Company, 1934), pp. 209 f.] though Nagel in his later books rejects the implication of operationalism.

14. Paul Edwards, "Atheism," in *The Encyclopedia of Philosophy, Vol. I,* Paul Edwards, editor-in-chief (New York: Macmillan and The Free Press, 1967),pp. 174–189.

Appendix A

REPORT OF THE COMMISSION FROM THE
INTERNATIONAL CONFERENCE ON HUMAN ENGINEERING
AND THE FUTURE OF MAN
July 21–24, 1975, Wheaton College, Illinois

RATIONALE

We hold that all things are originated and sustained by the creative will and action of God, as the Scriptures teach. Therefore the world is neither to be deified nor vilified, but rather is to be accepted as a trust from God. Human stewardship includes the search for understanding of the world. The Christian may confidently engage in this search because all truth is God's truth.

God charged man with governing and developing His creation. Scientific investigation and application assist in fulfilling this divine mandate. Jesus summed up human responsibility in two commands: to love God with all one's being, and to love one's neighbor as one's self. Consequently, Christians should strive with compassion to ameliorate the host of evils and suffering which entered the world through the Fall.

Among the many accomplishments of science certain techniques of genetic, neurological, pharamacological and psychological modification of human beings have great potential to enhance or erode their capacity to fully love God, neighbor and self as directed by the Scriptures. Because human beings are both finite and sinful special care must be taken to use the tools of these technologies with humility and integrity, and to preserve and foster the freedom, dignity and spiritual responsibility of man, who is created in the image of God. Moreover, God calls for justice to be reflected by the laws of the state in its treatment of those potentially affected by this technology, as well as toward and by those involved in developing and applying the technology.

Because no one is reducible solely to his biological, psychological or behavioral dimensions, or any combinations thereof, the results to be expected from human engineering will be limited. While God may benefit humanity through such technological processes, salvation is effected only by the supernatural grace of God through Jesus Christ. Nevertheless, human technology ought to be used responsibly by Christians in carrying their concern for the needs of humanity.

PRINCIPLES

Much has been said in the past few years regarding the ethics of research and application of these technologies. In general, the techniques that were discussed at the conference, if appropriately applied, can be used to increase or restore man's physical and mental health. On the other hand, if used to excess, misapplied, or used in a careless or inconsiderate way, they can be harmful. In light of a Christian understanding of personhood, steps must be taken to insure respect for human rights and responsibilities:

1. We should consider available investigative procedures and treatments and carefully identify those which are applicable to a given individual's condition. Procedures with more drastic or irreversible effects must be more extensively justified by showing that beneficial results could reasonably be expected to outweigh deleterious effects. The underlying aim must be to improve the person's wholeness. To illustrate, psychosurgery applied to the treatment of a childhood behavior disorder resulting from a chaotic home environment is almost always a misapplication. Its use on a brain-damaged eighteen-year-old who impulsively and homicidally attacks any person who tries to direct his behavior might be appropriate.

2. Investigatory procedures, applications of technology and release of data potentially harmful to an individual should be subject to the informed consent of the person primarily affected. In cases of those lacking capacity for informed consent to be exercised, special safeguards should be provided to protect their rights and interests.

3. Since all persons are made in the image of God we should treat everyone's claim with equity. There should be no prejudicial consideration of any factor that sets one person apart from another. Christians have a special obligation toward those who are without power, and should insist on a fair access to beneficial technology for everyone.

4. The biblical principles of love and justice, among others, are essential bases for decision-making in this area. However, many choices regarding the application of these technologies do not follow easily from these guidelines. Often there are a variety of ethical concerns which bear on a single decision and pull us in diverse directions. Special concern should be given to conflicts between individual and social consequences of a particular decision. For example, genetic planning should consider, among other things, the implications of bearing and not bearing children, the risks of bearing children who may be seriously deformed, and the social consequences of caring for deformed children.

dn,14 RECOMMENDATIONS

Given the complexity and urgency of these issues, we urge governmental bodies, scientific and professional groups and the general public to accelerate their efforts to exchange information and concerns about these matters. Reports such as those prepared by the Subcommittee on Health of the Committee on Labor and Public Welfare of the United States Senate (May 1975), the National Academy of Sciences (1975), Hastings Institute, and other scientific, professional, legislative and religious bodies ought to be widely distributed to individuals and groups from a variety of training and orientations. We particularly urge those who are followers of Christ to become deeply involved in this dialogue and subsequent decision-making.

Within the scientific community much benefit would come from more extensive discussions of ethical matters. We, therefore, encourage the following steps:

1. The training of scientists in the ethical dimensions of research and application;

2. The increasing consideration of ethical issues in scholarly journals;

3. The development of conferences and books that would help sensitize the professionals to ethical implications and decision-making approaches;

4. The rapid and vigorous implementation of plans to sponsor conferences and projects on ethical aspects of human engineering technology by such funding agencies as the National Science Foundation's Ethical and Human Value Implications of Technology program. Such funding should include groups with relatively diverse *and* relatively homogeneous value orientations;

5. The provision of funds for research projects which deal directly with ethical dilemmas, and which reach across disciplinary boundaries. A current need for such study exists with the research on recombinant DNA molecules, with its many implications for human gene therapy.

Within the general public unnecessary alarm and ignorance of developments must be avoided. From the local level to the national arena, opportunity must increasingly be given for citizen review of research design and the application of human engineering techniques. These groups should look beyond the immediate activities of researchers and practitioners to consider the future implications of present inquiry. The legislative, executive, and judicial branches of government increasingly will need to deal with bio-ethics. Anticipating the implications of human engineering technology will, however, reduce the need for disrupting research progress with governmental moratoria.

The Christian has extensive opportunities to participate in public dialogue, employing the sensitivity of Christian values and the leading of the Holy Spirit. We, therefore, urge Christians in the spirit of love and service to make themselves available for review boards and dialogue bodies at all levels. Christian organizations, particularly the professional and academic societies, are urged to deal with the ethical aspects of human engineering in conferences and publications. Finally, we urge Christian colleges and institutions to develop their special calling to integrate Christian ethics with scientific concerns.

Appendix B

SUGGESTED READING

THE SPACE SCIENCES

Barbour, Ian G. *Issues in Science and Religion.* Englewood Cliffs, N. J.: Prentice-Hall; London, SCM Press Ltd., 1966.

Barfield, Owen. *Saving the Appearances: A Study in Idolatry.* New York: Harcourt Brace Jovanovich, 1965.

Boyd, R. L. F. *Space Physics: The Study of Plasmas in Space.* London: Oxford University Press, 1975.

Ponnamperuma, Cyril, and Cameron, A. G. W. *Interstellar Communication: Scientific Perspectives.* Boston: Houghton Mifflin Co., 1974.

Shipman, Harry L. *Black Holes, Quasars and the Universe.* Boston: Houghton Mifflin Co., 1976.

THE FAILURE OF THE GOD-OF-THE-GAPS

Alexander, Denis. *Beyond Science.* Philadelphia: A. J. Holman Co., 1972.

Barbour, Ian. *Issues in Science and Religion.* Englewood Cliffs, N.J.: Prentice-Hall, 1966.

Bube, Richard H. *The Encounter Between Christianity and Science.* Grand Rapids, Michigan: William B. Eerdmans Publishing Co., 1968.

_____. *The Human Quest: A New Look at Science and Christian Faith.* Waco, Texas: Word Books, 1971.

Jeeves, Malcolm A. *The Scientific Enterprise and Christian Faith.* London: Tyndale, 1969.

MacKay, Donald M. *Christianity in a Mechanistic Universe.* Chicago: Inter-
    Varsity Press, 1965.
————. *The Clockwork Image.* Downers Grove, Ill.: Inter-Varsity Press,
    1974.

MAN IN THE CONTEXT OF EVOLUTIONARY THEORY

Barbour, Ian G., *Issues in Science and Religion,* Englewood Cliffs, N.J.:
    Prentice-Hall, 1966.
Berry, R. J. *Adam and the Ape,* London: Falcon, 1975.
Bube, Richard H., *The Human Quest,* Waco, Texas: Word Books, 1971.
Morris, Henry M. *The Troubled Waters of Evolution,* San Diego: Creation-
    Life, 1974.
Schaeffer, Francis A., *No Final Conflict,* London: Hodder, 1975.

ENVIRONMENTAL PROBLEMS AND THE CHRISTIAN ETHIC

Black, John. *The Dominion of Man.* Edinburgh: Edinburgh University Press,
    1970.
Derrick, Christopher. *The Delicate Creation.* London: Tom Stacey, 1972.
Passmore, John. *Man's Responsibility for Nature.* London: Duckworth, 1974.
Taylor, John V. *Enough is Enough.* London: SCM Press Ltd., 1975.

THE AMBIGUITIES OF SCIENTIFIC BREAKTHROUGH

Baker's Dictionary of Christian Ethics. Edited by C.F.H. Henry. Grand Rap-
    ids, Michigan: Baker Book House, 1973.
Barbour, Ian G., ed. *Science and Religion: New Perspectives on the Dialogue.*
    New York: Harper & Row, 1968.
Berkouwer, G. C. *The Providence of God.* Grand Rapids, Michigan: William
    B. Eerdmans Publishing Co., 1952.
Clark, Gordon H. *The Philosophy of Science and Belief in God.* Nutley, New
    Jersey: Craig Press, 1972.
Henry, Carl F. H. *God, Revelation and Authority.* Vols. 1–2. Waco, Texas:
    Word Books, 1976.

MOLECULAR BIOLOGY IN THE DOCK

Herrmann, Robert L. "On Taking Vows in Two Priesthoods, Scientific and
    Christian." *Yale Journal of Biology and Medicine* 49, No. 5 (November
    1976): 455–459.

_____. "Genesis and Biogenesis." *Christian Medical Society Journal,* Winter 1970, pp. 10–17.

MacKay, Donald M. *The Clockwork Image.* Downers Grove, Ill: Inter-Varsity Press, 1974.

Monod, Jacques *Chance and Necessity.* New York: Vintage, 1971.

Stent, Gunther S. "An Ode to Objectivity." *Atlantic,* November 1971, p. 125.

DILEMMAS IN BIOMEDICAL ETHICS

Brody, Howard. *Ethical Decisions in Medicine.* Boston: Little, Brown and Co., 1976.

Edmunds, Vincent, and Scorer, C. Gordon, eds. *Ethical Responsibility in Medicine: A Christian Approach.* London: E. & S. Livingstone, Ltd., 1967.

Nelson, James B. *Human Medicine: Ethical Perspectives on New Medical Issues.* Minneapolis: Augsburg Publishing House, 1973.

Ramsey, Paul. *The Patient As Person.* New Haven: Yale University Press, 1970.

Wertz, Richard W., ed. *Readings on Ethical and Social Issues in Biomedicine.* Englewood Cliffs, N. J.: Prentice-Hall, Inc., 1973.

BIOLOGICAL ENGINEERING AND THE FUTURE OF MAN

Barbour, Ian G. *Science and Secularity: The Ethics of Technology,* New York: Harper & Row, 1970.

Fox, Renée C. and Swazey, Judith P. *The Courage to Fail: A Social View of Organ Transplants and Dialysis.* Chicago: University of Chicago Press, 1974.

Lappé, Marc, and Morison, Robert S., eds. "Ethical and Scientific Issues Posed by Human Uses of Molecular Genetics." *Annals of the New York Academy of Sciences* 265 (1976).

Milunsky, Aubrey, ed. *The Prevention of Genetic Disease and Mental Retardation.* Philadelphia: W. B. Saunders, 1975.

Motulsky, Arno. "Brave New World?" *Science* 185 (1974): 653–663.

Smith, W. Lynn, and Kling, Arthur, eds. *Issues in Brain/Behavior Control.* (New York: SP Books, 1976).

BRAIN RESEARCH AND HUMAN RESPONSIBILITY

Berkouwer, G. C. *Man: The Image of God.* Grand Rapids, Michigan: William B. Eerdmans Publishing Co., London: Inter-Varsity Press, 1962.

Eccles, Sir John. *Facing Reality.* New York: Longman, 1970. (An interactionist view.)

Eccles, J. C., ed. *Brain and Conscious Experience.* Heidelberg: Springer-Verlag, 1966.

Jeeves, Malcolm A. *Psychology and Christianity—The View Both Ways.* London: Inter-Varsity Press, 1976.

MacKay, Donald M. *The Clockwork Image.* Downers Grove, Ill., and London: Inter-Varsity Press, 1974.

PSYCHOLOGICAL KNOWLEDGE AND CHRISTIAN COMMITMENT

Allport, Gordon W. *The Individual and His Religion: A Psychological Interpretation.* London: Constable, 1951.

Argyle, M., and Beit-Hallahmi, B. *The Social Psychology of Religion.* London: Routledge and Kegan Paul, 1975.

Jeeves, Malcolm A. *Psychology and Christianity: The View Both Ways.* London: Inter-Varsity Press, 1976.

Mowrer, O. H. *The Crisis in Psychiatry and Religion.* New York: Van Nostrand, 1961.

Thouless, R. H. *An Introduction to the Psychology of Religion.* 3rd ed. London: Cambridge University Press, 1971.

THE SPIRITUAL DIMENSIONS OF SCIENCE

Barfield, Owen. *Saving the Appearances: A Study in Idolatry.* New York: Harcourt, Brace & World, Harbinger, 1965. (Paperback).

Coulson, C. A. *Science and Christian Belief.* Chapel Hill: University of North Carolina Press, 1955.

Hooykaas, Reijer. *Religion and the Rise of Modern Science.* Edinburgh: Scottish Academic Press Ltd., 1972, 1973. (Paperback).

MacMurray, John. *The Self as Agent.* London: Faber and Faber Ltd., 1953.

Polanyi, Michael. *Personal Knowledge.* London: Routledge and Kegan Paul, 1958, 1962; New York: Harper & Row, Harper Torchbooks, 1966. (Paperback).

THE LIMITS AND USES OF SCIENCE

Bridgman, Percy. *The Logic of Modern Physics.* New York: Macmillan Co., 1927.

_____. *The Way Things Are.* Cambridge, Mass.: Harvard University Press, 1959.

Burtt, Edwin A. *The Metaphysical Foundations of Modern Science.* New York: Harcourt, Brace and Co., 1925.

Clark, Gordon H. *The Philosophy of Science and Belief in God.* Nutley, N. J.: Craig Press, 1964.

Reichenbach, Hans. *Modern Philosophy of Science.* London: Routledge and Kegan Paul, 1959.

Sullivan, J. W. N. *The Limitations of Science.* New York: Viking Press, 1933; Mentor, 1957.